Political Culture of Language: Swahili, Society and the State

Ali A. Mazrui

Institute of Global Culture Studies (IGCS)
Binghamton University

Alamin M. Mazrui

Department of African-American and African Studies
The Ohio State University, Columbus

Studies in Global Africa

Published by
The Institute of Global Culture Studies (IGCS)
Binghamton University, The State University of New York
Binghamton, New York
1999

First edition published as *Swahili State and Society: The Political Economy of an African Language* by East African Educational Publishers Ltd., Nairobi, Kenya in association with James Currey Ltd., London, England, 1995.

Copyright © Ali A. Mazrui and Alamin M. Mazrui, 1999
This edition is published by *The Institute of Global Cultural Studies* at Binghamton University, Binghamton, USA, 1999.

Library of Congress Cataloging-in-Publication Data

Ali A. Mazrui and Alamin M. Mazrui, *Political Culture of Language: Swahili, Society and the State.*

1. Language   2. Africa   3. Swahili
4. Culture   5. Politics   6. Mazrui

ISBN 1-883058-06-6
Second edition
Third print, 1999

Studies on Global Africa

sponsor

Society for Global Africa

Executive Committee

Ricardo René Laremont   Ali A. Mazrui   Parviz Morewedge

Published by

Institute of Global Cultural Studies
Director: Ali A. Mazrui

Binghamton University, State University of New York
Binghamton, New York, USA
1999

ACKNOWLEDGMENTS

This book is a product of many interactions. The two authors are themselves products of Swahili culture and civilization, and learnt about the role of the Swahili language from both within and outside Swahili culture itself.

Former colleagues of Ali Mazrui in East Africa who contributed to the work included Henry S. D'Souza, formerly of Kenyatta University in Kenya, Ahmed Mohiddin, and the late Pio Zirimu of Makerere University in Uganda. Former colleagues of Alamin Mazrui included Khelef A. Khalifa, who extended Alamin the hospitality of his home in Lamu when Alamin was co-authoring the book, the late Kadenge Kazungu, Kimani wa Njogu of Kenyatta University, Rocha Chimerah of Egerton University, and Ibrahim Noor Shariff, who had many ideas about the role and destiny of the Swahili language over the years.

This book is also indebted to the resources made available by Binghamton University of the State University of New York, for publications of this kind. This help has included research and editorial assistance, and the technical preparation of the text.

For permission to print the second edition of this text, we are indebted to East African Educational Publishers Ltd., Nairobi, Kenya, and to James Currey Ltd., London, England. We wish to express our appreciation to the late Omari H. Kokole, the secretary of the Society for Global Africa (SGA) for the inclusion of this text in the (SGA) series, to Parviz Morewedge for his commitment and encouragement to publish this book, and to Timothy Gray and Ruzima C. Sebuharara for their detailed assistance in the preparation of the manuscript.

This edition of the book contains more recent data and information on developments in the political culture of Swahili in the region, ranging from the situation in Uganda since the adoption of its new constitution, to the linguistic implications of the fall of Mobutu Sese Seko in what was then Zaire. The political culture of Swahili continues to unfold in the crucible of East African history.

Ali A. Mazrui
Institute of Global Cultural Studies
Binghamton University
Binghamton, New York, USA

Alamin M. Mazrui
Department of African-American
and African Studies
The Ohio State University
Columbus, Ohio, USA

TABLE OF CONTENTS

Introduction

The spread of Kiswahili in Eastern and Central Africa has taken place against a background of the interaction between church and state and between economics and politics. Missionaries, merchants and administrators, politicians as well as educators, have all played a part in this drama of linguistic spread.

We propose to draw a sharp distinction in this book between Kiswahili for political and administrative purposes on one side and Kiswahili for economic functions on the other. But the story of the language touches not only politics and economics, but also religion. We shall address ourselves to all these three domains of social experience — spiritual considerations, affairs of the state and considerations related to the business of earning a living and to the balance of cost and benefit.

We shall further argue that the role of Kiswahili as an economic medium is, in some respects, older than its role either as a political or religious medium. After all, the language initially spread as a result of the expansion of trade in Eastern Africa. We hope to demonstrate that the role of Kiswahili as an economic medium has been the most spontaneous and the most natural of its three historic functions. Because the spread of Kiswahili for economic purposes has been the most spontaneous, it has also depended least on formal education and lessons in schools. Where Kiswahili is needed purely for purposes of trade, marketing, and employment, the language has not fired the imagination of educators. Certainly in Uganda in the last sixty years or so, Kiswahili has played a major role in important sectors of the economy, but this role has not persuaded successive Ugandan educational authorities to introduce the language formally in schools on any significant scale. Yet the economic role of Kiswahili has been important in horizontal national integration, fostering contacts across ethnic groups at the grassroots level. The political role of Kiswahili has, on the other hand, promoted vertical integration, creating links between the elite and the masses.

It is when Kiswahili is needed either for a political function or for religious purposes that educational policy-makers become inspired, and governments or missionaries move with dispatch towards giving the language a role in the formal structures of training and socialization.

Let us now look more closely at these different dimensions, but in the context of the broad historical perspective.

CHAPTER I

Kiswahili and the Politics of Change

This book is about Kiswahili, not merely in politics nor simply in the wider process of social change, but more specifically in those aspects of change whose direction is compatible with the present stage of human knowledge and which does justice to the potentialities of the human person both as a social creature and as an innovative being.

In the context of the role of Kiswahili in Eastern Africa, this direction of change can be concretized in a number of specific social processes. First, the wider the arena of social interaction that a person is involved in, the closer that process is to the kind of change that does justice to the potentialities of the human person as a social creature. Thus, an individual constrained only within his or her village has not as yet experienced the full-scale of his or her potentialities as a social creature. Secondly, an individual who feels comfortable only in his or her clan is being still held back from full realization of his or her potentialities as a human being. Thirdly, an individual whose allegiance is incapable of transcending ethnic affiliations has yet to experience the human potentialities inherent in a more complex network of allegiances and competing loyalties. And finally, an individual whose horizons are limited to the borders of his or her own country or society is not yet sensitized to the international implications of social existence.

In this connection, therefore, we first inquire whether Kiswahili has played a role in expanding the capacities of East Africans as social creatures. We begin by examining especially the impact of Kiswahili on processes of "detribalization" in the societies of Eastern Africa.

1. Kiswahili and Detribalization

Some of the strongest and most persistent loyalties in Africa are still ethnic. What role has Kiswahili played in influencing these ethnic loyalties?

Our first argument is that ethnic loyalties do not simply disappear, but are gradually absorbed into a wider network of allegiances. From this point of view "detribalization" is, therefore, not a process by which people stop thinking of themselves as Luo, or Baganda, or Bakongo, or Chagga. There is little evidence yet in Eastern Africa that those who are associated in "ancestry" with those particular groups have stopped thinking of themselves in terms of those groups. On the contrary, there is some evidence of increasing rather than diminishing ethnic consciousness for the time being.

"Detribalization" has, therefore, to be seen in a somewhat different context. Firstly, it could take the form of changes in custom, ritual and rules, and a shift towards a more cosmopolitan style of life. In *behavior*, a particular Muganda or Luo may no longer be guided by the heritage of values and rules of his or her rural, ethnic community, but in *loyalty* and identification the person may be even more ferociously a Muganda or Luo than ever. It is, therefore, possible to have declining "ethnic behavior" as one becomes increasingly cosmopolitan, but stable or even increasing ethnic loyalty in terms of emotional attachment. The question, therefore, arises whether Kiswahili has played a part in this sense of "detribalization."

The other sense of "detribalization" concerns the emergence of new loyalties, not necessarily to supplant older ones, but more often to supplement them in complex ways. Those new loyalties could be in terms of social class, religious affiliation, racial identity, or national consciousness. The question, therefore, arises whether Kiswahili has played a part in making the network of loyalties among East Africans more complex and more diversified.

Our answer in this little book is that Kiswahili has indeed facilitated both senses of "detribalization." In terms of diversifying social attachments, it has done this through its impact on class formation, its role in the diffusion of Christianity and Islam, its function in politicizing racial consciousness among Blacks in Eastern Africa, and the part it has played in creating new forms of national consciousness among the inhabitants of each of the countries of Eastern Africa.

We shall discuss in the next section of this contextual essay the issues of class formation more fully. But it is relevant to remember that Kiswahili has significantly facilitated the transformation of many East Africans from peasants to proletarians, from independent rural cultivators to members of the urban workforce.

But, an even earlier role played by Kiswahili in supplementing East African allegiances is its role in Islamization and Christianization. As we shall illustrate in later chapters, Kiswahili was at first deeply associated with the legacy of the Mosque before it was later mobilized to serve the purposes of the Church. This was particularly so in those countries which later came to be known as Kenya and Tanzania. The coastal regions of those countries especially were substantially Islamized several centuries before the European penetration. Kiswahili facilitated social intercourse among Muslims from different ethnic groups and regions, and gradually built up a comprehensive culture of its own over and above language as a mere medium of communication. Swahili culture was born — with its own form of Islam, its own worldview, its own dress culture, its own cuisine, its own ethics and aesthetics. There was a danger that this would itself become another parochial form of ethnicity. This possibility was averted by two factors — the universalistic orientation of Islam and the fact that Swahili culture was itself a child of multiple heritage combining and synthesizing African, Arab, Indian (especially in food culture) and other elements. At the same time, the language itself was providing further communication between the Waswahili (Swahili people) and other groups, and was contributing to the expanding network of affiliations of the peoples of the coast of Eastern Africa.

With the coming of the Christian missionaries in the later nineteenth century and their activities from then on, Kiswahili gradually acquired the additional role of becoming a language of Christian mission.

At first there was reluctance on the part of some missionaries to use Kiswahili since it had been so substantially associated with Islam. But the very fact that it had evolved a vocabulary of Middle-Eastern monotheism and had already been carrying the burden of the heritage of the Old Testament in its modified version in the Qur'an improved the credentials of the language as a medium of Christian proselytism. This role, once again, helped to broaden the social and human horizons of East Africans beyond the confines of their ancestral ways.

In the process of "detribalization", the role of Kiswahili is also linked to the process of urbanization. Certain forms of urbanization have the effect of expanding the scale of social interaction. Urbanization in Eastern Africa has also been a major factor behind the erosion of rural ethnic custom and ritual, though it has not necessarily eroded ethnic loyalty and identity. The groups from different ethnic origins have intermingled in places like Dar es Salaam, Lubumbashi, Mombasa and Jinja. Many of the customs of the rural areas have declined in these urban or semi-urban conditions. But members of the different ethnic groups, who have quite often organized themselves to meet the needs of their ethnic compatriots, have interacted with those compatriots in their own ethnic languages and have often felt the pull of ethnic loyalty in the scramble for limited opportunities and resources in the cities and towns. Rural ethnic behavior may have declined in the cities, but ethnic loyalty has persisted.

Kiswahili has been a facilitating factor behind such urbanization, and has served as a *lingua franca* among the different ethnic communities.

It has also been quite often the most important language of the workplace and the marketplace in the towns. Once again, this is a role that has both expanded the network of allegiances and eroded some ancestral traditions of village life.

The towns and cities also became (after the second World War) major centers for the new politics of African nationalism. A growing race-consciousness was spreading among East Africans. They were sensing not merely their own original ethnic identity as Kikuyu or Acholi or Samburu. They were also recognizing in a new way that they were a people sharing a history of exploitation and domination by people belonging to other "races." It is important here to distinguish between race-consciousness and racism. Race-consciousness is, at the minimum, an awareness in a politicized fashion of one's membership of a particular "race." Racism, on the other hand, is usually a hostile or contemptuous attitude towards people of other races. The rise of nationalism in Eastern Africa was more a case of politicized race-consciousness than a case of racism against Europeans. What is clear is that Kiswahili played an important part in the new phenomenon of African nationalism. Africans in Dar es Salaam, Zanzibar, Mombasa, and Nairobi heard speeches from the new breed of African politicians, agitating for African rights including by the 1950s the right of self-determination and independence. Politics in Kenya, Tanzania, and parts of Zaire became more and more national partly with the communicative facility of Kiswahili as a *lingua franca*.

In addition to the racial boundaries of the new nationalism in East Africa, there were also the emerging territorial boundaries. East Africans were thinking of themselves not merely as a people belonging to the African continent, but also as Tanganyikans, Ugandans, Kenyans, Congolese, and the people of Ruanda-Urundi. A new complex relationship based on territorial nationality was in the process of being born—and Kiswahili played its part in the process.

Yet another role Kiswahili has played in "detribalization" in

East Africa lies in the emergence of national armies and security forces. Within the King's African Rifles in colonial East Africa, Kiswahili became the language of command. As we shall later indicate in this book, recruitment into the armed forces was substantially trans-ethnic as well as trans-territorial. Soldiers enlisted from Uganda served in Kenya and vice versa.

Ethnic intermingling in the barracks, accompanied by new military routines and drill, contributed towards the erosion of more localized forms of ethnic custom and ritual within each group. For a while it was also assumed that ethnic mixture in the armed forces would culminate in an integrated *esprit de corps* among the soldiers transcending their ethnic ancestry. The first form of "detribalization", in the sense of reduced observance of the more rural ethnic customs and ritual, was indeed realized in the barracks. But the second form of "detribalization", in the sense of declining loyalty and allegiance to one's ethnic compatriots turned out to be much more difficult to achieve than had once been assumed.

The experience of the Ugandan army was particularly revealing from that point of view. After the British withdrew from Uganda, the "Nilotes" recruited into the armed forces were all too conscious of their separateness from many of the Bantu communities in the country, and were especially alienated from the Baganda. And after Amin captured power in January 1971, the divisions among the Nilotes themselves, in spite of years of intermingling in the barracks, widened catastrophically. Thousands of Acholi and Langi soldiers lost their lives in the aftermath of Idi Amin's coup. Their ethnic rivals were the Kakwa and related communities, in alliance for a while with the Lugbara. All these groups, in turn, had for so long been communicating with each other as soldiers, partly in Kiswahili. The language had remained the *lingua franca* of the armed forces within Uganda, but the task of conquering ethnic hostility was too great to be accomplished in a generation or two. Kiswahili needed a longer spell within the Ugandan armed forces if its integrative mission was to make adequate progress.

The political decline of the Baganda in Uganda, then, and the rise of the soldiers helped to give greater political importance to Kiswahili in Uganda during Amin's era. The Baganda were at one time among the greatest opponents of the promotion of Kiswahili in the country. The soldiers became, almost on the rebound, the greatest champions of Kiswahili in Uganda. The political fortunes of the language were, for better or for worse, aided both by the decline of the Baganda and by the rise of the soldiers to political power.

Yet there was one nagging worry throughout Idi Amin's presidency. Just as the Afrikaans language had come to be associated with *apartheid*, was Kiswahili in Uganda going to be identified with militarism? Was military rule going to be so hated in the Uganda of the future, that the hatred would be extended to Kiswahili as the language of the soldiers? The children of Soweto in South Africa refused to learn Afrikaans because it was the voice of *apartheid*. Were Ugandan kids one day going to refuse to learn Kiswahili because it was once the language of barracks?

On the whole, the analogy is distant though not entirely far-fetched. In any case, partly because Kiswahili has its ancestry more along the coast of Tanzania and Kenya than in the ethnic regions associated with Ugandan soldiers in the 1970s, it is not easy to identify the language with some of the particular ethnic groups that defended the worst years of military rule in the country. Kiswahili would, therefore, gain from the political impact of the soldiers on the country and escape the wrath of those who were brutalized by the soldiers. The feelings for a while may indeed have been mixed, but Kiswahili had become too strong a linguistic factor in East Africa to be kept out of the most central areas of national life in Uganda. In a sense, then, Kiswahili continued to play an integrative role in the Ugandan army while gaining converts in the society at large.

The collapse of Idi Amin's regime did not bring an end to the association of Kiswahili with the Ugandan militariat. What did happen was the transformation of the military equation precipitated in part by the return of Milton Obote to power and the subsequent resistance against his regime by forces of Yoweri Museveni. Both Amin and Obote belonged to the Nilotic ethnic groups of northern Uganda, and the Ugandan armed forces had, until then, been predominantly Nilotic. The rise of Museveni's National Resistance Army (NRA) in militant opposition against the Obote (II) government quickly came to assume a macro-ethnic dimension. As the NRA consolidated its base in the Bantu-speaking south, Obote's army increased the proportion of its recruits from the predominantly Nilotic north. For a while, then, a predominantly Bantu army was pitted in a bloody confrontation with a predominantly Nilotic army.

But, precisely because both the Bantu-speaking and Nilotic-speaking regions of Uganda are ethnically heterogenous, Kiswahili continued to serve as a medium of inter-ethnic communication in both armies. In the barracks of Obote's military and in the liberated zones of the NRA Kiswahili continued to facilitate the expansion of the circle of social interaction. It was in tribute to this "detribalizing" and integrative role of Kiswahili in the military that the language was declared the official language of the army after the NRA came to power in 1986.

The potential danger of Kiswahili being rejected by Ugandans due to its association with Amin's tyranny, was now counter-balanced by more positive prospects as a result of the NRA's liberation efforts. As the editor of Uganda's *Weekly Topic* (of October 1, 1986) put it, "Faced with a practical problem of communication and unity while in the bush, the NRA was bailed out by Swahili." The association of Kiswahili with the tradition of post-colonial liberation in Uganda's military history, therefore, may increase its potential contribution towards various aspects of the process of "detribalization".

In the Democratic Republic of Congo (DRC), or what was hitherto

Zaire, though Kiswahili has long been a major player in inter-ethnic communication in the eastern part of the country, its role in the military was limited to the early years of Belgian colonialism. What was then the Congo Free State initially relied heavily on mercenaries from various parts of Africa to maintain its armed forces. In this way, trans-national *lingua francas*, like Kiswahili and Hausa, came to serve as important vehicles of inter-ethnic interaction that aided in expanding the social horizons of the African army recruits. Kiswahili was, in fact, used as a language of instruction for the troops in Katanga and the Oriental Province until World War I. When the "Force Publique," as the army was then called, began to recruit within the colonial territory, Kiswahili was eliminated in the armed forces in favor of Lingala.

As for Kiswahili within the armed forces of Kenya and Tanzania, the record has been relatively integrative without the massive ethnic convulsions in Uganda. The army, the police, and the para-military forces in Kenya have all utilized Kiswahili as the primary language of command. So, of course, have the security forces of Tanzania including the National Service which recruits (for limited periods) young people from all parts of the country.

Throughout the colonial period recruitment for the armed forces drew mainly from that large section of the African population that had little or no educational training, and whose linguistic competence was limited to non-European languages. Kiswahili became virtually the only possible medium of inter-ethnic communication for this population. Senior positions in the armed forces were almost invariably held by Europeans themselves who, nonetheless, preferred to communicate with their African subordinates in Kiswahili. Recruits into colonial armies often included Africans from neighboring states. For a while, therefore, Kiswahili in the armed forces of colonial East Africa facilitated not only inter-ethnic communication, sometimes across national boundaries, but also inter-racial communication. The army had thus served as a crucible within which the role of Kiswahili in expanding the social horizons of African officers had assumed a demographically trans-continental dimension.

Since independence, at least in Kenya and Uganda, there has been a decrease in the role of Kiswahili in inter-racial communication in the barracks and an increase in the use of English in inter-ethnic interaction. More and more high school and university graduates with a reasonable command of English are now joining the army. The "detribalizing" role of Kiswahili in the lower ranks is now being increasingly complemented by a similar role of the English language at the higher ranks of the armed forces. Kiswahili though continues to be the main language of social and professional interaction between these two military classes.

When, therefore, we are assessing the role of Kiswahili in broadening the social horizons of East Africans, we must include its different functions within the armed forces, as well as its role in those other areas we mentioned — religious conversion, race consciousness, national identity, urbanization, and as we shall soon explore more fully, class-formation. East Africans have come closer to doing justice to their potentialities as social beings and have enriched the network of their allegiances partly through the facilitating services of the Swahili language.

2. Kiswahili and Class-Formation

In the previous section we looked at change in terms of the loosening up of ancestral and parochial bonds under the influence of new cultural horizons. Let us now look at change in terms of a transition from the bonds of biological reproduction to new ties of economic production. The bonds of biology relate to mating and kinship, husbands and wives, parents and children, brothers and sisters. The ties of economic forces of production, on the other hand, relate to social and economic roles in the business of making a living.

Kinship itself can be either literal consanguinity, or social myth, or social metaphor. When kinship is literal consanguinity, we are referring to direct relationships of descent and lineage. This is clearly the case in a nuclear family, but is also often the case in an extended family, and even in a clan.

When kinship is a social myth we are referring to a presumed descent from common ancestry, often fervently believed in by the members of the group, but with less than adequate evidence of authenticity. Myths of origin among African "tribes", often claiming in part some kind of shared ancestors, are a case of kinship as a social myth.

Kinship as metaphor arises in situations where a large collectivity uses the symbolism of the family to enhance cohesion, in figurative terms, without claiming literal consanguinity or presuming it as a myth. Thus, when upon the death of Charles de Gaulle, it was announced in Paris that "today France is a widow", the metaphor of a great leader as the husband of his nation was being invoked.

Kinship as metaphor also occurs in such concepts as "Mother-country" or "Fatherland" and "Founding Fathers". Theories of race in history have also often included kinship either as a myth or as metaphor converting millions of members of a particular "race" into some kind of family *writ large*.

The expansion of social horizons need not entail the disappearance of family allegiance, nor the ties of the clan, the bonds of ethnicity, the consciousness of racial affinity, nor the supreme metaphor of "patriotism". But the process probably has to include some important moderation of those allegiances by the class factor in society. Ethnicity in Africa is still mainly rooted in the forces of biological reproduction; class, on the other hand, is part of the new forces of economic production. Africa is gradually moving from a culture of the primacy of kinship to a culture of the primacy of class. The question then arises, what role has Kiswahili played in that transition in Eastern Africa?

In the hands of the Arabs of the coastal city states in Eastern Africa, especially from the eighteenth century onwards, Kiswahili was an aristocratic language, rich in religious imagery and linguistic Arabisms, rich in poetry and rhetoric. In places like Lamu, Pate, Kismayu, and Pemba, the highly Arabized variety of the language was becoming a medium of elegance, eloquence, and polite culture. There was also a simplified Kiswahili for discourse with the *Washenzi* or barbarians. The Waswahili of one century or two centuries ago sometimes manifested tendencies similar to those associated with the Chinese to the present day — that those who were outside their own culture were basically barbarians! For quite a while then, the city states of the coast of Eastern Africa could indulge themselves in this form of cultural arrogance, enriching their own version of Kiswahili into a medium of high culture, but not yet establishing with other coastal communities relationships of equity or equality except with those who were converted to Islam or with those with whom the Waswahili intermarried.

Late in the nineteenth century came the Germans and established their own rule in parts of East Africa. If the aristocrats of Pate, Lamu, Zanzibar, and Tanga had used Kiswahili in part as the language of high culture in contrast to the ways of the *Washenzi*, the Germans decided to make Kiswahili a buffer language between their own culture and the African ethnic groups over whom they exercised dominion. Unlike the French, the Germans did not want their colonial subjects to be proficient in the ruling language. To share a language with one's menial subject was to narrow the social distance between him and the master. Africans presuming to speak German were often regarded as linguistic upstarts. Authority was best maintained by stressing both status and cultural distance. Kiswahili provided the Germans with the buffer solution. Why not spread Kiswahili among the natives of different ethnic groups to enable them to communicate with each other and, more importantly, to receive orders from above in a shared intermediate language? Kiswahili became a *medium* in more than one sense — in the sense that it was a means of mediation and communication between people, but also in the sense of being a middle language ranked between the language of the rulers above and the "tribal vernaculars" below.

Although France did attempt to compete for parts of Eastern Africa in the nineteenth century, it made virtually no progress in those parts of the sub-region where Kiswahili was spoken. French attitudes to social distance were fundamentally different from those of the Germans. Far from seeking to prevent their colonial subjects from becoming proficient in French, France actually promoted the policy of assimilation, however inconsistently. While the cultural arrogance of the Germans asserted that no native was good enough to speak German, French cultural arrogance took the form of the assertion that no native was good enough *until* he spoke French.

The French language did indeed spread in parts of the Swahili world — especially in DRC, Rwanda, and Burundi. But the French language arrived in these societies through the Belgians rather than the French. And this itself had important linguistic implications.

The Belgians at home in Europe form a nation with two languages — Flemish and French. In their colony, the Belgian Congo, it was for a while touch and go whether it would be Flemish or French that would finally triumph. Of the two European languages French was both feared and admired by the Flemish Belgians resident in the Congo. Since Flemish culture was partly Germanic, it shared some of the German conceptions of linguistic distance between the subject and the ruler. Flemish-speaking Belgians were not keen to transmit their language to the Congolese. French in parts of the Belgian Congo was at times itself a buffer language sandwiched between Flemish above and African languages below. The spread of French in DRC has been almost by default — benefitting from the narrow chauvinism of the Germanic legacy with its distrust of any attempt to narrow the linguistic distance between the master and the subject. The schools were controlled by Flemish Belgians.

But Kiswahili was also spreading in Eastern and Southern Congo. As independence approached, a quarter of the population of DRC could speak Kiswahili at some level or another. Thirty years later the proportion is nearer to a third of the population of DRC.

The three most important African languages of the country have become Lingala, Kikongo, and Kiswahili. Kiswahili was the most wide-spread language in the economically rich parts of DRC, especially Shaba Province (formerly Katanga).

Indeed, at the time of independence, it seemed that the three major African languages each rested on a different kind of power. The fortunes of Kiswahili in the country seemed to rest on the economic richness of the provinces where it was spoken. The fortunes of Kikongo rested on the political centrality of the Bakongo and their apparent access to political power. The people had even contributed their own name to the country as a whole.

As for the fortunes of Lingala, they were tied in part to the potentialities of military power in DRC. The armed forces in the country had been recruited disproportionately from Lingala-speaking regions. The initial balance in favor of Lingala-speakers during the era of the Belgians has been consolidated since independence.

Soon after independence the question hanging over the fortunes of the three African languages was whether it would be economic power (in Katanga) or the legacy of political power among the Bakongo, or the new military power among Lingala-speakers, that would finally prevail.

The fortunes of Kiswahili were for a while linked to the fortunes of Moise Tshombe, the Katangan leader who attempted to pull out the mineral-rich province from the Congo and form a separate country. If he had succeeded, Kiswahili would have continued to prosper within Katanga, but its impact on other areas of the former Belgian Congo would have been drastically reduced. A separate Katanga could not linguistically enrich central DRC, let alone northern DRC. The failure of Tshombe's bid to separate Katanga from DRC helped to ensure that Kiswahili would remain a major language of DRC as a whole.

But that very failure of Katanga's secession was part of the evidence that economic power alone could not prevail over military power. The wealthy part of the country was forced to remain part of the country.

In the initial years of independence, the Bakongo seemed to be still a critical element in the political equation under President Kasavubu. But the final triumph of General Mobutu helped to demonstrate that in African conditions, perhaps more than in Chinese, power resided in the barrel of the gun (Lingala) rather than in the political platform (Kikongo) or the copper mines (Kiswahili).

In the mid 1970s President Mobutu Sese Seko even began to consider the possibility of pushing Lingala to the front as the national language of DRC (then Zaire). Its importance was enhanced by its aesthetic dynamism as a language of song. Lingala acquired an influence well beyond the borders of DRC — men and women were dancing to it in the night clubs of Nairobi, the private parties of Kampala, the secret lounges of Dar es Salaam, and the streets of Lagos. In fact, one of the most important influences exerted by DRC on other parts of Africa has been through Lingala music and song. A strange combination of military power and sheer musical rhythm has given Lingala its credentials in its competition with Kikongo and Kiswahili. The three languages remain poised for cultural competition within the grand arena of turbulent DRC.

If the Germans believed that no native was good enough to speak German, and the French believed that no native was good enough unless he or she spoke French, the British with their usual genius for muddling through fluctuated between the two solutions. Like the Germans, the British invested a good deal of effort in the promotion of Kiswahili; but, unlike the Germans and more like the French, they also invested a good deal of effort in promoting their own European language. Many British people in the colonies discouraged their domestic workers from addressing them in English however fluent the workers might be, and insisted on speaking to the workers in their own native language however incompetent the British speakers might be. On the other hand, British educational policy-makers prepared the ground for the emergence of the *Afro-Saxons*, Africans steeped in English culture and language.

In Eastern Africa the British agonized for a while about the role of Kiswahili. Should it be suppressed and discouraged as a rival to the English language? Or should it be promoted as something superior to "tribal vernaculars"? We shall discuss in subsequent chapters the outcome of these dilemmas.

But stratification in Eastern Africa was not merely between the ruling imperial power and the subject peoples, but also in terms of new social classes. In both Kenya and Tanzania, Kiswahili played a significant role in the history of proletarianization, the emergence of modern industrial or urban working classes. Kiswahili facilitated labor migration in Eastern Africa and, as we indicated, very often became the primary language of the workplace and the marketplace.

In Kenya the most important Kiswahili-speaking city was for a long time Mombasa. The city was also virtually the birthplace of militant collective-bargaining in Kenya and the utilization of strike-action.

A number of factors went towards making Mombasa a breeding-ground for organized labor agitation and relatively effective collective-bargaining. One factor concerned the role of Mombasa as East Africa's most important port. Like dockworkers in a number of countries elsewhere, including many other parts of Africa, dockworkers in Mombasa became "leaders in labor organizing and protest".

The first significant urban strike took place in July 1934 among the dockworkers in Mombasa. Sharon Stichter has compared Mombasa with Nairobi from the point of view of industrial action during the colonial period. Mombasa experienced four general strikes in 1939, 1947, 1955, and 1957. Nairobi, on the other hand, experienced only one general strike in 1950 — and even this had more direct political causes (Sharon Stichter, 1975:33).

The ethnic mixture of the labor force in Mombasa, at least in the colonial period, was more diverse. While very few coastal people trekked into the interior of Kenya to look for jobs in those years, many people from "up-country" descended on the coast for employment. This affected Kiswahili in two ways. The ethnic mosaic in Mombasa against the background of Swahili culture made the language more necessary than ever in this hive of labor agitation and class-consciousness. Secondly, many of the workers from "up-country" had come from so far that they tended to invest considerable time in their jobs in Mombasa, if they had them, and thus, had time to improve or even enrich their Kiswahili. By contrast, workers in the capital city of Nairobi were disproportionately short-term employees who worked for wages for a limited period and then went back to the land in the nearby "tribal reservations". As Stichter put it:

> Over half of Mombasa's workforce were Kikuyu, Luo, Baluhya, Kamba and other long-range migrants from up-country. The time, effort, and money that had to be invested in transportation made long-distance migrants more dependent than short-distance ones on the wages they could make, and typically, they stayed in employment for longer lengths of time. In Nairobi, on the other hand, places of employment were scattered throughout the city. The bulk of the workforce were short-term Kikuyu, Embu, and Meru migrants from the nearby reserves. (1975:31)

The Nairobi pattern in those colonial days was in part a continuation of the legacy of target workers— people who looked for jobs with relatively short-term specific goals in mind (like earning enough to buy a bicycle) and then returning to the reserves or the villages to resume their role as cultivators. From the point of view of linguistic stability, target workers, by definition, were not in a multi-language context long enough to enrich and stabilize their command over the *lingua franca*.

In contrast, the Luo and Kamba that migrated all the way to Mombasa were forced by geographical distance to stay longer in their role as wage-earners (as distinct from their alternative role as independent cultivators at home). And since Mombasa was in any case part of the heartland of Kiswahili in Kenya, these questions of labor longevity intermingled with issues of linguistic stability and acculturation.

In Dar es Salaam, across the border, a similar interaction between proletarianization and Swahilization was taking place. Dar es Salaam, like Mombasa, was of course a port; and also like Mombasa, it was part of the heartland of Swahili culture. And thirdly, like Mombasa, Dar es Salaam was a magnet attracting workers from long distances, holding them for long periods, and Swahilizing them in the process. Once again, the interplay between working conditions in a port and diversified ethnicity both sharpened class-consciousness and necessitated an effective *lingua franca*. Labor unrest, following World War II, culminated in the Tanzanian strike of 1947. In the words of John Iliffe:

> The strike was the high point in the dockers' history. They initiated it. They won impressive gains both in their working conditions and in their organization and confidence. Briefly, they led the most wide-spread protest in Tanzanian history between the end of the Maji Maji rising and the formation of Tanu... Meanwhile, the strike had begun to spread up-country along the railway line. Railway workers in Morogoro, Dodoma, and Tabora walked out... The next day they were joined by their colleagues at Kilosa and by sisal workers at Morogoro ...

> The astonishing success of the seething discontent it demonstrated, undoubtedly influenced...wage increases variously estimated at 40-50 percent of existing pay,...finally pushing the dockers' wages well above the price increases since 1939... The 1947 award made the dockers a priviledged group among Tanzanian workers, the best paid, most formidable labor force in the country. It was won by the first real exercise of African power in Tanzania since the end of Maji Maji—an exhilarating and enlightening experience for those who participated. (1975:62-65)

Once again urbanization, proletarianization, and Swahilization converged—giving Kiswahili one more role in the emerging process of class-formation in East Africa.

In Uganda also, Kiswahili had its proletarianizing role. This took two major forms. One concerned the immigration of workers from neighboring countries, especially from Kenya. Trade unionism in Uganda was partly the product of labor migration from Kenya. Luo workers, especially, organized themselves and sought to involve Ugandan workers in the new techniques of collective-bargaining and economic leverage. The *lingua franca* between the immigrants and the Ugandan workers was more often Kiswahili than Luganda.

The other role that Kiswahili played concerned migrant labor from northern Uganda into the city of Kampala and the industrial center in Jinja. Again, on balance, northern Ugandans and Kenyan workers operating in Ugandan cities utilized Kiswahili as the major medium of the workplace and the marketplace. Indeed the spread of Kiswahili in Uganda was due much more to migrant workers than to priests and school teachers.

3. Kiswahili and Political Participation

The third aspect of our concern with the process of change is the growing involvement of the people in public affairs and policy-making at different levels. The precise mode of mass involvement may vary from country to country, from ideology to ideology. Liberal political systems may put an emphasis on participation in the periodic elections of parliamentarians or their legislative equivalents, as well as elections of executive and sometimes judicial officials. Socialist systems put greater stress on participation in party cells, and elections concerned with party officials and auxiliaries. But regardless of ideology, most political systems strive toward expanding popular participation in some sense.

But where does Kiswahili come into this? We must first remind ourselves that the first prominent phase of liberalism in Eastern Africa during the twentieth century might well have been the last ten years of colonial rule. This is particularly true of those countries of Eastern Africa that were once ruled by Great Britain. In the last ten years of colonial power African nationalists could agitate for self-government and independence, often with the support of important members of parliament in London. These leaders were at times arrested and even imprisoned, but on the whole, there was a level of openness and frank agitation in the last decade of colonial rule which stood out in marked contrast to previous decades and certainly in marked contrast to more recent times in independent Africa.

Kiswahili, as it evolved into the primary language of politics in Tanzania and Kenya especially, was part of the process through which the masses in those countries became increasingly involved in national agitation for African rights. A national political constituency emerged partly because a national *lingua franca* was operating in those societies.

In Kenya, the Mau Mau emergency (1952-1960) created additional complications. The Mau Mau insurrection against the

British was primarily by the Kikuyu to some extent aided by the sister communities of the Embu and the Meru and, to a lesser extent, by other Kenyan communities. The British colonial rulers decided to insulate the Kikuyu from the mainstream of the political process in the course of the emergency as a way of depoliticizing them. This relative insulation of the Kikuyu in the 1950s also partially arrested their Swahilization. There was a temporary retreat to bonds of ethnicity under the pressure of counter-insurgency techniques inaugurated by the British. Kikuyu isolation deepened Kikuyu identity, lessened Kikuyu involvement in national affairs, and slowed down the process of Kikuyu Swahilization.

On the other hand, the Mau Mau emergency increased Luo's visibility in national politics. And since trade unionism in Kenya was substantially Luo-led, the Mau Mau emergency created a fusion between proletarian economic movements in Kenya on the one side, and nationalistic political movements on the other. Class-consciousness and the new race-consciousness were in alliance, partly because leadership in both movements was in part in the hands of the same people.

The most illustrious figure to emerge in this dialectic between proletarianism and African nationalism was the late Tom Mboya. He was a trade union leader who rose to become Kenya's most eloquent political spokesperson in the last decade of British rule. Mboya was an orator both in English and in Kiswahili. Internationally, his impressive command of the English language was a major factor behind his impact on liberal opinion in the United Kingdom and the United States. But domestically in Kenya, it was his command of Kiswahili which gave him access to transethnic mass opinion and created for him an impressive national constituency. Luo's political leadership in the 1950s prepared the ground for Kikuyu political ascent in the 1960s.

The Mau Mau emergency in Kenya came to an end officially in 1960. A year later, Jomo Kenyatta was released. In 1963, the country became independent and Kiswahili once again was called upon to play a role in national politics. Kenyatta's own credentials as a national leader were greatly enhanced by his impressive command of Kiswahili.

And yet in terms of language policy, the first decade of Kenya's independence witnessed very little change from the old British pattern. The English language continued to be the primary official language except perhaps in broadcasting. The Voice of Kenya led the way in popularizing the image that Kiswahili was the national language while English was the official language.

It was not until 1974, more than ten years after independence, that Kenyatta took a major step in changing the status of Kiswahili. He ordered that debates in parliament from then on be conducted exclusively in Kiswahili. As we shall indicate later, the move perhaps deserved more careful planning than it had received. There was even a case for a while of having a bilingual legislature with simultaneous translation. But Mzee Kenyatta ordered instant Kiswahili in the *Bunge* (parliament).

In fairness to Kenyatta, however, his move was perhaps prompted by what appeared like covert opposition against his efforts to encourage the gradual Swahilization of his government. In fact, as early as 1964, Kenyatta demonstrated his desire to Swahilize the parliament by addressing it in Kiswahili. After reading his prepared English speech, Kenyatta stated:

> Bwana spika, mimi nataka kusema maneno kidogo kwa Kiswahili kwa sababu mimi natumaini kwamba wakati si mrefu katika nyumba hii yetu tutaweza kuzungumza Kiswahili ambacho ni lugha yetu. Sasa tukiwa tuna uhuru wetu kamili itakuwa tunajitia katika utumwa wa lugha za kigeni katika mashauri yetu yote, na kwa hiyo ndugu zanguni, mimi nilitaka kusema hivyo maana kila kitu kina mwanzo wake. (Republic of Kenya, 1965: Column 8)

Mr. Speaker, I would like to say a few words in Kiswahili as it is my expectation that in the near future in this August house we shall be able to conduct our discussions in Kiswahili which is our language. Now that we have our complete independence, we would be submitting to foreign language enslavement [if we continue to use English] in all our deliberations;and so, comrades, that is all that I wanted to say, because everything has its beginning.

The matter came up again in parliament in 1969 in the form of a motion moved by Kamwithi Munyi, the member of parliament for Embu East. The motion was formulated as follows:

That in view of the fact that His Excellency the President, Mzee Jomo Kenyatta, has always been appealing and encouraging the people of Kenya to be proud of their own culture and their traditional richness, this House calls upon the Government to make immediate plans to declare Swahili as an official language which will be used not only in offices, but, subject to suitable amendment of the Constitution of Kenya, our Parliament as well. (Republic of Kenya, 1969: Columns 2509-10)

After some extensive debate, however, the motion was substantially amended to read:

That in view of the fact that His Excellency the President, Mzee Jomo Kenyatta, has always been appealing and encouraging the people of Kenya to be proud of their own culture and their traditional richness, this House calls upon the Government as soon as practicable to declare Swahili along with English as an official language which

> will be used not only in offices, but, subject to suitable
> amendment of the Constitution of Kenya, in our Parliament
> as well. (Republic of Kenya, 1969: Column 2771)

Though this amended motion was finally passed, little came out of it in
terms of practical steps toward its implementation.

Sensing the opposition in the House of Representatives,
Kenyatta decided to use another platform, that of the ruling party, the
Kenya African National Union (KANU), in its advocacy of Kiswahili
as the official language of the country. In its meeting of the National
Governing Council of April 1970, KANU passed a resolution that
set 1974 as the year in which Kiswahili would be fully adopted as the
official language of the country following a three-phase plan of action
(*The East African Standard*, April 7, 1970). It was when nothing had
been done to implement this resolution by the target year of 1974 that
Kenyatta made the dramatic move to declare Kiswahili as the sole language
of parliament.

As it turned out, the decision was much less disruptive than
some might have feared. It is true that some members of parliament
who had previously commanded high prestige as orators in the English
language were now cut down to size when performing in Kiswahili.
On the other hand, other speakers that had previously been mediocre
when using the English language in parliament now rose rapidly into
major artists in rhetoric and eloquence in Kiswahili. Some
restratification occurred in parliament in terms of oratorical ranking
as a result of the change in the medium of parliamentary discourse.

This restratification was perhaps fair and understandable. But
there were also anomalies arising out of the peremptory way in which
Kenyatta ordered the change from English to Kiswahili in parliament.
After some eight months of experimentation with Kiswahili as the
only language of parliament, some members moved that since the
official language of the executive wing of the government and the

judiciary was still English, all legislation, whether proposed or actual, should appear in the English language. The bill proposing such a change was finally adopted, and the Constitution was accordingly amended in February 1975. Kiswahili thus remained the language of debate in the legislature, but the legislation itself now came before parliament written in the English language. Documents written in English were thus made subject to debate in Kiswahili. This at times had complications of its own, from phrase to phrase, clause to clause.

Another anomaly concerned the dichotomy between the language of the constitution and the language of politics of Kenya. As we have indicated, the language of practical politics nationally had become overwhelmingly Kiswahili. From speeches at mass gatherings to oration in parliament, Kiswahili had become the supreme language of political communication in the country.

And yet, the official version of the constitution as fundamental law is in the English language. A constitutional point which comes before the courts has to be resolved by interpreting phrases and words in the English version. What a particular clause of the constitution means can be resolved by a judge who understands very little Kiswahili. Indeed, the judicial system of Kenya is based on the assumption that many of the most senior judges might be completely illiterate in Kiswahili. And thus, the anomaly persists — the supreme language of politics in Kenya is not the language of the supreme law of the country.

Yet another paradox in the Kenyan situation concerns the language requirement for candidates standing for parliamentary election. The original requirement at the time of independence was competence in the English language. In 1974, as we indicated, Kiswahili became the language of debate in parliament. Legislators whose credentials at election time were based partly on competence in English were now called upon, virtually without warning, to perform in Kiswahili. Moreover, no action was taken to change the linguistic qualifications demanded of candidates in the elections which were to follow. Candidates still had to demonstrate competence in the English language, and did not have to demonstrate competence in Kiswahili, in spite of the fact that both languages were needed for effective parliamentary business. Each member of parliament needed a capacity to read English, but not necessarily to speak it; and a capacity to speak Kiswahili, but not necessarily to read it. Much of the legislation continued to arise before parliamentarians written in the English language, while the debate which followed was conducted in Kiswahili.

Partly because both English and Kiswahili continued to be necessary qualifications in the Kenyan parliament, Mzee Kenyatta's decision to make Kiswahili the medium of parliamentary debate had less effect on broadening political participation than it might have had. If linguistic qualifications for membership of the Kenyan parliament had been based more purely on competence in Kiswahili, this would immediately have broadened the number of people eligible to be candidates for parliament. This follows from the simple statistics that the number of Kenyans competent in Kiswahili is much higher than the number of those who are competent in the English language.[2] The full Swahilization of the Kenyan legislative process would, therefore, have considerably broadened the general area of elite-recruitment (i.e., recruitment of additional people into the political establishment of the country).

The role of Kiswahili in Kenya's parliament that was established by Jomo Kenyatta was further weakened barely a year after Daniel Arap Moi came to power. Hitherto, Kiswahili was the sole medium of parliamentary debate. In 1979, however, the constitution was amended to allow oral debate in the National Assembly to be conducted in either Kiswahili or English. Standing orders of the assembly, however, provided that a question posed in Kiswahili could not be answered in English, and vice-versa.[3] A further amendment of the constitution required that a parliamentary candidate will have to prove at the date of nomination that he or she has a high enough proficiency in both written and spoken Kiswahili and English to take an active part in the proceedings of the National Assembly. This is the substance of Article 34(c) of the Constitution of Kenya. But precisely because subsequent changes continued to require competence in both Kiswahili and English, political participation in the parliament could not be expanded enough to include those who were not proficient in English.

Across the border in Tanzania, the parliament, or *Bunge*, was indeed Swahilized almost all the way. As we shall indicate in later chapters, the Swahilization of the political process in Tanzania has resulted in greater participation. Kiswahili has made it possible to mobilize more people into the political and decision-making processes of the country. The fact that the ruling party of Tanzania has been more active than the ruling party in Kenya has helped to enrich Tanzanian Kiswahili in terms of political vocabulary and metaphor. A dynamic political system often enriches the language in which it conducts its business.

The situation in Uganda has been different. Until the soldiers first captured power in January 1971, Kiswahili was more a language of economic than political participation. As we have indicated, and as we shall further elaborate subsequently, Kiswahili helped the expansion of the modern wage sector of the economy and facilitated the emergence of a modern working class. But in practical politics the language was hardly utilized in national politics in the years between independence in 1962 and the military takeover in 1971.

Almost by definition, Amin's military takeover was a reduction of political participation by the masses. Parliament and political parties were abolished, and even student politics gradually ground to a standstill.

And yet, paradoxically, this "shrinking of the political arena" (Nelson Kasfir, 1976) in Uganda was accompanied by an expansion of the use of Kiswahili in national life. Radio and television were ordered to use Kiswahili for the first time as one of their languages; the new president, Idi Amin, used Kiswahili much more often in his speeches than his predecessor had ever done; and the government formally conferred upon the language the status of a national language.

The soldiers meanwhile, precisely by being in power, increased the use of Kiswahili in their own contacts with the general public. Partly because of the political considerations of communication with the armed forces, and partly because the prestige of Luganda had declined among non-Baganda, more and more people were learning Kiswahili. The paradox therefore persisted — the arena of political activity had shrunk in Uganda and the arena of Kiswahili had expanded.

But the return to civilian politics in the 1980s, while expanding the arena of popular participation, reduced Kiswahili's role in the national political life of the country. The restriction of the military to the barracks also reduced Kiswahili's contact with the society at large. The victory of Yoweri Museveni's National Resistance Army (NRA) against the government of Milton Obote in 1986, however, gave Kiswahili a new impetus in Uganda's national life. The extent to which this will broaden political participation in the country, however, is a matter that is still unfolding in spite of the fact that the latest (1996) Constitution of Uganda continues to be silent about the place of Kiswahili in the national life of the country. Museveni himself is probably the most fluent president in the Kiswahili language that Uganda has ever produced. But he has so far shown little inclination to apply his Kiswahili skills in political mobilization in Uganda.

In the meantime, much of Africa is in an important transition towards a more liberal political order. The relentless resolve of the African peoples themselves and the dramatic changes in global politics have led to an unprecedented widening of political space. All these changes have introduced a dynamism in the politics of the respective Eastern African countries that is likely to expand the political horizons of Kiswahili. Growing political liberalism may ultimately have the effect of enhancing Kiswahili's potential as an instrument of mass political participation in Eastern Africa.

4. Kiswahili and Secularization

The fourth aspect of change which concerns us in this book relates to the declining significance of religion, both as an explanation of natural phenomena and as a basis of social behavior. In this regard, religion sometimes plays a dialectical role in the process. In East Africa, as indicated, universalistic religions like Christianity and Islam facilitated change by broadening the social horizons of people from various ethnic groups and by diversifying their network of allegiances and affinities. But that aspect of change which seeks to do justice to the present stage of human knowledge and to the innovative potential of human beings can be thwarted by Christianity and Islam as effectively as by ethnic religions. These universalistic religions widened the horizons of East Africans by enabling them to know more about the outside world and to develop social links with fellow Christians or fellow Muslims which sometimes transcended ethnic or racial links. But in terms of explaining natural phenomena through supernatural intervention, the universalistic religions were sometimes as dogmatic as the ethnic religions they sought to replace.

Kiswahili began as basically an Islamic language. This was due to a number of factors. One concerned the definition of the *Waswahili*, the Swahili people (singular: *Mswahili*). A debate has sometimes occurred as to whether accepting or professing Islam is a defining characteristic of an *Mswahili*, or whether it is merely an accompanying characteristic. If it is a defining characteristic, then presumably nobody continues to be an *Mswahili* upon being converted to, say, Christianity; but, if Islam is merely an accompanying characteristic of the *Waswahili*, we are discussing a correlation rather than a definition. We are suggesting that the great majority, if not all the *Waswahili*, happen to be Muslims — just as they happen to have been born in Eastern Africa. But the son of a Swahili family who is born in Nigeria and then returns to East Africa as a baby with Kiswahili becoming his mother-tongue, would still be a *Mswahili* in spite of being born outside Swahililand. Similarly, a *Mswahili* Christian or a non-believer would not cease to be a *Mswahili* because of that. Islam thus becomes an attribute that *usually* accompanies the *Waswahili*, but it is not part of their definition. It is more defensible to assert that the *Waswahili* are those to whom Kiswahili is the mother-tongue and whose culture has been influenced significantly by Islam.

Islam as a cultural influence is of course different from Islam as a religion embraced in its entirety. Many Lebanese Christians, especially among the poor, have been considerably influenced by Islam while still remaining Christian. Similarly, there are many Moroccan Jews whose culture has been influenced by Islam while remaining very Jewish in belief, ritual, and dogma. We would, therefore, suggest that at the very minimum, the definition of the *Waswahili* requires that we include an Islamic influence upon their culture, as well as the fact that they are people to whom Kiswahili is the mother-tongue.[4]

Of course, the great majority of those who speak the Swahili language are not themselves *Waswahili* — just as the great majority of those who speak the English language are not themselves English. Native speakers of Kiswahili are outnumbered by non-native speakers by a ratio of more than thirty to one.[5] And since Kiswahili is still expanding in East Africa, the proportion of native speakers of the language will for a while become even smaller. Then there will come a time when future generations of those who are today non-native speakers will themselves be new native speakers. The chances are that some of the ethnic languages of East Africa will in time "die out" and be replaced by Kiswahili. This would take a number of generations, but it seems to be one inevitable consequence of the success of a major *lingua franca*. Whether by that time influence by Islamic culture will still be a relevant aspect of the definition of Waswahili is something which only the future can fully reveal. All we know for the time being is that the Islamic factor has been of crucial definitional importance among the native speakers of the language so far.

Another element which has established links between Kiswahili and Islam is the influence of the Arabic language upon Kiswahili. Some estimates would put words of Arabic derivation as constituting over twenty percent of Kiswahili's basic vocabulary. In many ways Arabic has been to Kiswahili what Latin has been to the English language — a source of a great variety of loan words.

But Arabic is the language of the Qur'an and is, therefore, very susceptible to Islamic imagery and connotation. This has helped enrich Kiswahili, alongside borrowings from Bantu and non-Bantu languages. The word for God in Kiswahili (*M'ngu* or *Mungu*) comes from Bantu, whereas the word for angels (*malaika*) comes from Arabic. The word for the heavens (*mbingu*) comes from Bantu, whereas the word for Earth, especially when used religiously (*Ardhi*) comes from Arabic. The word for a holy prophet (*mtume*) comes from Bantu, whereas the word for a devil in a religious sense (*shetani*) comes from Arabic. Curiously enough, the word for paradise and hell (*pepo* and *moto*) come from Bantu, whereas the word for the hereafter as a whole (*akhera* or *ahera*) comes from Arabic.

What about this world of the here and now? How do the two linguistic "parents" of Kiswahili — Bantu and Arabic — address themselves to the immediate world? By having a word from each language for the same thing. Thus, this world of ours is both *ulimwengu* (from Bantu) and *dunia* (from Arabic).

A wider range of illustrations could be added to these, showing an important interplay of meaning and symbolism between two universes of religious experience — the traditions of the Bantu and the legacy of Islam.

The third major linkage between Kiswahili and Islam emerges from an important literary accident of history — that a disproportionate number of the greatest classical poets of Kiswahili were either very religious themselves or very knowledgeable about Islam. These were the *Ulamaa* (the learned ones) of places like Lamu and the old Mvita (now part of Mombasa). A significant section of the early written literature of Kiswahili was certainly rich not only in Islamic imagery and allusion, but often also with Islamic theology and catechism.

Because so much of the literary dynamism and creativity of classical Kiswahili was concerned with Islamic issues, the language has as a whole once again sensed the impact of the different nuances of Islamic metaphor and intellectual concern.

But the secularization of Kiswahili has been underway in the twentieth century for a variety of reasons. One factor concerns the major promoters of the language in the twentieth century. The Germans, the British, and more recently governments such as those led by Presidents Julius Nyerere, Ali Hassan Mwinyi and Benjamin Mkapa of Tanzania and Presidents Jomo Kenyatta and Daniel Arap Moi of Kenya, found Kiswahili important and useful — but primarily for goals which were secular in nature. Thus, the proportion of roles that Kiswahili was being called upon to play in society has been shifting more decisively in the direction of non-religious roles.

And even the gradual utilization of Kiswahili for spreading the Christian gospel had secularizing consequences. After all, European Christianity by the twentieth century was part of a civilization in which religion was in the retreat and modern science on the ascendant. The Christian missionaries who used Kiswahili for propagating faith also used their educational institutions for transmitting Western secular ideas, skills, and concepts. The subjects taught in ostensibly missionary schools included not merely Bible knowledge or religious studies, but also such subjects as physics, mathematics, and physical geography. The higher levels of the subjects were taught of course in English rather than in Kiswahili. What should be noted is that Christian missionaries were as much couriers of secular skills and values as they were champions of religious principles and beliefs. The increasing use of Kiswahili for communicating Western civilization helped to secularize the language.

But in the same manner, the language was also helping to secularize the rest of the society in which it operated. Social change on one side and linguistic change on the other constantly reinforced each other. On one side, the linguistic change is a mere reflection of the broader social mutations in a given cultural system. But on the other hand, language itself, precisely by being the basic medium of communication among human beings, helps to deepen the wider changes that a society undergoes.

The Islamic factor continues to be a major part of the vocabulary and imagery of the Swahili language. But as the language has spread well beyond the boundaries of the people that produced it, and as it has been called upon to serve the needs of other religious systems and other worldviews, the language is definitely undergoing a process of dis-Islamization. The proportion of Islam within it is declining and, at the same time, the language is helping to promote a civilization in Eastern Africa in which religion of any kind plays a less fundamental role than it did a century or so ago.

Kiswahili has continued to borrow words from Arabic, as well as increasingly from European languages. But the words obtained from Arabic are now more likely to be political than theological, secular than religious. Thus, words like *jamhuri* (republic), *katiba* (constitution), and *raisi* (president) are part of the new contributions from Arabic to political Kiswahili.

Once again, the multiple heritage of Kiswahili emerges from the juxtaposition of concepts drawn from different sources. While the word for president (*raisi*) is from Arabic, the word for parliament (*bunge*) comes from Bantu. While the word for politics (*siasa*) comes from Arabic, the word for economics (*uchumi*) comes from Bantu. The army (*jeshi*) is from Arabic; the police (*polisi*) is from English; the people (*watu*) is a word from Bantu; and the masses (*umma*) is a concept from Arabic. The interplay between African, Arabic and European languages reveals a basic receptivity in Kiswahili which is part of the secret of its impressive success. The receptivity once helped to clarify and illuminate religious experience. That receptivity has now been called upon to help in fostering a secular civilization.

5. Kiswahili in Science and Technology

But a higher stage of the process of secularization, especially since the nineteenth century, is the stage of the scientific method and of relatively advanced technological culture. How has this affected Kiswahili and its role in East African societies?

The first thing to note is that the most advanced form of science and technology in recent times has come to East Africa through European cultural and political penetration. As a result, the most appropriate languages for scientific and technological discourse *in the first instance* have been English (in Kenya, Tanzania, and Uganda), German primarily until the end of the first World War (in Tanganyika and Ruanda-Urundi) and French (through the activities of the Belgians in the old Belgian Congo or Zaire — now renamed the Democratic Republic of the Congo — and in Rwanda and Burundi).

Kiswahili as a language of administration benefitted from the policies of the European rulers; but Kiswahili, as a language of education, was permitted to remain relatively underdeveloped. The Germans, the British, and the Belgians called upon the language to serve some specific political ends and purposes, but in the educational system, Kiswahili was used only in the first few classes of formal schooling. It is true that the British nevertheless did more for African languages in their own colonies than the French did in theirs.

But in spite of the fact that the British record in taking African languages seriously in the educational system was much more impressive than the record of virtually any other European power, it fell far short of giving Kiswahili a chance to evolve and develop into a language of scientific discourse and analysis.

No language is inherently incapable of handling modern science and technology. In a paper entitled "Swahili in the Technical Age," Professor Mohamed Hyder, then a lecturer in zoology at the University College in Nairobi, posed the problem in quite stark terms. He asked whether it was possible to write a serious scientific paper in Kiswahili on the subject of "The Effect of Thyroid Stimulating Hormone on the Radio-Active Iodine Uptake in Beef Thryoid Tissue *In Vitro*." His answer was that if a serious attempt were made to develop a "technical limb" to Kiswahili, this was indeed possible. The title of the paper would, it was true, include terms like *thairodi, homoni, ayodini, redioaktivu,* and *in vitiro*. However, Dr. Hyder went on to assert that:

> There is no good reason why this development of a "technical
> limb"... of Swahili through the Swahilization of such terms
> should weigh heavily on our consciences. Examination of any
> technical or scientific journal in English, French, German,
> Russian, or Chinese shows clearly that such technical terms
> are really international in usage. Look up the word "thyroid"
> or "radio-active" in any of these languages and you would
> find that apart from the token digestive processes exerted on
> them, they are practically the same the world over. (1966:6)

In a *Presence Africaine* lecture delivered in November 1961, Pierre
Alexandre, the French linguist, linked this issue more specifically to
the scientific utility of the European classics:

> It is wrong to say that African languages are a barrier to
> the teaching of science and technical subjects. The
> syntactical structure of those known to me would not
> provide any major obstacle to the pursuit of logical
> reasoning. The absence of technical terminology in the
> vocabulary is all the more easy to remedy since, in fact,
> the international technical terminology is based on an
> artificial assembly of Greek and Latin roots. The Parisian
> who speaks of a "telegram" rather than "far-off writing"
> is expressing himself in Greek, in the same way as a Duala
> who speaks of "telefun." (1963:21)

Alexandre argued that he knows of no syntactical structure in African
languages familiar to him that would seriously inhibit their
development as languages of scientific discourse. One could go further
and point out that the Japanese language was developed as a language of
scientific discourse in spite of syntactical difficulties seemingly more acute

than might be encountered in Kiswahili. In the opinion of Inatomi Eijiro:

> ...Japanese [are] devoid of "self-consciousness"...as [evidenced by] the lack of clear distinction between the parts of speech in Japanese as contrasted with the European languages [in the latter, all sentences are composed of individual words] each independent of one another... In Japanese, on the contrary, there are some characters that can be clearly distinguished as forming independent "parts of speech" and there are also not a few that cannot be strictly separated from other words... A Japanese sentence is a composite whole and not an aggregate of individual words or phrases. (1967:234-5)

John Whitney Hall relates these difficulties to the educational process in Japan:

> Despite the remarkable success which the Japanese had in modernizing the language, the retention of the ideographs (Kanji) perpetuated a host of educational problems. Some observers have concluded that the complexity of the Japanese language has been a formidable barrier to early elementary education and has restricted the rapid and exact communication of ideas either within the culture or from outside it. The habits of rote learning required in mastering the characters, it is also claimed, have been carried over into other fields of learning and have tended to encourage uncritical acceptance of officially approved ideas and dogmas... (1965: 409)

Herman Kahn then refers to the general ambiguity of the Japanese language — "an emotionally rich ambiguity." He contrasts this with the relative concreteness and specificity of the English language: "Many Japanese have recognized this, and the Japanese Nobel Prize winning physicist Yukawa has stated several times that he personally finds it difficult to think scientifically and precisely in Japanese and much easier to do so in English" (1970: 56-57). Kahn also states that it is rather difficult for the Japanese to prepare original material in written form.

> It is, therefore, much easier to emphasize the spoken word and face-to-face exchanges in business and professional communication, leaving the written word more for artistic, literary, and emotional purposes. There is little activity in Japan that corresponds to the enormous interchange of correspondence in most American governmental or private offices — indeed, many Japanese secretaries do not take dictation. (1970: 57)

In spite of these considerable syntactic and cultural constraints, the Japanese nevertheless managed to convert the language into a major medium of technological discourse and study. On the basis of the characteristics attributed to Japanese, it would seem that its problems in coping with the vocabulary of Western-derived scientific discourse are greater than those which might be encountered if Kiswahili were subjected to the same process of elaboration. In other words, the structure of Kiswahili is closer to the structure of those European languages which carry the main complexities of modern science than Japanese was when it was challenged to undertake the demands of the new technological age.

It may be true, of course, that English is structurally better designed to accommodate the development of scientific terminologies than Kiswahili. Mohamed H. Abdulaziz (1989: 37-38) identifies two features which make English more suited than Kiswahili to the creation of scientific and technological vocabulary. First, the process of lexical compounding is achieved less easily in Kiswahili than in English. Facilities of compounding and a broader range of affixes provide English with an infinite possibility for forming nomenclature. Secondly, English is said to be a highly nominalizing language while Kiswahili tends towards a greater use of verbal constructions. This difference gives English an edge over Kiswahili precisely because much of the scientific and technological vocabulary belongs to the nominal category.

Nonetheless, over the centuries, Kiswahili has demonstrated a remarkable capacity to adopt linguistic items from languages that are as far apart as Germanic and Semitic. It has been able to Swahilize both simple and compound forms from the English language, and is in the process of expanding its own nominalizing potential. In short, Kiswahili has been flexible enough to respond creatively to the new linguistic challenge of the scientific age.

And yet today it is a socio-linguistic impossibility for East African scientists to assemble together and discuss their scientific problems primarily in an African language. The entire training of an African scientist, following the colonial experience, has been overwhelmingly in a European language. Thought, oral discussion, and writing in physics, chemistry, zoology, or related sciences have to be done in the European language in Eastern Africa. In Japan, on the other hand, in spite of the problems of syntax and culture, it is usual and not merely possible for scientists or engineers to assemble and conduct the bulk of their professional business in Japanese.

One of the major questions now confronting Kiswahili is whether the governments of East Africa will be prepared before long to invest their resources, time, and effort into making Kiswahili a language that can cope with scientific discourse. Of all the indigenous languages of Eastern Africa, Kiswahili is perhaps the best candidate for such an investment. Its history of adapting and integrating contributions from other languages, its capacity to be flexible in form, its distribution across several countries of Eastern Africa, touching in varying degrees and at different levels the lives of over fifty million people — all these factors have made Kiswahili large enough in scope and adjustable enough in structure to justify the effort to transform it into black Africa's first modern scientific language.

All this concerns the issue of whether to and how to bring Kiswahili itself to a level that can cope with the present state of technical and scientific knowledge. But what about the role of the language in "technicalizing" and "scientificating" the society as a whole?

Four forms of technology especially have to be borne in mind in this regard. One is the broad area of the technology of production, from the tractor on the farm to the factory in the city. Secondly, there are various activities ranging from nutrition to maternal and child health care, which constitute a technology of reproduction. Thirdly, there is the technology of destruction — military technology especially. Fourthly, there is the technology of communication, from the printed word to television and satellite transmission. What has been the role of Kiswahili in these four forms of technology?

In terms of technology in the countryside in cultivation and the organization of agriculture, the role of Kiswahili started off by being rather modest. After all, village communities usually interacted with each other in their own ethnic languages. A *lingua franca* is less of a necessity there than it is in large multi-ethnic situations in the towns.

But in recent times, Kiswahili has become more important in proportion to the increased use of extension officials and advisors going to different farms in different linguistic areas to advise on techniques of production and organization. Both in Tanzania and in Kenya the increased central planning of agriculture and the expanding use of technical advisors for farmers has begun to enhance the role of Kiswahili in rural counseling. Its use on radio programs in both countries on matters important to farmers is also an aspect of this role in rural production.

Secondly, the growth of cooperative movements for farmers has also contributed to the expanding use of Kiswahili outside the framework of the urban economy. There are times when cooperatives operate in the context of a single ethnic community in the main, but multi-ethnic cooperative efforts for farmers have grown in scale and importance since the 1950s in different parts of Eastern Africa. In those countries where Kiswahili was already playing a role in other spheres, the language has acquired additional roles in cooperative production and marketing.

Thirdly, there is the phenomenon of village consolidation both in Tanzania and Kenya. Again, this consolidation began by being mainly in areas of a single language or more than one related ethnic languages. In Tanzania, this later took the form of what were for a while called "ujamaa villages." But with the increased consolidation of both social services and joint production in such enlarged rural communities, Kiswahili began to find new targets for penetration. Scattered homesteads in isolated parts of Tanzania were, for a while, almost insulated from the processes of Swahilization in the rest of society. But when those single farming homesteads were more or less compelled to link together with other homesteads and be integrated into new communities, the Swahilization process then started.

Then there is the role of Kiswahili in the Democratic Republic of Congo and the extractive industries in former Katanga (now Shaba). A technical vocabulary in Kiswahili has emerged related to the business of mining. These extractive industries have attracted workers from different parts of the country, though for some years the fluctuations of world trade and the tensions of politics in places like Shaba led to a considerable exodus from the mining areas.

The technology of reproduction is concerned not only with sexual reproduction, but also with physical reproduction. The science of family planning, and the various birth control devices and methods and their implications, fall in the realm of the technology of sexual reproduction. The technology of physical reproduction, on the other hand, concentrates on keeping the body healthy and functioning and includes the science that deals with issues like maternal and child health care, nutritional value of various foods, preventing dehydration caused by diarrhea, precautionary measures against AIDS and other sexually-transmitted diseases, treatment and prevention of malaria, and so forth. Through the electronic media and community clinics Kiswahili has played an important role in disseminating aspects of the technology of reproduction, especially in Kenya and Tanzania.

With regard to the technology of destruction, we have already referred to the role of Kiswahili as the language of the armed forces in Tanzania, Kenya, and Uganda. And to the extent to which armies involve modern equipment and modern technology, which in turn need at least some minimal technical and technological skills, they have constituted part of the avenue of penetration into Africa for the western world's technology of destruction.

The vocabulary needed for handling some of these skills among soldiers in East Africa has helped to technicalize Kiswahili. The words are often borrowed from the English language, and are then Swahilized and used as part of the basic verbal equivalent in the armed forces in relation to repairing tanks, or reassembling the parts of a machine gun, or discussing the potentialities of a surface to surface missile. African armies then are almost certainly part of the development of Kiswahili as a language that can cope with the technical parts of the discourse of the twentieth century.

As for the role of Kiswahili in the technology of communication, this partly relates to its functions in wireless and electronic media. The language's most important role on television is played in Kenya rather than anywhere else. This is partly by default — until recently mainland Tanzania resisted the temptation to introduce television into the country. Socialist austerity on the mainland was partly linked to abstinence from television.

Zanzibar, on the other hand, not only has television, but has installed color television virtually before anybody else in Eastern Africa. Although Zanzibar was at least as "socialist" in rhetoric as the rest of Tanzania, the regime there did not regard this particular electronic medium as a danger to ideological purity. Kiswahili, therefore, found a role within that medium in this former Arab Sultanate.

Uganda, after Amin captured power, did not even pretend to be socialist. On the contrary, it turned its back on Milton Obote's experimentation with the "Move to the Left." But while losing socialism, the country gained Kiswahili. Within two weeks of Amin's capture of power, Kiswahili was used as one of the languages on radio and television in Uganda. Uganda has since also decided to move in the direction of Zanzibar with regard to the installation of color television.

Privatization in the electronic media in Kenya, however, seems to have given English greater prominence in television. The government owned Kenya Broadcasting Corporation (KBC) has operated a bilingual channel, screening programs in both Kiswahili and English. But the privately owned Kenya Television Network (KTN) and Stellavision have shown programs that are exclusively in the English language. At the moment, the chances that there will be a television station that can counter-balance KTN and Stellavision by featuring Kiswahili programs alone, seem rather remote.

The most important language for the radio in the region as a whole is Kiswahili. There are more programs in Kiswahili, listened to by more people, than there are programs addressed in any other African language in Eastern Africa. This is particularly so when we include broadcasting from foreign countries abroad in Kiswahili, beamed to Eastern Africa. Whenever any country in Europe, Asia, or the Americas is considering introducing a program in an African language for its overseas services, the first candidate usually is either Kiswahili for Eastern Africa or Hausa for West Africa. Of these two major indigenous languages, Kiswahili still has an edge in terms of the number of broadcasts from foreign countries utilizing it. These range from the Voice of America to All-India Radio, from Radio Moscow to the British Broadcasting Corporation, from Radio Peking to Cairo Radio.

Telephone operators in Tanzania and Kenya are invariably at least bilingual — in Kiswahili and English. As for the telephone conversations themselves, within Tanzania the majority of telephone calls before independence, such as there were, were conducted in the English language. Since independence, there is a heavy preponderance of telephone calls in Kiswahili. This is partly because of the shift in power and the emergence of new elites with access to telephones — elites who turned more and more to Kiswahili than to English in their discourse.

In Kenya, English still has an edge over Kiswahili as a language of telephone conversations, but English has probably been losing ground. A high proportion of telephone conversations in Kenya are also in ethnic languages. Because the presence of Indians in Kenya among the commercial elites is economically significant, many phone calls are also in Indian languages.

International telephone calls have a high preponderance of English language conversations. But telephone calls in Kiswahili between East Africa and the Arab world have increased quite dramatically since the 1960s. This is partly because more and more East Africans travel between Arab capitals and their own homes for business reasons, or on holiday, or for family reasons. This last factor gives us the second major reason why telephone calls in Kiswahili between East Africa and the Persian/Arabian Gulf have increased — the significant migration of native speakers of Kiswahili from Zanzibar, mainland Tanzania, and coastal Kenya in search of either economic opportunities or political refuge in the oil-rich Arab countries.

In previous centuries, it was the Arabs that penetrated Eastern Africa and helped to Arabize certain aspects of East African culture, especially the Swahili culture itself. But since the 1960s, the process of counterpenetration by the Waswahili into the culture of the Persian/ Arabian Gulf has gotten underway. This process has been aided by, firstly, the Zanzibar revolution of 1964 which resulted in the exodus of many Arabs and Waswahili in search of new homes and new opportunities in the Arab world and elsewhere. A second factor that facilitated the small, but significant, Swahili migration into the Gulf states is the very fact that those states were newly rich with oil and seemed economically promising to the adventurous from Eastern Africa.

The third factor concerns the relatively developed skills of the Waswahili, especially when combined with competence in the English language, as contrasted with the educational underdevelopment of the eastern Arabian states. Countries like Oman and the United Arab Emirates were in need not only of high-level skills, but even of basic clerical and functionary skills. By a strange destiny, the Waswahili from Zanzibar, on the one side, and Palestinians in exile, on the other, became major functionaries in different parts of the Persian/Arabian Gulf, filling the educational void that existed there before oil wealth necessitated the importation of new skills.

Kiswahili in the streets of Muscat, or even in the Foreign Office of Abu Dhabi or in the lounge of the Abu Dhabi Hilton, is no longer a surprising language to hear. The interplay between the technology of communication in the modern era, on one side, and the vicissitudes of politics and economics, on the other side, have resulted in the counterpenetration of Swahili culture into the old conservatism of Arab tradition in parts of southern and western Arabia.

As for Kiswahili and the printed word, it is already the most important indigenous publishing language in Eastern Africa as a whole. More school books are printed in Kiswahili than in any other African language, more novels, more pamphlets, and increasingly more academic books. Amharic in Ethiopia had previously been ahead in terms at least of educational books, but it has been overtaken by the new and vigorous publishing ventures in Kiswahili, especially in Tanzania and Kenya.

In written journalism too, Kiswahili is already the most important African language of news communication in Kenya and Tanzania.

Journalism in local languages in Uganda, however, is still dominated by Luganda. Newspapers in Kiswahili have often had an interterritorial market in the region (politics permitting from year to year). Tanzanians and Kenyans have read each other's Swahili newspapers whenever the politicians have permitted their importation. And Uganda continues to receive Kiswahili newspapers from Kenya on quite a regular basis.

What emerges from all this is that Kiswahili is indeed an active participant in the new technology of communication, and has enabled East Africa to utilize that technology more effectively than it would have been able to do had it lacked a *lingua franca*, like Kiswahili. As we indicated, Kiswahili has also been involved, for better or for worse, in the new technology of destruction — providing a medium for the armed forces, and acquiring a lexical competence in the analysis of military hardware. As for Kiswahili's role in the technology of production, it has ranged from agricultural counseling in Tanzania and Kenya to its role in the organization of mining in the Shaba Province of the Democratic Republic of the Congo, from the language's role in creating a modern working class to its function within agricultural cooperative movements in the region. And its involvement in educating East Africans about human health and sexuality has given Kiswahili a place in the technology of reproduction. Once again, Kiswahili finds itself linked in a variety of ways to the emerging culture of new technology, organization, and ultimately science itself.

6. Conclusion

We have attempted to explore in this essay the involvement of Kiswahili in the whole process of change in a direction which is compatible with the present stage of human knowledge and which does justice to the human person both as a social animal and as an innovative being.

Detribalization can be part of the process of expanding human capacities to socialize beyond kith and kin. Kiswahili's role in broadening the horizons of East Africans and enriching the complexities of their loyalties and allegiances must, therefore, be deemed relevant to this aspect of change.

But basic to some of these issues is the whole dialectic between the economic forces of production and the biological forces of reproduction. Eastern African societies have been experiencing a gradual transition from kith and kin loyalties (a product in part of biological consanguinity) to class loyalty (a product of the means of economic production). And Kiswahili has been a significant factor in the emergence of class consciousness in these societies.

Thirdly, we related change to expanding participation by the populace. We paid special attention to both economic participation by the people and to political participation at the national level. Kiswahili has facilitated economic participation in multi-ethnic workplaces, and has helped to promote political participation as a national language of persuasion, bargaining, and intrigue.

Finally, we addressed ourselves to the issue of change as something deeply linked to science and technology. Change in a direction which is compatible with the present stage of human knowledge makes science and technology important points of reference in measuring that direction. The European colonial powers helped in developing Kiswahili as a language of administration, but they fell far short of helping it to become a language of education and scientific analysis. Kiswahili is probably the most eligible single African language anywhere in black Africa for transformation into the first indigenous African language for modern science and technology. From the evidence of those who have studied Japanese, it would also seem that Kiswahili is more adaptable and more flexible for such a conversion than Japanese ever was. And yet, Japan has managed to become one of the major technological powers of all time, while conducting a substantial portion of its technological discourse in its own native language, duly technicalized.

It may not be very long before East Africans find the political will to invest in Kiswahili as a test case of whether technological advancement is ever possible in Africa without westernization. Must access to modern science and technology be exclusively through the alien gates of European languages? Can the African masses ever begin to participate in the culture of modern science and technology without making it available, at least in part, in an African language?

The issue is not one of turning one's back on European languages. Western leadership in science and technology is likely to last well into the next century. Africans will continue to need important stimulus from Western, as well as other foreign sources. But technological and scientific interdependence requires that Africans in turn begin to make a contribution to the new world culture of the future. That contribution is unlikely to "do justice to the African as an innovative being" unless efforts are made to do justice to African cultures as cultures of potential innovation. The development of Kiswahili itself, on one side, and the contributions of Kiswahili to the development of East African societies, on the other, are part of Africa's preparation for a fuller involvement in a world culture which is indeed compatible with the present stage of human knowledge, which facilitates the human person to realize the full potentialities of a social creature, and which opens the gates of creativity for the human person as an innovative being.

CHAPTER II

History of Kiswahili

1. From Pre-Colonial Times to the Maji Maji Rebellion (1905)

The language itself goes back at least to the tenth century. According to Rajmund Ohly (1973), the language originated sometime before the tenth century. Somewhat in agreement with Ohly, Derek Nurse and Thomas Spear place the birth of Kiswahili sometime after 500 AD and suggest that by the ninth century an early form of Kiswahili was probably already in use throughout much of the East African Coast (1985: 49). Oral Swahili sources place the origin of the language at even an earlier period. But the bulk of the evidence would seem to suggest that the language remained overwhelmingly a coastal phenomenon until about two hundred years ago. The beginnings of trade into the interior have been traced to the last quarter of the eighteenth century. It was not until Seyyid Said bin Sultan established full residence in Zanzibar in 1832 and consolidated the al-Busaidy sultanate on the islands, that trade with the interior of the continent developed more substantially. The momentum of this trade was also a momentum of linguistic spread.

There were obstacles to internal trade which in turn served as obstacles to the further spread of Kiswahili. In some parts of Eastern Africa militantly protective communities acquired the reputation of hostility to foreigners and were thus able to keep away many an enterprising merchant from the coast. The Maasai in both Kenya and Tanganyika acquired this martial reputation and, therefore, served as a hindrance both to the expansion of trade and the spread of Kiswahili, especially in Kenya. Sometimes it was periodic warfare between particular groups that discouraged commercial activity and large-scale economic contacts.

A third factor concerned economic anthropology, *per se*. There were communities in East Africa that were not inclined towards economic exchange or towards any kind of entrepreneurship. Resistance to entrepreneurial activities was sometimes primordial, derived substantially from ancestral beliefs and values. There were communities in East Africa that relied on herding their own cattle and augmenting them through raids rather than trade. There were other communities that were minimally based on subsistance, cultivating their own ground, without feeling the impulse for surplus and exchange. Even the Kikuyu, who showed quite early considerable signs of entrepreneurial skills in their relations with their neighbors before colonization, were for quite a while uncooperative in their relations with traders from afar. Merchants from the coast found Kikuyuland inhospitable for either trade bases, marketing, recruitment of porters, or replenishment of supplies. The Kamba, on the other hand, were actively trading far from their own homes in the same period, and for a while appeared to be far more entrepreneurial than the Kikuyu and among the most enterprising of all the Bantu communities of this part of the continent.

As the nineteenth century unfolded, trade expanded. Settlements inhabited by large numbers of people drawn from different linguistic groups increased, and the need for a *lingua franca* also arose.

The slave trade, especially in the second half of the eighteenth century and much of the nineteenth century, also played a part in the dissemination of Kiswahili. In Eastern Africa, the Arabs were particularly active in the slave trade and had their own African agents in different parts of the region. As the slave trade was regarded simply as an additional area of economic activity, it ought to be seen as part of the total impact of economic considerations on the spread of Kiswahili. Those who used Kiswahili for purposes of trade and commerce ranged from the Kamba to the Mijikenda, from the Nyamwezi to newly arrived immigrants from the Persian Gulf. All these are instances of economic spontaneity in relation to linguistic spread.

These were the days when the language could claim no special hold on the imagination of educators.

An orthography, based on the Arabic script, had already come into being among the Arabs, the Waswahili, and the Mijikenda of the Coast. Kiswahili poetry goes back several centuries and had previously used this orthography. But, while many studied these poems as works of art in Eastern Africa, and others as media of religious instruction, actual preoccupation with the teaching of the language, as such, was still something awaiting fulfillment in the future.

The poets and religious instructors in the mosques played an important role in enriching the language, but at this stage it was still pre-eminently the merchants and traders who spread the language. The dissemination of the language entailed some "dilution" as the distance grew between its place of origin and its new locale of economic function. The Swahili culture remained overwhelmingly a phenomenon of the coastal areas, but Kiswahili found more purely technical functions in the marketplace. The spread of Kiswahili at this stage must, therefore, be seen as a phenomenon almost entirely independent of schools and other structures of training and education.

In addition, it might be said that three wars were particularly important in the history of Kiswahili in East Africa. One war was the Maji Maji Resistance in German Tanganyika which broke out in 1905. The second important war for the evolution of Kiswahili was World War I, and the third was World War II.

The Maji Maji Resistance against German rule in Tanganyika was, in a sense, the first trans-ethnic mass movement in the modern history of Tanganyika. It was a movement both because of its scale and because of the ideological content behind its assertiveness. Both the scale and the ideological content afforded a fundamental role for Kiswahili in its slow process of conquering Tanganyika.

As regards the scale and ideological content, John Illife has captured the significance of this particular episode in the history of the region.

> Maji Maji was quite different from the early resistance which
> the Germans had faced when occupying Tanganyika, for that
> had been local and professional — soldiers against soldiers
> — whereas Maji Maji affected almost everyone in the
> colony... In the long term, the movement may have provided
> an experience of united mass action to which later political
> leaders could appeal... Maji Maji became a mass movement
> because it acquired an ideological content which persuaded
> people to join and fight. (1969: 25)

Illife discusses the use of religious symbols in the movement. He mentions
the thrust of the "integration of diverse peoples." He also mentions the
rapidity with which the revolt spread.

> Within a fortnight, nearly all the peoples surrounding the Rufiji
> valley, from Kilosa to Liwale, were in revolt... [In another
> two months] most of the peoples south of the line from Dar
> es Salaam to Kilosa and thence to the northern tip of Lake
> Malawi were in revolt. (1969: 19-20)

The Maji Maji Resistance was important for the future of Kiswahili, both
because Kiswahili featured as a trans-ethnic medium of communication
among the rebels and because German policy concerning political
penetration included a linguistic policy which favored Kiswahili even more
after the war than it had done before.

Among the nationalist fighters in the Maji Maji war, Kiswahili was
mainly organizational rather than inspirational. It made it possible for different
people to communicate with each other. Even the *Nywinywila,* the
whispering campaign used to communicate the ideological substance of
the movement, relied heavily on Kiswahili. And yet, to the extent that the
Maji Maji Resistance was a religious movement inspired by belief in
invulnerability, Kiswahili did serve some inspirational functions, though the
status of the language may have been somewhat rudimentary in most parts

of Tanganyika at that time.

A student of the history of Kiswahili, Mohamed Hassan Abdulaziz, has drawn attention to the significance of Maji Maji in the genesis of trans-ethnic and egalitarian movements in Tanzania; and he has placed Kiswahili at the heart of this process. In Abdulaziz's words:

> Swahili has played a very significant role in the development of political values and attitudes in Tanzania. Its integrative qualities have influenced the style of Tanzania politics, especially its non-tribal and egalitarian characteristics. All movements of national focus have used Swahili as an instrument for achieving inter-tribal unity and integration. The Maji Maji war of 1905-07 against German colonial rule drew its support from different mother-tongue speakers who already possessed a rallying force in Kiswahili. (1971: 164)

In a statement to the United Nations Fourth Committee in 1956, Julius K. Nyerere described the Maji Maji war as the final act of violent resistance by his people which had begun in 1885.

> For fifteen years, between 1885 and 1900, my people, with bows and arrows, with spears and clubs, with knives or rusty muskets, fought desperately to keep the Germans out. But the odds were against them. In 1905, in the famous Maji Maji Rebellion, they tried again for the last time to drive the Germans out. Once again, the odds were against them. The Germans, with characteristic ruthlessness, crushed the Rebellion, slaughtering an estimated number of 120,000 people. (1966: 40-41)

In its anti-German rhetoric, Nyerere's statement belonged almost to the same oratorical genre as Winston Churchill's wartime speeches. But what matters from our point of view here is Nyerere's conception of the Maji

Maji war as the final attempt to deal with German occupation by violent
rebellion: his assumption that the primary resistance of 1885 belonged to
the same category of social phenomena as the final trans-ethnic mass
movement of 1905. In fact, the Maji Maji war was not the last of the
movements of primary resistance starting from 1885, but rather the first of
the really nationalist mass movements of Tanganyika. Illife's emphasis on
the distinctiveness of scale in the Maji Maji Resistance, and the trans-
ethnic ideology which seemed to animate it in spite of other religious
differences, is indeed well taken. And because the Maji Maji Resistance
was the first nationalist mass movement of modern Tanganyika, it also
offered the first nationalist role to Kiswahili in that country.

Prior to the revolutionary eruption of Maji Maji, German colonialism
found itself in a state of predicament with regard to the language question
in its East African dominion. It definitely needed an inter-ethnic language
of colonial administration, but the policy-makers were reluctant to allow
German to play that role. It was feared that German would be a key to
European sources of knowledge and may, subsequently, serve the ends of
African subversion against colonialism.

Kiswahili, on the other hand, was regarded as a reservoir of Islamic
spirit and a dangerously potential agent of inter-ethnic African unity against
German rule. According to one colonial ideologue of the time, H. Hansen,
Islam and Kiswahili together constituted not only the mortal adversaries
of Christianity, "but also, in Africa, the unrepentant enemies of colonial
politics" (quoted by Charles Pike, 1986: 231). In a sense then, the Maji
Maji war was merely a confirmation of some of the worst fears of at least
a section of the German colonial establishment about the unifying role of
Kiswahili and Islam in East Africa.

All in all then, the ambivalence towards the promotion of the German
language, and the fear of an Islamic linguistic force of resistance supposedly
inherent in Kiswahili, led to a rather indecisive administrative position with
regard to German colonial language policy. The result was that before the
Maji Maji war, no extensive efforts were made to promote either one of

the two languages in what was then German East Africa.

Yet, it was quite clear to the Germans that the tide of Kiswahili spread was so strong that, in terms of sheer pragmatism, it made a lot of sense to accord it an official status in meeting the local communicational needs of colonial administration. But then, how was German colonialism to deal with the danger of Islam that was bound to Kiswahili? It was Carl Meinhof, a prominent German linguist of the time, who ultimately provided what seemed like a solution to this "problem." During the 1905 Colonial Congress, Meinhof proposed that Kiswahili be dis-Islamized by replacing the Arabic script, which had been used for centuries in writing Kiswahili, with the Roman script and Arabic loan words with German terms (Charles Pike, 1985: 224). In this way Kiswahili was thus going to be purged of its Islamic component to render it a more suitable tool for colonial consolidation and a less potent force of African resistance.

The existence of an anti-colonial Kiswahili literature in the Arabic script was probably seen as a vindication of Meinhof's position. The Kiswahili journalistic venture, *El-Najah*, and the 1908 widely spread Kiswahili letters, supposedly from Mecca, both written in the Arabic script, openly agitated against German colonial rule (Charles Pike, 1985: 230). For a while colonial Kiswahili literature in the Roman script almost seemed to be pitted in opposition against an anti-colonial Kiswahili literature in the Arabic script.

Whatever the case, the immediate shock of Maji Maji was on the Germans themselves. Whatever complacency there might have been in German colonial policy was now shattered. The Germans decided minimal control of the hinterland of Tanganyika was no longer a sensible strategy. In the words of John Illiffe, "...Maji Maji compelled a greatly increased German involvement in terms of political energy. The minimal aims of early colonial rule gave way to purposive colonial policy" (1969: 28).

The decision to embark on a more comprehensive program of political penetration inevitably reinforced those aspects of German policy which were already strengthening the role and functions of Kiswahili in

Tanganyika. The Germans had decided before the Maji Maji war that Kiswahili was going to be the language of administration, and efforts were already underway to document the language using the Roman script. Settlers and missionaries had also entered the great endeavor to make Kiswahili an effective *lingua franca* while, at the same time, attempting to dis-Islamize its vocabulary. The endeavor was partly a recognition of the role which Kiswahili had already assumed in this regard, and partly a commitment to make this role more efficient and more extensive for colonial ends.

The first newspapers in Kiswahili came barely three or four years after the full establishment of German rule. *Msimulizi* came into being in 1888, and *Habari za Mwezi* probably came into being in 1894. Later on, *Pwani na Bara* came into being under the auspices of the German Protestant Mission. The first issue consisted of four pages with an article on the Kaiser's birthday and a note on the Nyamwezi chief, Mirambo. The newspaper also contained statistics on the number of lions and leopards killed. In the same year, the German Catholic Mission produced its Kiswahili newspaper, *Rafiki*.

All this was part of the earlier colonial commitment to the promotion of Kiswahili. This commitment received an added impetus following the Maji Maji war and the German realization that administration in the rest of the country had to be much tighter and more responsive than it had been before the war.

> By 1914, the Administration was able to conduct much of its correspondence with village headmen in Swahili; indeed, letters not written to the Administration in either Swahili or German were liable to be ignored. This was one feature of German Administration which proved of great value to their successors, the British, and evoked a good deal of approval in later years. The Report on the Territory for 1921, for example, stated "...the late German system has made it

possible to communicate in writing with every Akida leader
and village headman and, in turn, to receive from him reports
written in Swahili. (Wilfred Whitely, 1969: 60-66)

What had happened was again a rather ruthless determination by the
German administration, not only to "pacify" the natives, but also to centralize
the system of administration in their colony. And centralization included
ease of linguistic communication. The fortunes of Kiswahili in Tanganyika
were greatly facilitated by the Maji Maji Resistance both as a pioneer in
mass organization and in its impact on German colonial policy in Tanganyika
for the subsequent decade.

2. From World War I to World War II

World War I and its aftermath were also of importance for the
fortunes of Kiswahili in East Africa. During the war itself the language
helped to emphasize fratricidal aspects in the violence between local
peoples themselves. The East African Coast especially was torn by the
simple fact that the Germans, occupying the southern part of the Coast,
were fighting the British, occupying the northern part of the Coast, and
Kiswahili was the language of cultural and economic intercourse down the
seaboard as a whole. Both the Germans and the British recruited into their
armed forces local people who would not otherwise have been at war
with each other, and who, in the case of the Coast, were a people culturally
and linguistically related to each other. Along the coast Kiswahili was
indeed used for inspirational purposes during the war, but its major function
in the East African region as a whole was still basically functional and
organizational.
World War I may have affected the destiny of Kiswahili in the Belgian
Congo (or what is today, Zaire) in a different direction altogether. As a
result of trade relations between the coast and the interior of Eastern Africa,
Kiswahili had established its presence in the eastern part of the Congo

sometime prior to the inception of European colonialism. When the region fell under King Leopold II of Belgium, and copper mining was introduced on an industrial scale, the language became an important medium of inter-ethnic communication not only within the mines, but throughout the mine extracting area. And the World War appears to have posed no threat to this *lingua franca* status of Kiswahili in the mining region.

Where the war may have influenced the fortunes of Kiswahili was in the military. As indicated earlier, the Belgians relied heavily on mercinary soldiers from other regions of Africa during the early phase of their colonialism. Later, however, there was a change in policy and the recruitment for the army began to rely on the more local (Congolese) pool. World War I may have been one of the factors that led to this change in recruitment policy. Because of the war and the events leading to it, each imperial power now had to depend more exclusively on populations under its direct colonial control for its military manpower.

This change in recruitment pattern in the Belgian Congo had the effect of de-Swahilizing the army. Lingala now gradually moved in to replace Kiswahili. Though Kiswahili was probably spoken by as many Congolese nationals as was Lingala, the latter seems to have established itself over a wider geographical area in the country. Lingala then had an edge over Kiswahili in an army that recruited widely throughout the Belgian colonial territory of the Congo.

More important than the actual war itself, for the future of Kiswahili in Eastern Africa, however, was the *outcome* of World War I. The defeat of Germany and the assumption of administrative authority in Tanganyika by Great Britain, had long-term repercussions not only for Tanganyika, but for East Africa as a whole. From a linguistic point of view, the triumph of the British over the Germans was a mixed blessing for Kiswahili. The British as a colonial power were, in their attitude to language, different both from the French and the Germans. The French were tied to a missionary vision to disseminate their culture and spread their language. Because of that vision, the French were among the least tolerant of colonial powers in their attitude to local cultures. The Germans, on the other hand, were not particularly keen on fostering the German language among their subjects. They sometimes even regarded it as presumptuous that a "lower breed" of people should seek to express themselves in German. The French tried to create a mystique of France by popularizing the French language; the Germans were tempted to create a mystique of Germany by isolating their language from the squalor of popular comprehension and making it mysteriously and powerfully distant. The French wanted to be admired for their culture. The Germans preferred to be respected for their power. Hence, the French policy of assimilation came into being, while the Germans emphasized mysteries of social distance. It was, therefore, basically presumptuous for an African to aspire to Germanhood in culture.

In addition, as we have indicated, German administration regarded it as inefficient to have to deal in too many different languages all over the colonial territory. There was, therefore, a case for singling out one medium or a few major media to be used for administrative purposes and letting some of the others decay or die by administrative disuse.

The British were in an intermediate position between the Germans and the French. They believed in the ideology of indirect rule and its cultural appendages. They conceded a certain right of survival to indigenous cultural ways and indigenous languages. They even set up committees to coordinate the growth of key languages in their colonial territories. The East African Inter-territorial Language Committee was a case in point during British colonial rule. But the British also believed, with some ambivalence, in bestowing the gift of the English language on at least the elites of the colonial territories.

As a generalization, we might then say that the British favored a native acquisition of English a little more than the Germans had once favored a native acquisition of German; and the British were more tolerant of smaller African languages and more prepared to put up with lingusitic plurality than either the Germans or the French.[6]

The fortunes of Kiswahili within Tanganyika suffered a little, though by no means fatally, when the country shifted from German control to British control. The British toleration of smaller languages, to the extent that it was greater than the German, slowed down the spread of Kiswahili as a *lingua franca*. The British, leaning towards promoting the English language to the extent that it was greater than the German leaning towards promoting the German language, again affected adversely the fortunes of Kiswahili within Tanganyika. Indeed, the spread of the English language under British rule had the effect of relegating Kiswahili to the status of second-class language even among Africans themselves. In the words of Wilfred Whitely:

> Whereas in German times the acquisition of Swahili represented a first stage toward participating in Government through membership of the junior Civil Service, no further stage in this participation could be achieved through the language. The next stage involved the acquisition of English and for this reason, Swahili was seen increasingly by Tanganyikans as a "second-class language" (1969: 61-62).

Educational policy was framed under the British on the basis of a declining utilization of Kiswahili. The language was used as a medium of primary school education, but became only one subject among several at secondary school, and disappeared completely even as a subject in higher education.

> As time went on the difference in the quality and quantity of secondary school materials and teachers was clear evidence to pupils, if to no one else, of the inferior status of the language. Institutions designed primarily for East Africans made no provision for the study of Swahili while their use of English simply confirmed East Africans in their belief that it was on this language that they should concentrate their sights. While Swahili newspapers were plentiful, the glossy magazines were in English. (Whitely, 1969: 62)

Of course if Tanganyika had been entrusted as a League of Nations' mandate to the administration of France, the fortunes of Kiswahili would have suffered even more drastically. French culture would have made of Kiswahili an even more second class language than it became under British rule. What is apt to be overlooked is that within Tanganyika the language would probably have fared better, and developed faster, as a national language enforced by the colonial power had the Germans remained in control.

But while the fortunes of Kiswahili as a language of Tanganyika might thus have suffered when the country fell under British rule, the fortunes of Kiswahili as a language of East Africa probably improved. With the outcome of World War I being what it was, it was now conceivable for Kenya, Uganda, Zanzibar, and Tanganyika to develop on the basis of increasing regional integration. Among the most unifying of factors in modern Africa has been the factor of being ruled by the same colonial power. Tanganyikans are much closer today to Kenyans and Ugandans than they would have been had Tanganyikans been German-speaking, while Kenyans and Ugandans were English-speaking. Regional organizations, like the East African High Commission, and its successors right up to the now defunct East African Community would not have been conceivable if there had continued to be a German East Africa in this part of the continent. The very concept of an East African Federation, hotly debated as it was for decades, would not have featured realistically if Tanganyika had been the colony of a European power other than Britain which had colonized Kenya and Uganda.

Not least significant of the consequences of World War I was the fact that Zanzibar and Tanganyika now shared the same imperial power, Great Britain. Zanzibar, as the heartland of what later became standard Kiswahili, maintained its ease of communication with Dar es Salaam as the capital of Tanganyika. The dissemination of Kiswahili through East Africa as a whole received an additional boosting by the very fact that the Sultanate, then still relatively powerful, shared the same metropolitan "protecting" power as what later became mainland Tanzania. Indeed, the very union between Tanganyika and Zanzibar in 1964 might well have been inconceivable if the island and the mainland had reached the 1960s under the impact of two entirely different colonial powers.

The outcome of World War I was also an important factor behind the emergence of the very concept of *standard Kiswahili*. Because the British now controlled Kenya, Uganda, Zanzibar, and Tanganyika, the idea of standardizing Kiswahili became viable. Rivalries between the colonial powers themselves over which dialect to choose for such an enterprise ceased to be relevant after the ouster of the Germans. In 1925, an education conference was convened by the Governor of Tanganyika and held in Dar es Salaam. This became an important landmark in the development of the idea of standard Kiswahili orthography. In 1926, a number of proposals were made concerning spelling and word-division in Kiswahili. Meanwhile, the 1925 conference had led to the establishment of a Central Publishing Committee. This body now demanded to be fully informed about projected textbooks for schools in an endeavor to avoid unnecessary duplication.

Kenya was also groping for some kind of standard orthography. It was in January 1928 that an inter-territorial conference held in Mombasa confirmed the decision to adopt the dialect of Zanzibar as the basis of standard Kiswahili. The Universities Mission to Central Africa had recommended the Zanzibar dialect in competition with the Church Missionary Society who were advocating the dialect of Mombasa. Again, the whole enterprise of choosing a dialect from British controlled East Africa as the basis of standard Kiswahili became viable partly because Tanganyika was not controlled by another power. The range of dialects to choose from would have been reduced to that of Mombasa and Zanzibar alone if a divided imperial presence had been an additional factor in the linguistic situation in East Africa.

On January 1, 1930, the Inter-Territorial Language Committee came into being at last. This committee became a paramount mechanism in the process of standardizing Kiswahili throughout the region, as well as promoting regionally usable literature in the language.

In Uganda, Kiswahili was still relatively underdeveloped as compared with Tanganyika and Kenya. But even in Uganda, the fortunes of Kiswahili began, perhaps haltingly, to take a turn for the better following the defeat of Germany in Tanganyika. In the 1920s, Kiswahili in Uganda had at first seemed to be receding completely into the background. In 1925, A.W. Smith had observed that in Uganda "probably no person would favor the teaching of Swahili; Luganda is making headway in the provinces at the expense of the vernaculars."[7]

In 1926, special committees on language policy recommended that three languages be promoted in schools in the country. In the north, Acholi should be used as the medium of instruction; in parts of the eastern province, Teso should be the medium; and in the rest of Uganda, Luganda should continue to dominate. Kiswahili did not feature very prominently in this planning. The full significance of Tanganyika's new status as a Mandated Territory under Britain had taken longer to reveal its implications for Uganda than it might have done. It was nearly seven years after World War I before Governor William Gowers of Uganda made the first major bid to pull Uganda into the mainstream of Kiswahili.

> Gowers argued that since Tanganyika had become a British mandated territory and communication in East Africa had improved, Uganda could not afford to isolate herself by ignoring Swahili which was understood in Kenya, Tanganyika, and as far as the Congo... The possibility of federation [in East Africa] must have made the Swahili issue a matter of urgency for Gowers. But he confined his arguments to a more general discussion of the need for Uganda to integrate herself with general developments in East Africa, and to the educational advantages of Swahili. (Fay Gadsden, 1971:4)

The question of coordinating, if not integrating the armed forces and the police of East Africa, had also been examined. The King's African Rifles had sought to recruit across ethnic boundaries within the region. On a global scale, the number of troops to be recruited from East Africa was indeed quite modest, but the recruitment covered a diversity of linguistic backgrounds. The King's African Rifles had already had to face the issue of the language of command even before the war. The issue was not absent even in the First World War when East Africa was the scene of battle between Britain and Germany over the possession of German East Africa, Tanganyika. But with the imminence of the Second World War and the possibility of wider recruitment once again, the problem of a suitable language of command, effective enough for a multi-linguistic unit of the armed forces, assumed a new persistence.

In the ultimate analysis there were three possibilities — first, a policy based on using a number of ethnic languages; secondly, a policy based on adopting English; and thirdly, a policy based on utilizing Kiswahili. The multi-ethnolinguistic solution had a number of disadvantages. Unlike the West African languages, such as Hausa and Yoruba, the native speakers of indigenous languages in East Africa were more modest in population. Even the larger ethnic groups, like the Kikuyu and the Baganda, were at the time little more than a million each, whereas Yoruba speakers in West Africa — let alone Hausa speakers — were to be counted in several millions.

There was the related argument that military command based on ethnic languages would bedevil the issue of promotions within each linguistic group. The officers commanding Baganda soldiers might need themselves to be Baganda; the officers commanding Acholi soldiers might need themselves to be Acholi. If they were not drawn from the same linguistic community, the officers would need to be versed in the appropriate language.

The adoption of English would help this problem of communication across ethnic lines, but would inevitably drastically reduce the sector of the population from which the soldiers could be recruited. In the 1930s and 1940s, only a small proportion of the population of the East African countries spoke even rudimentary English, and those who spoke it well would look towards recruitment as officer cadets from the beginning. The King's African Rifles knew they had to recruit from a wide section of the population of East Africa and could not at the time afford to have this area circumscribed by an insistence on some knowledge of the metropolitan language.

The third possibility centered on adopting Kiswahili as the language of the armed forces. This would eliminate the problem of each linguistic community producing its own officers and non-commissioned officers. An Acholi could command an army consisting of Akamba, Baganda, and Wadigo. Both boundaries between ethnic groups and boundaries between colonies within the same region would no longer need to be constraining factors in recruitment. It is true that knowledge of Kiswahili was not uniformly distributed throughout the region. Some ethnic communities spoke it better than others. Some colonial territories preferred a more sophisticated version of Kiswahili than others. But a basic *lingua franca,* somewhat rudimentary, was already evolving. The armed forces could take advantage of the availability of such a *lingua franca* and could, in turn, strengthen its functions by providing, if need be, further courses in Kiswahili in the barracks.

In Uganda, Kiswahili joined Luganda as one of the official languages of Uganda in 1927. But it was not for long. Missionary distrust of Kiswahili as an "Islamic language," Baganda suspicion of it as a rival to Luganda, and a sincere worry among educationalists that the introduction of Kiswahili into Uganda schools would be a retrograde step, all conspired to force the language out of the mainstream of life in Uganda.

But there was one area of national life where Kiswahili retained an official role. This was in the security forces. Kiswahili remained a language of command in the police and in the King's African Rifles. Both the fortunes of Kiswahili, and the spirit of regionalism in East Africa, became part of the history of the armed forces. It is to this factor that we must now turn.

The man who was one day to become the first military ruler of independent Uganda, Idi Amin, claimed he knew military service in Burma during World War II. This fact was symbolic of a wider phenomenon.

It might be said that military service contributed to the rise of a political awareness in Africa as a whole because of two important factors — the very factor of expanding horizons of experience in areas far away from home, and the factor of learning new skills of a technical kind in the armed forces. Both factors contributed to the frustrations of ex-servicemen in West Africa. The expanding horizons obtained as a result of seeing other parts of the world and of knowing the white man as a fellow soldier in combat, and of seeing his weaknesses as well as his strengths at close quarters, began the process of humanizing the white man and of discovering that he was indeed fallible.

The factor of learning new skills, on the other hand, contributed to a sense of frustration after demobilization. The skills newly acquired were not always easy to utilize profitably outside the armed forces in the Africa of those days.

It is partly because of these factors that in the history of nationalism in Africa as a whole, ex-servicemen throughout West Africa after World War II contributed to the general feeling of unrest which remained unassuaged, if it was not stimulated, by the mild constitutional reforms of the mid- 1940s in West Africa. In a country like Nigeria it was not "surprising to find ex-servicemen among the more militant leaders of the nationalist movement during the post-war period" (Dennis Austin, 1956: 14).[8]

In Kenya's history too, a whole chapter stands out with the title "The Role of the Ex-Soldier in Kenya's Political History." On one side, we have the role of *European* ex-servicemen in the conversion of Kenya into a country with white settlers — with all the political repercussions which that entailed. As far back as World War I, the War Council of Kenya concerned itself not only with the war and problems of conscription (in which East Africa led the way in the Empire), but it sought to strengthen the European position in particular by devising a Soldier Settlement Scheme for the post-war period (George Bennett, 1963: 38-39).[9]

And at the end of the Second World War the Kenya government and the British government announced an agricultural settlement scheme for soldiers released from the armed forces — "men and women of pure European descent, who were thus eligible to farm in the area reserved for Europeans, and whose war services a grateful country wished to recognize" (Michael Blundell, 1964: 63). What emerges from this is the importance of what Blundell called "soldier settlers" as a factor in the land question of Kenya's history.

As for the role of the African ex-servicemen in East Africa's history, one Kenya settler who served with Africans abroad has suggested that the first signs of nationalism in East Africa are discernible in the African *askari*. The *askari* was at least prompted to ask why only Europeans were officers in the East African army and why the food scales were different between white and black soldiers. As in West Africa, though less dramatically, "the first real seeds of African nationalism were sown in the later years of the war, when the African just began to question the traditional differences between himself and the white man" (Blundell, 1964: 58).[10]

From Uganda, as we have indicated, young Idi Amin may have known military service in Burma. And young Edward Mutesa, while studying at Cambridge, toyed with the idea of serving with the forces in Malaya. But it was not merely national awareness which was fostered by military experience. In the case of East Africa there was also the emergence of regional consciousness, complete with the promotion of Kiswahili among all members of the security forces of Uganda, Kenya, and Tanganyika. This sense of pan-regional consciousness was facilitated partly by the method of recruitment into the King's African Rifles. Recruitment was conducted all over East Africa, but it did not follow that Ugandan soldiers would serve only in Uganda, Tanganyikans in Tanganyika, and Kenyans in Kenya. On the contrary, an important aspect of policy was its trans-territorial dimension. In the police and the army, perhaps even more than any other services, two factors were combined — an attempt to maintain a balance in the number of people recruited from each territory and an attempt to minimize the significance of the territorial origins of a new recruit in determining where he was to serve. Again, it is worth remembering that Idi Amin experienced military service in Kenya during the colonial period. And even after the Uganda coup of January 1971, there was still in the security forces of Uganda personnel from the other two countries.

The role of Kiswahili in making such "joint command" feasible, and in facilitating inter-territorial recruitment into the armed forces, was indeed critical. From the Maji Maji Rebellion to Amin's coup, the fortunes of Kiswahili had in part been linked to military history and the warrior tradition.

3. Kiswahili as a Medium of Education

The entry of Kiswahili into the mainstream of formal education in East Africa on any significant scale did not come until European countries colonized this region, and missionaries infiltrated African societies. The great debate then got underway about media of instruction for Africans, the comparative merits of Kiswahili as against what were called "vernacular languages" and the comparative merits of Kiswahili as against the English language. The debates which began at the beginning of the century are continuing to the present day. The great competition on one side was between English and Kiswahili as the *lingua franca,* and on the other side it was between Kiswahili and more localized indigenous African languages.

This debate, especially when it touched upon the fundamental issues of educational policy, became quite often an issue between church and state in a colonial situation. It is to the ramifications of this grand dialogue, half-religious and half-political, that we must now turn.

A rather simplistic, but nevertheless, suggestive distinction needs to be made in this regard. This is the distinction between training the mind of the colonized African, on the one hand, and converting his soul, on the other. Colonial policy-makers in the administrative field at their most enlightened viewed education as a medium for the training of the African mind; but the Christian missionaries viewed education as a method of winning the African soul. In reality, there was a good deal of overlap between these two concepts and, in practice, they were rarely sharply differentiated. But it is still true to say that the missionaries in those early days were especially concerned about "spiritual transformation," the elimination of "heathen tendencies," and the spread of the gospel itself. The secular colonial policy-makers, on the other hand, were beginning to be interested in producing some levels of indigenous humanpower for some of the practical tasks of here and now. The settler policy-makers were also interested in legitimizing colonial rule itself to the outside world by providing education as an instrument of modernization, rather than as an aid for spiritualization.

In fact, in the initial stages of colonial rule matters pertaining to education were often left in the hands of missionary societies. But increasingly the various colonial administrations became concerned that the mission schools were too narrowly focused on the spiritual at the expense of the intellectual and the cultural. It was also feared that the over-emphasis on Christian education might render certain African communities even more suspicious of the school. In a letter to Bishop Hirth, a colonial administrator in Ruanda-Urundi once wrote:

> I freely admit that I believe that, at first, attempts at religious instruction and attempts at conversion must be dropped; but I also think that by wisely using his influence, the teacher who gains is the one who knows how to enthral his students; in this way, a school prepares the way for Christianity without religious instruction. Even the Tutsi, who probably still will not be moved to adopt Christianity for a long time, will be subjected to Christian influence which they will receive unnoticeably and inescapably through the school. (Quoted by W.M. Roger Louis, 1963: 184)

What this colonial officer was trying to suggest, then, was that if school instruction was used simply as a tool to proselytize it would defeat not only the missionaries' own religious goal, but also the goal of education in general. The struggle between missionaries, administrators, and settlers for control of the school curriculum, then, became a feature of colonial interest in African education in several parts of Africa.

Kiswahili too became involved in this debate between the soul and the mind, between the spiritually-oriented missionary activist and the modernizing colonial administrator. Because Kiswahili developed within an Islamic culture, and borrowed many Arabic words, the language initially carried considerable Islamic associations. Many of the individual loan words from Arabic were inevitably influenced by these prior associations. And many terms connected with religious experience, ranging from the concept of the hereafter to the idea of praying, carried overtones or undertones derived ultimately from Islamic practice and thought.

Some of the earliest evidence of colonial hostility towards Kiswahili on account of its association with Islam came from Tanganyika under German rule. According to Marcia Wright:

> In Germany, Director Buchner proved to be an unrelenting foe of Swahili, going so far in a speech before the Kolonialrat in 1905 as to declare that it was irredeemably mixed with Islam that every expedient ought to be employed to obstruct their joint penetration... Buchner's opposition to Swahili was adopted and expanded by Julius Richter, a member of the Berlin Committee. Richter delivered a diatribe during the Kolonial Kongress in 1905 against the pernicious influence of Islam everywhere in Africa. Isolating East Africa as the scene of the worst danger, he envisaged a mosque alongside every coastman's hut, and took the official support for Swahili to be blatantly pro-Islamic. (1971: 113)

This opposition to Kiswahili from a section of the German colonial establishment, however, seems to have had little to do with Kiswahili's potential to capture the souls or train the minds of the African subjects. As indicated earlier, it seems to have been based on the belief that Kiswahili's Islamic orientation was an essential bond of African cooperation against the consolidation of German colonialism. But after the Maji Maji war and Carl Meinhof's prescription to de-Islamize Kiswahili, the German colonial administration virtually doubled its efforts to promote the language in various domains of its dominion. Kiswahili was thus found to be an adequate medium to cater for the interests of missionaries, administrators, and German civilization at large.

Equally important as a sociolinguistic feature of the education system in German East Africa, was the rivalry between the English language and German. The presence of English was seen as a direct threat to the establishment of German cultural control over its colonies:

> For many Germans it was not so much the spector of African languages, Swahili included, but the spector of English which most upset their visions of *Deutschtum*. Throughout the German colonial empire it was English, in one form or another, which they confronted. The "English problem," as Brumfit pointed out, was not confined to missionaries in East Africa, but also included many people in the Indian communities as well... The colonial newspaper reported that the English language must be driven out of East Africa, and only German and Swahili should be used. (Charles Pike, 1985: 22)

Inter-imperialist rivalry, then, led to a rather ironic position in German colonial circles with regard to the language of African education. A Germanic language, English, was a threat to the promotion of a sister culture of the Germans, but a Bantu language, Kiswahili, could be transformed to play precisely that role. In general, then, when it comes to the issue of language of instruction, the Germans seemed more pre-occupied with the broader area of culture and power than with the more specific dichotomy between the soul and the mind.

Where the linguistic debate between the soul and the mind came to feature quite prominently in Eastern Africa is in the region of British rule. In the earliest days of European colonization and evangelism, the association of Kiswahili with Islam was not held against Kiswahili by the Christian missionaries. On the contrary, quite a number felt that since both Islam and Christianity were monotheistic religions drawn from the same Middle Eastern ancestry, and sharing a considerable number of spiritual concepts and values, Kiswahili would serve well for the conversion of indigenous Africans to Christianity precisely because Kiswahili could already cope with the conceptual universe of Islam. As early as 1850, Dr.J.L. Krapf was already campaigning for Kiswahili as a language of evangelism. Its status as a *lingua franca* and its rich reservoir of religious concepts relevant to Christianity, made Kiswahili in the eyes of Rev. Krapf an ideal language for East African Christianity. The only aspect of Kiswahili that Krapf found objectionable was its use of the Arabic script which, if left to continue, would leave a wide door open to "Mohammedan proselytism among the inland tribes which may hereafter be Christianized and civilized" (J.L. Krapf, 1850: 170). It was partly due to this fear that Krapf initiated the use of the Roman script in writing Kiswahili; otherwise Krapf was solidly in support of Kiswahili as a medium of Christian evangelism.

By contrast, "vernacular languages," like Luganda or Luo, were too saturated with associations and connotations drawn from an indigenous religious experience much further removed from Christianity than Islam was. The utilization of "vernacular languages" for Christian proselytism carried the risk of conceptual distortion greater than that posed by Islam. Echoing Rev. Krapf, therefore, Bishop E. Steere concluded: "Neither there is any way by which we can make ourselves so readily intelligible or by which the Gospel can be preached as soon or so well than by means of the language of Zanzibar" (E. Steere, 1870: Preface).

Bishop Steere, the Reverend Krapf, and Father Sacleux are among the missionaries who not only championed the use of Kiswahili for the

Christian gospel, but also made substantial contributions towards the systematic study of the language (W.Whitely, 1969: 15-17).

In Uganda, Bishop A. Mackay records in November 1878: "Fortunately, Swahili is widely understood and I am pretty much at home in that tongue, while I have many portions of the Old and New Testament in Swahili. I am thus able to read frequently to the king and the whole court (of Buganda) the word of God" (Mackay, 1898: 103).

There was also a feeling of using Kiswahili at least as a transitional medium for the Gospel, linking European Christian vocabulary with African ethnic languages. O'Flaherty records translating tales and such-like, and teaching many Baganda catechumens the skill and art of translating from Kiswahili into Luganda. Other Christian missionaries also used both Kiswahili and Luganda for devotional purposes. This was certainly the great transitional period, using Kiswahili as a linguistic medium which would gradually modify and influence the religious vocabulary of "vernacular languages," and bridge the conceptual gap between European theological language and the indigenous spiritual universe in Africa.[11]

For a brief while Christianity came to be identified partly with a knowledge of Kiswahili and the ability to read in that language. But as this identification began to get underway, a new swing of opinion was also becoming discernible. Certainly in Uganda, a movement to replace Kiswahili altogether with Luganda became quite strong. The old Swahiliphile views of Mackay were coming under increasing challenge, and the ancient association of Kiswahili with Islam was now regarded as *ipso facto* dysfunctional to Christianity. In the words of Bishop Tucker in Uganda:

> Mackay...was very desirous of hastening the time when one language should dominate Central Africa, and that language, he hoped and believed, would be Swahili... That there should be one language for Central Africa is a consummation devoutly to be wished, but God forbid that it should be Swahili. English? Yes! But Swahili, never. The one means the

> Bible and Protestant Christianity and the other
> Mohammedanism... sensuality, moral and physical
> degradation, and ruin... Swahili is too closely related to
> Mahammedanism to be welcome in any mission field in
> Central Africa. (Mackay, 1908: 215)

In fact, Mackay's support for the English language was hedged with a number of reservations and these reservations were widely shared by other missionaries. As far as the missionaries were concerned, Kiswahili was deficient for spiritual purposes as compared with the "vernaculars." On the other hand, as far as colonial administrators were concerned, Kiswahili was suspect when compared with the English language, rather than with "vernaculars."

Among the missionaries, the so-called "Livingstonian principle" began to hold sway. This was the principle that in the final analysis each African community could be consolidated in its Christianity by the efforts of its own indigenous members and by using the conceptual tools of its own indigenous cultures. Kiswahili became suspect precisely because it had developed into a *lingua franca*. A *lingua franca* was deemed unfit to reach the innermost thoughts of those undergoing the conversion to Christianity. There was also the argument that a child should in any case be educated initially in its own language. For example, a resolution passed at the eighth meeting of The Executive Council of the International Institute of African Languages and Cultures in 1930, states:

> We are of the opinion that no education which leads to the
> alienation of the child from his ancestral environment can be
> right, nor can it achieve the most important aim of education
> which consists in developing the powers and characters of
> the pupil. Neglect of the vernacular involves the danger of
> crippling and destroying the pupil's productive powers by
> forcing him to express himself in a language foreign both to
> himself and to the genius of his race. (Quoted by

F.J.Clatworthy, 1971: 117)

Sentiments similar to those quoted above also came to influence educational language policy in what was then the Belgian Congo. In fact, the issue of Kiswahili's Islamic association does not seem to have concerned Belgian authorities in the Congo at all. This might be explained, in part, by the fact that Congo's Kiswahili was highly creolized, assuming a life that was somewhat different from the Kiswahili of the East African Coast, and, in part, by the absence of an Islamic population that was large enough to challenge the asendancy of Christianity in the region.

More paramount in the Belgian mind — whenever there was some concern with the education of the native — was the question of the medium of instruction most suitable for African education. A section of missionaries and colonial administrators felt that educational interests of the African child would be served best by using French as the medium of instruction. Using arguments of what is seemingly most practical in the situation, others argued for the use of one or more of Congo's *lingua francas*. Father Hulstaert, on the other hand, was of the opinion that using a language of instruction other than the mother-tongue was a reversal of values. He further espoused the Livingstonian principle in favor of preserving the mother-tongue for evangelical purposes (Edgar Polome, 1967: 305). Underlying the educational factor, then, was still the question of how best to handle the business of winning the souls. In the end, however, Belgian Congo settled for a solution that was deemed most pragmatic. It adopted Congo's four *lingua francas* — namely Lingala, Kiswahili, Kikongo, and Tshiluba — for early primary education and retained French for the higher levels.

In the rest of Eastern Africa Westermann's educational theories exerted a considerable influence at this time. He advanced the following thesis:

Mental life has evolved in each people in an individual shape and proper mode of expression; in this sense we speak of

the soul of a people and the most immediate, the most adequate
exponent of the soul of a people is its language. By taking
away a people's language, we cripple or destory its soul and
kill its mental individuality... Any educational work which does
not take into consideration the inseparable unity between
African language and African thinking is based on false
principle and must lead to the alienation of the individual from
his own self, his past, his traditions, and his people. (Quoted
by T.P. Gorman, 1974: 449)

For a while longer there were still administrators willing to put up a strong
fight in defense of Kiswahili. From the state's point of view, there were
indeed significant advantages from a *lingua franca*. Administration could
be facilitated, regulations would be available in fewer languages, and district
officers and commissioners could be moved to different parts of the country
without having to learn the local "vernacular" in each case. In Tanganyika,
that is what the Germans, after some hesitation, proceeded to do.

In areas controlled by the British, the policy of leaving the
control of education to the missionary orders was more
marked than was the case in French colonial territories, for
example, or more relevantly, in Tanganyika during the period
of German occupation. Indeed, the relative success of the
German government in establishing government schools at
which future members of the administrative service were
educated in Swahili, according to a consistent policy, facilitated
the spread of Swahili in Tanganyika as the language of
administration and as the *lingua franca*. (T.P. Gorman, 1974:
405).

In British East Africa also, there were, for a while, strong voices
championing the administrative virtues of a *lingua franca* like Kiswahili.
Particularly noteworthy was Governor W.F Gowers of Uganda (as we

noted earlier) who submitted an incisive memorandum to the Secretary of State for the colonies, saying:

> Kiswahili should be adopted as the *lingua franca* throughout a considerable portion of this Protectorate for the purpose of native education in elementary schools, and on the lines adopted in Tanganyika... Kiswahili is the only vernacular language in East Africa which can prove in the long-run anything but an educational cul-de-sac, in Uganda as in Kenya and Tanganyika...

Governor Gowers compared the arguments for Luganda, Kiswahili, and English as educational and administrative media and concluded that in the Bantu-speaking districts of Uganda, "Kiswahili should be introduced as an extra subject in lieu of English."

In the same memorandum he had earlier argued against the suggestion that English should be utilized as the *lingua franca* and against the contention that English could as easily be learned by non-Bantu "tribes" as could a Bantu language. Gowers feared "the dissemination of a barbarous jargon of English," and asserted that "for mutual comprehension between Europeans and Africans... inter-communication should be in an African vernacular, even if it not be the local tribal dialect (i.e., Swahili) than in so-called English" (W.F. Gowers, 1927).

A year later, in 1928, the Colonial Report included references to measures which had been adopted to introduce Kiswahili as the dominant language for educational and administrative purposes throughout a considerable area of the Protectorate. The Annual Report of the Education Department for 1929 also confirmed the vigor with which the new policy was being implemented.

But champions of Kiswahili underestimated the opposition which would soon be released. Kabaka Sir Daudi Chwa, hereditary guardian of the cultural heritage of the Baganda, inevitably felt bound to oppose the introduction of Kiswahili as the official native language of Buganda. The

Baganda's opposition, in alliance with the missionaries and their belief in "ultimate conversion through the vernacular," began to organize against the Swahili policies. In spite of the establishment in 1930 of an inter-territorial (Swahili) Language Committee, the Ugandan bishops, both Protestant and Roman Catholic, submitted a long and weighty memorandum to the Colonial Secretary in London through the Governor of Uganda. The burden of the memorandum was to demolish the arguments for Kiswahili as the official native language, and put a strong case for Luganda.

The Education Department included in its 1931 Annual Report, a rebuttal of the bishop's memorandum. Controversy grew. Then a Joint Committee on Closer Union in East Africa was set up and evidence was taken on language matters, as well as other things.

By a curious destiny, the Baganda were suspicious of Kiswahili partly because they were suspicious of the white settlers of Kenya. The very arguments of administrators in favor of Kiswahili as a *lingua franca* created in the minds of many Baganda the fear of being incorporated more fully into an East African protectorate encompassing Kenya as well as Uganda. The Baganda began to feel the Swahilization of their country would be part of the political process of its Kenyanization. And the power of Kenya resided in the hands of the settlers. When the Baganda gave evidence to the Joint Committee on Closer Union in East Africa, their opposition to Kiswahili formed part of their opposition to closer union in the region. In fact, the only people who gave evidence in London to the Joint Committee were Luganda speakers. The views of the country were not sought on an ethnically representative basis.

It was out of the Joint Committee's report and verdict that Uganda's language policy evolved. Luganda had, at the formal level of utilization for administrative and educational purposes, won against Kiswahili. The Baganda themselves were used extensively as administrators in areas other than their own, and their language was often utilized as a medium of instruction not only in Buganda, but in some of the other Bantu areas for a while.

But in terms of broader policy-making, the missionaries generally had succeeded in making the "vernacular languages" in both Kenya and Uganda the medium of elementary education except at the Coast. Those administrators in favor of a *lingua franca* had lost that round.

On the other hand, both the missionaries and the administrators agreed after a while on the importance of using the English language at the higher levels of education and promoting it. The administrators now saw in the English language a more effective medium of "training the African mind" than Kiswahili just as the missionaries, at least in Kenya and Uganda, had found "vernacular languages" better instruments of "cultivating the African soul" than Kiswahili. In fact, by 1953 a colonial report, the Binns Report, could argue: "The existence of Swahili in Kenya and Tanganyika and its place in school teaching is unfortunate, for it seems to have affected adversely the teaching both of vernacular and English. It comes in-between the study of these two languages as an element confusing the educational picture" (Nuffield Foundation and Colonial Office, 1953: 81). It looked as if Kiswahili was progressively losing both to the more localized languages of the regions and to the English language. The educational system seemed to be by-passing Kiswahili, except along the Coast of Kenya, and sharing instead "local vernaculars" and the imported metropolitan language itself.

The administration's enthusiasm for Kiswahili as a *lingua franca* waned further when the growth of national consciousness and anti-colonialism in East Africa began to benefit from the availability of a grassroots trans-ethnic language like Kiswahili. Political consciousness was now regarded as a dangerous "post-war epidemic" extending from the Gold Coast to Uganda and Kenya. Educational policy-makers in the region moved more decisively against "over-promoting Swahili." In the words of a Ugandan scholar, Tarsis B. Kabwegyere:

In the light of...the African awakening in the post-war period, it is not unreasonable to assert that the stopping of Kiswahili was a strategy to minimize intra-African contact. In addition, intensive anglicizing followed and East African peoples remained separated from each other by a language barrier... What this shows is that whatever interaction was officially encouraged remained at the top level and not at the level of the African populations. That the existence of one common language at the level of the masses would have hastened the overthrowal of colonial domination is obvious. The withdrawal of official support for a common African language was meant to keep the post-war 'epidemic' from spreading. (1974: 218-219)

As independence approached it was not only Kiswahili that was gradually pushed out of the educational system as a medium of instruction. The so-called "vernacular languages" that had been regarded as essential for harnessing the intellectual potential of African students while preserving their customs, ideals, and self-respect soon followed the fate of Kiswahili. By 1952, Kiswahili had, of course, completely disappeared from Ugandan schools partly because of Baganda pressure on the colonial government. The influential Baganda had regarded Kiswahili as a serious threat to their own language, Luganda. And in what was later to become the Democratic Republic of Congo — formerly Zaire — French was adopted as the medium of instruction for the entire country in the 1962 educational reform, replacing Kiswahili, Kikongo, Lingala, and Tshiluba which, until then, were the main media of instruction up to the third grade in various parts of the country.

Since the National Resistance Movement (NRM) government of Yoweri Museveni came to power in Uganda, hopes have rekindled that Kiswahili may once again find its way back to Ugandan schools. In 1989 there was a Ugandan mission to Tanzania to "find out how best they could facilitate the teaching of Kiswahili in Uganda, as well as how much help they could get from Tanzania ... [Meanwhile] in collaboration with the

Ministryof Education and Kakoba National Teachers College near Mbarara, CHAKU (Chama cha Kiswahili Uganda), or the Uganda Kiswahili Association, has started training teachers who will teach it to adult learners" (Ireri Mbaabu, 1996:109). A military intervention, therefore, may have created new opportunities for Kiswahili in the educational set up in Uganda. Will the coming to power of Laurent Kabila and his movement affect the fortunes of Kiswahili in a similar manner in Congolese schools? The situation in Congo continues to unfold.

In Kenya, until 1952, Kiswahili was still the medium of instruction in the first three years of primary education in those areas of the country in which it predominated as a native tongue. But in 1957, the Ministry of Education created the Nairobi Special Centre with the specific objective of promoting English medium instruction under the name of New Primary Approach (NPA). This development essentially ended Kiswahili's role as a medium of instruction.

The Nairobi Special Centre was to look into ways of addressing the problem of high failure rate in both primary and secondary school education that was supposedly caused by poor command of the English language. As would be expected, after some investigatory work, the Centre recommended that English be used and adopted as a medium of instruction from the very beginning of primary education. It argued that such a move would not only eliminate the problem of offering instruction in many languages that lacked instructional materials, but it would also avoid the negative learning effects that are bound to result from the transition from African languages to English language instruction.

Thus, on the eve of independence, English was already on an irreversible march to replace Kiswahili and other Kenyan languages, as media of instruction, at all levels of education throughout the country. After this, Kiswahili never regained its status as an instructional language and, in fact, was to remain no more than an optional school subject for more than twenty years of Kenya's independence.

Immediately after independence there was some hope, in fact, that the colonial linguistic legacy would at least be challenged. That was after the so-called Ominde Commission under Professor S.H. Ominde, was set up to survey the country's educational resources and advise the government on the formulation and implementation of national educational policies. But far from coming up with any proposal to reform the English language policy, the Ominde report actually reaffirmed the importance of using the language as an instructional medium throughout the school system. It did, however, suggest that, in view of Kiswahili's unifying role in the region, it should be made a compulsory subject in Kenya's primary schools (Republic of Kenya, 1964: 60-61). But even this modest recommendation on Kiswahili remained unadopted.

In 1975 yet another task force, the Kenya National Committee on Educational Objectives and Policies, was set up to identify more realistic goals for the country's rapidly expanding educational system. The report of this Committee essentially attempted to recreate a more substantial place for Kiswahili as well as for other Kenyan languages in Kenya's school curriculum. Recommendation 101 of the report proposed that "dominant" local languages be used as media of instruction in the first three years of primary school before they are replaced by English in subsequent years. Recommendations 107 and 141, on the other hand, sought to make Kiswahili a compulsory and examinable subject in primary and secondary schools (Republic of Kenya, 1976). But it was not until 1984, after Kenya adopted the 8-4-4 educational system (i.e., eight years of primary education, followed by four years of secondary education, followed in turn by four years of university education) that the recommendations on Kiswahili were finally implemented.

In essence, then, if European colonial governments were once debating about which language was best for capturing the African soul and which for cultivating the African mind, independent African governments had now decided that European languages were best for both their souls and their minds.

Among the Eastern African countries it was only Tanzania, in fact, that seriously attempted to change the colonial linguistic legacy. To a more modest extent, the British continued to pursue some of the policy objectives of the Germans insofar as Kiswahili was concerned. The language was used in the lower administrative levels and, except in Asian schools which used Indian "vernacular" and English, Kiswahili was used as a medium of instruction up to the fifth year of primary education.

This colonial language policy in education was, of course, not endorsed with unanimity. The Phelps-Stokes Commission, for example, was wary of the rate of the spread of Kiswahili in schools. It warned:

> There is a danger that the claims of both the vernacular and European languages shall be overshadowed by the ease with which the people learn a *lingua franca* such as Swahili... The vernaculars, therefore, have a vital claim to recognition in the school system. The advantages of a knowledge of a European language should also be seriously considered. The ease with which Swahili can be transmitted should not be permitted to exclude, at least in all higher schools, a knowledge of English or some European language which not only gives access to officers of government, but spreads the influences of civilization among the natives... (J. Jones, 1925: 192)

In 1955 the East African Royal Commission was even more antagonistic towards the position of Kiswahili in education. It considered the teaching of Kiswahili as a second language as a "complete waste of time and effort" and tried to justify the expansion of English as a demand of the African peoples themselves. According to the report of this commission:

> The African is very keen on learning English which is his gate of entry to a new world and we think that the teaching of English should begin in as low a class as possible and should become a medium of instruction as early as can be followed by pupils. (1955: 184)

Despite the opposition to Kiswahili from sections of the colonial administration, however, the language had taken strong roots at least in early primary African education in what was then Tanganyika.

On the eve of independence there were "three types of primary schools: Kiswahili-medium schools, English-medium schools, and Asian-vernacular-medium schools. All three types of schools began at the primary level with different languages though they followed a common syllabus with the school leaving examination in English. Kiswahili was introduced as a subject in schools where it was not a medium" (Zaline M. Roy-Campbell, 1992: 121). At independence, however, in quest for a more integrated school system, the Asian vernaculars were replaced with Kiswahili and English as media of instruction, and Kiswahili was made a compulsory subject in former "European schools."

It was not until 1967 after the launching of the Arusha Declaration and the adoption of Julius Nyerere's developmental policy of "Education for Self-Reliance," that Kiswahili was made the medium of instruction throughout the primary level of all government-sponsored schools. Education for self-reliance was designed to provide an education for life that would be relevant to the needs of the Tanzanian nation and which would not alienate the educated from the masses. Its focus was primary education as the availability of secondary and post-secondary education was still restricted to a relatively small section of the population. The initial consolidation of Kiswahili at the primary level of education, then, was partly prompted by the intended scope of the policy of education for self-reliance.

Cognizant of the fact that teachers may not be well prepared for the task of teaching in Kiswahili, the language was also introduced as a medium of instruction in teacher training colleges that concentrated on primary education. An anomaly that has persisted to this day, however, is that many texts used in these colleges continue to be in English while oral instruction is exclusively in Kiswahili (Y.P. Msanjila, 1990).

Despite the heavy focus on primary education, however, the

government started hinting at the possible extension of Kiswahili as a medium of instruction to post-primary education as early as 1969. In its 1969-74 developmental plan, for example, the government anticipated that:

> ...the division between Swahili education at the primary level and English education at the secondary level will create and perpetuate a linguistic gulf between different groups and will also tend to lend an alien atmosphere to higher education, making it inevitably remote from the problems of the mass of society. (United Republic of Tanzania, 1969: 152)

It was feared that the transition from Kiswahili-medium instruction in primary schools to English-medium instruction in secondary schools would have some debilitating effects on students. Educational problems were expected to arise because:

> ...children, on entering secondary school, will now have to shift to study in a new language, at the same time as taking on more difficult sets of subjects...as government moves over to the complete use of Swahili [therefore] it will become more and more inappropriate to have the secondary and higher educational system operate in English. (United Republic of Tanzania, 1969: 152)

This statement was read as an explicit expression of the Tanzanian government's intention to replace English with Kiswahili in post-primary education.

The 1969-74 plan, however, hastened to add that such a shift cannot be made overnight and that sufficient amount of time must be provided for the preparation of instructional materials:

> The major barrier to a shift to Swahili-medium will be lack of

teaching materials in Swahili. This lack cannot be made up overnight... Therefore, there must be long-term planning for such a shift with adequate commitment of resources to prepare for the change ahead of the intended implementation, so that adequate materials will be available in Swahili for the students at that time. The problem involved in mounting this effort and the complexities that are likely to arise during the transition period are such that it will be subject of a specially selected team who prepare proposals for the timing of the necessary steps and lay out a programme for the preliminary stages. (United Republic of Tanzania, 1969: 153)

This challenge was immediately taken up by various agencies of the government in preparation for the planned change in medium of instruction at the post-primary educational level. The Institute of Kiswahili Research and the Kiswahili National Academy (BAKITA) started developing technologies for subjects like mathematics, physics, chemistry, and biology while the Institute of Education coordinated the production of instructional materials. By 1975, materials had been written for political education, geography, commerce, mathematics, history, agriculture, and domestic science. In addition, technical vocabulary had been developed for economics, biology, chemistry, technical education, and physics (Zaline M. Roy-Campbell, 1992: 161). Despite all this activity in preparing instructional materials, however, by the early 1980s there was little evidence that the government was making any concrete plans for a medium shift in the country's secondary schools.

In 1980, Julius Nyerere set up a Presidential Commission on Education to review the state of education in Tanzania and make appropriate recommendations for reform for the next twenty years. In 1982 this commission came up with its report in which it argued:

In order that the nation is able to develop its culture and ease the understanding of most of the populace at the different

stages of education after primary education without the
encumbrance of a foreign language, it is recommended that...
*firm plans be made to enable all schools and colleges in
the country to teach all subjects using Kiswahili beginning
with Form I in January 1985 and the University
beginning 1992.* (United Republic of Tanzania, 1982: 209)

Instead of adopting the recommendations of this report, however, the
government seemed more inclined to consolidate the position of English in
its educational system. In 1984, two years after the release of the report
of the Presidential Commission on Education, the government argued that
"both Kiswahili and English will be used as media of education. The
teaching of English will be strengthened at all levels. Kiswahili will be the
medium of education at post-primary levels where the teaching of Kiswahili
as a subject will also be strengthened" (United Republic of Tanzania, 1984:
19).

As this position came under criticism from some educationists and
intellectuals, Julius Nyerere, then still the President of the country, found it
necessary to intervene with the following statement:

English is the Swahili of the world and for that reason must
be taught and given the weight it deserves in our country... It
is wrong to leave English to die. To reject English is foolishness,
not patriotism... English will be the medium of instruction in
secondary schools and institutions of higher education
because if it is left as only a normal subject it may die. (Quoted
by Zaline M. Roy-Campbell, 1992: 188)

With these sentiments at the highest echelon of the government, Tanzania
began to prepare the ground for the British sponsored English Language
Teaching Support Project whose central objective was to reinvigorate the
language as an instructional medium in secondary schools. This project
was ultimately launched in 1987.

On the other hand, early in 1998, the Tanzanian government and the Dar es Salaam.City Commission were locked in a controversy over the introduction of English as a medium of instruction in the city's primary schools. The government was opposed to attempts to phase out Kiswahili as a language of instruction in primary schools, which city authorities began in 1998, on the ground that the move would create a disparity in the preformance of pupils in rural and urban schools. But the government's position was criticized by parents increasingly seeking educational opportunities for their children beyond the country's borders where proficiency in English is considered a definite advantage (*The EastAfrican*, Feb 2-8, 1998).

Despite these moves to consolidate the position of English in post-primary education, however, and to extend it to the primary level, the position of Kiswahili in the Tanzanian society at large is not likely to suffer. Tanzania has continued to harness the national integrative potential of Kiswahili that was first discovered during its struggle against German colonialism and which was later found essential in its quest for egalitarianism. And it is to the interaction between Kiswahili and national integration that we should now turn.

4.   Kiswahili and Economic Integration

As Kiswahili was given the political cold shoulder both in up-country Kenya and in Uganda during the colonial period, the language spread in these areas in spite of the educational and language policies which were adopted. A major process involved concerned the role of the language as an economic medium. This is when the language became necessary in the fields of employment, trade, and the whole process of urbanization in contemporary East Africa.

Class-formation in the region touched upon the competition between Kiswahili and the English language as national media. The English language in the region was still a medium to be acquired at school. The prestige of the imperial language converted it into a resource which was relevant for class-formation. As East Africa approached independence, and both colonial policy-makers and missionary paternalists sought to facilitate the emergence of an educated elite, the balance of influence and power was beginning to shift significantly in the direction of those who had acquired the cultural symbols and educational skills derived from the imported metropolitan civilization.

Opportunities for the educated and the semi-educated were disproportionately located in the urban areas. The relationship between the English language and urbanization was, therefore, different from the relationship between Kiswahili and urbanization. Rural boys who had been educated enough to speak and write English were moved to the cities in order to capitalize on their new skills. It might even be argued that these boys joined the migration to the urban centers because they were already equipped with the potentially profitable English language.

On the other hand, many rural boys who were not so well educated and wanted to go to the cities to look for employment as porters or domestic workers, proceeded to acquire some competence in Kiswahili in order to facilitate their own individual urbanization. To some extent this was a reversal of cause and effect. The educated went to the cities because they had already acquired the English language; the less educated acquired Kiswahili because they wanted to move to the cities. The acquisition of European linguistic skills provided motivation for further migration to the urban areas; whereas in the case of the less educated, it was often the prior desire of moving to the cities which provided the motive for studying Kiswahili in the first place.

This is, of course, an over-simplification of a set of phenomena which were and continue to be sociologically complex. But the distinction being made is still defensible if we think of the educated class as *rural misfits* forced by their very qualifications at times to migrate to the cities; whereas the less educated with a smattering of Kiswahili begin by being *urban misfits* and improve their Kiswahili as part of the process of adjustment.

The educated are deemed to be rural misfits sometimes by their own families. Many parents go to considerable trouble and sacrifice to send their children through school. Fees have to be paid, books acquired, in some cases uniforms have also to be purchased. Rural families, otherwise deeply deprived, nevertheless put their trust in the future and proceed to make sacrifices for their children's education. The last thing such parents would welcome when the day of graduation comes would be to see their children still on their own little plot of land, seeking to earn a living in the rural areas in ancestral ways, instead of exploring wider opportunities beyond the green fields. By the time the youngster has been through school and articulated that ultimate difference of the command of the English language both orally and in writing, his or her family's expectations are in the direction of office work in the urban areas or, at any rate, something which could not have been done but for the sacrifice of putting a child through school. It is in this sense that the educated in African villages become to some extent rural misfits and are, therefore, under sociological pressure to seek white-collar respectability far from home.[12]

But the less educated, too, sometimes feel the pressure of seeking to improve their lot in the urban areas. Sometimes it might be because there are too many sons to have adequate land for cultivation together in the rural areas; or sometimes because there are too many women who would be otherwise underemployed unless the men go to the cities to earn and supplement the income of the extended family. Many an African husband works in a town while his wife cultivates his land in the village. The movement towards those urban centers increased the need for a *lingua franca* among the diverse groups. Kiswahili, even in parts of East Africa where it was completely ignored by the educational system, found its own momentum of spreading partly under the impact of these processes of urbanization.

Although no adequate comparative work has been done, it seems probable that East African cities by the nineteen-seventies are more multilingual, given their relatively small sizes, than West African cities. There are large urban centers in West Africa that are overwhelmingly uni-lingual. They constitute the points of demographic congregation for ethnic communities that are themselves large, sometimes numbering several million.

But East Africa has, on the one hand, fewer and smaller urban centers and, on the other hand, smaller ethnic communities. The few towns and cities, once communications improve enough, begin to draw from a larger range of linguistic groups than would be the case in, say, the old Eastern Nigeria or Western Nigeria.

In the case of some of the East African cities, communications with the rural areas are still so modest and rudimentary as to retard the full realization of linguistic diversity. But as these communications improve, the tendency will be towards greater multi-ethnic diversity in East African cities than in comparable urban areas on the west coast of the continent. It may already be true that, once we allow for the difference in size, there is greater ethnic and linguistic diversity in Jinja than in Ibadan, in Mombasa than in Accra. All these are approximations which have not as yet been computed, nor have any comparative studies been adequately undertaken. But the combination of smaller linguistic groups in East Africa and fewer towns and cities would seem to indicate a *trend* towards greater linguistic diversity in East African towns than in many West African ones.

If such trends are correct, the case for a trans-ethnic medium in East African cities is proportionately stronger. Part of the triumph of Kiswahili in East Africa may lie precisely in the fact that the great majority of East African ethnic groups and communities are so small. Few ethnic groups in East Africa top the four million mark in population, whereas language groups in West Africa are in some cases in terms of ten or twenty million people. West Africa, therefore, has been less successful than East Africa in evolving an adequate *lingua franca,* apart from the English language and its pidginized varieties.

Hausa is to some extent a *lingua franca* in West Africa, but it suffers from the handicap of being the native language of a group already large enough and powerful enough to be feared by others. The acceptability of Hausa as a *lingua franca is,* therefore, retarded precisely because those who speak it as a first language are already so numerous and, in any case, because there are rival groups almost comparable in size and with languages and cultures of their own, rich enough to be regarded as the true equals of Hausa.

In East Africa, the smallness of the group that speaks Kiswahili as a mother-tongue improves the chances of the language being accepted by others. In Kenya, less than a million people speak Kiswahili as a first language in a population of nearly thirty million.[13] This limited number of native speakers, and the smallness of the great majority of other linguistic groups in the country, have interacted especially towards giving Kiswahili an expanding role in the life of the nation.[14]

In Uganda, the privileges of the Baganda during the colonial period, and the fact that they were the largest group in the country, contributed to the spread of Luganda beyond the immediate confines of the kingdom. In spite of this factor, and in spite of the increasing indifference of colonial and educational policy-makers towards Kiswahili, and in spite of the continuing inertia with regard to language policy during the years of independence, Kiswahili spread fairly widely in Uganda under the impetus of urbanization and migrant labor. These two latter phenomena of urbanization and migrant labor, though closely related, were not identical. Urbanization included deruralization, the severance of ties among some sectors of the urban populations from their ancestral rural roots. Migrant labor, on the other hand, could at times be merely a case of the rural-urban continuum, a process by which husbands labored in towns while wives cultivated the land, a process by which some maintained continuing spiritual and economic communion with their villages. Kiswahili received a new lease of life, in the face of the hostilities of the missionaries and the Baganda, as a result of these twin processes of the growth of towns and cities and the mobility of the working force.

The political economy of Kiswahili in Uganda has resulted in its being disproportionately a language of men rather than women. Kiswahili and Luganda competed in the great marketplace of human communication. By 1972, fifty-two percent of Uganda men were able to hold a conversation in Kiswahili, but only eighteen percent of the women. Indeed, there were more Ugandan men who could conduct a conversation in Kiswahili than Ugandan men who were competent in Luganda. And yet, the percentage of Ugandans who could conduct a conversation in Luganda was higher than that of Kiswahili speakers mainly because Luganda speakers included a high proportion of female native speakers of the language. In general, many more men than women learn a second language, in any case. In the case of both Kiswahili and English in Uganda, the 1972 statistics indicate that the number of male speakers of each language was well over twice the number of female speakers. But in the case of Luganda, the number of male speakers, though considerably more than that of female speakers, was nevertheless significantly less than double. This was because of the three languages, only Luganda had large numbers of native female speakers.[15]

A lot has, of course, transpired in Uganda since 1972 that has led to a major flux and depletion of the population. The 1972 figures, then, may have little value in the Uganda of today. Nonetheless, in both Uganda and Kenya, it is still possible to speculate that Kiswahili has continued to have a greater proportion of male than female speakers. This is because a number of the processes that favor the acquisition of Kiswahili, like rural-to-urban migration, employment in the urban workforce and recruitment into the armed forces, have continued to be predominantly male-oriented. In Tanzania, on the other hand, the language is so widely spread, in any case, that these male-oriented processes are not likely to have a significant effect on the male/female ratio of its speakers.

On the question of language and gender specifically, the West African experience may be somewhat different from that of East Africa. The West African phenomenon of market women, in particular, may have served as a counter-balance to the male-oriented economic processes that contribute to the acquisition of a *lingua franca,* like Hausa. Of course there are market women too in East Africa, but the phenomenon tends to be much smaller in scale and, geographically, much more localized in comparison with the situation in West Africa. West African "market women" constitute an economically formidable force, and they traverse large distances, often across national boundaries in search of goods and markets. The political economy of West Africa, therefore, may have created a greater gender balance with respect to the acquisition of Hausa, for example, than is the situation in East Africa with respect to Kiswahili.

The growth of trade unionism in East Africa added a new and important organizational role for Kiswahili independently of educational policy. The wage sector of each East African economy was expanding, and the workers after World War II began to experiment with collective-bargaining. In Uganda a significant proportion of the workforce came from Kenya, and trade unionism in Uganda was, for a while, partially led and controlled by Kenyan immigrants. The importance of Kiswahili was enhanced in a situation where the labor force was not only multi-ethnic, but also international. So closely associated with workers and the beginnings of proletarian organization was Kiswahili in Uganda that the social prestige of the language among the more aristocratic Baganda declined even further. The language was deemed to be one for "lower classes" of society, and a language of the migrant proletariat. The social prestige which Kiswahili enjoyed in Tanzania, with all the associations of a complex culture and political society, was conspicuously absent in Uganda. Many of those who did speak the language did not speak it well. The Kiswahili of Uganda was indeed basically a language for the workers, functionally specific and non-versatile, and, for those reasons, more limited in scope. Nevertheless, the need for the language as a medium of organizing the workers in these early stages of the growth of trade unionism must be counted as one of the major aspects of the political economy of Kiswahili.

These new functions of Kiswahili in East African society were integrative at the horizontal level. We define horizontal integration simply in terms of social communication and interaction across geographical and ethnic divisions of the society as a whole. We define vertical integration as a process of interaction between different strata of the society, especially between the elite and the masses. To the extent that Kiswahili served as the main language of trade unionism and organized labor, and facilitated social communication between workers and peasants from different geographical areas and ethnic groups, the language was performing horizontally integrative functions. To the extent to which these functions were expanding the wage sector of the economy, facilitating the circulation of money across the country as a whole, promoting a consciousness of a national economy, and defining the boundaries of the national marketplace of goods and labor, Kiswahili was involved in the critical process of economic integration within each of the East African countries.

In Kenya, even the shift of the capital from Mombasa to Nairobi later enhanced Kiswahili's potential as a mechanism for horizontal economic integration. At first, the decision to transfer the capital seemed to be a blow against the spread of Kiswahili. After all, if Mombasa was no longer the hub of national life in the country, the impact of Mombasa's language on the rest of the society seemed to be minimal.

> By the beginning of the century ... the administrative focus of the East African Protectorate had moved away from the coastal area, Nairobi replacing Mombasa as the headquarters of the Uganda railway in July 1899. In 1907, the capital of the Protectorate was moved from Mombasa to Nairobi and there is not doubt that this transfer diminished the influence on Kenya's development of the coastal Swahili culture that became so important in Tanzania's history. (T.P. Gorman, 1974: 389)

While it may be true that the spread of the Swahili culture was adversely affected by the shift from Mombasa to Nairobi, it is by no means certain that the spread of Kiswahili suffered with this transfer. On the contrary, it is arguable that the relative centrality of Nairobi increased the spread of the *lingua franca* on a national level. What happened to many non-Baganda workers in Kampala did not happen to many non-Kikuyu workers in Nairobi. Because the Baganda under the colonial administration had been a privileged group and were allowed to retain considerable influence and prestige, their language in turn commanded derivative prestige, and many of the workers who came into the capital of Uganda felt they had to learn Luganda. Indeed, Kiganda culture favored the linguistic and cultural assimilation of newcomers. In one or two generations, many workers who were descended from non-Baganda became, to all intents and purposes, native Luganda speakers and were absorbed into the body politic of Buganda.

The Kikuyu in colonial Kenya, on the other hand, though comparable to the Baganda in size and proximity to the capital, were not a privileged group. On the contrary, they were often the most humiliated and exploited of all groups because of their nearness to the white settlers of Kenya.

The Kikuyu also performed some of the most menial tasks even in towns very far from their own areas. These tasks ranged from sweeping the streets of Kisumu to emptying latrine buckets in Mombasa.

For the non-Kikuyu workers pouring into Nairobi there was relatively little incentive to perfect their familiarity with the Kikuyu language. Many non-Kikuyu workers did indeed learn some Kikuyu, but not for reasons of improving their social status in Nairobi or enhancing their chances of a good job. Kiswahili in Nairobi had an easier time in the competition with the Kikuyu language than it had in the competition with Luganda in Kampala. By the time of independence, very few Kikuyu politicians addressing public audiences in Nairobi regarded it as sensible to use the Kikuyu language. This was in marked contrast to Baganda politicians addressing public meetings in Kampala, who normally used Luganda in preference to both Kiswahili and English.

Mombasa itself continued to be a Swahili metropolis, continuing to grow in size and attracting an expanding non-coastal population. Though second in size to Nairobi by the time of independence, Mombasa was nevertheless large enough to be bigger than either the capital of Tanzania or Uganda. Nairobi was linguistically pluralistic with a widespread use of the Kikuyu language and the English language. But on balance, Kiswahili had been gaining ground at least as the *lingua franca* for horizontal integration and increasingly as a medium also for vertical integration in select areas of social change.

What remains remarkable is the extent to which these new functions of the language in Kenya, as a whole, evolved in spite of the relative indifference of educational policy-makers and quite often in spite of their actual hostility to Kiswahili. What all this reveals once again is how economic necessity for a particular language in a given sociological situation could generate the spontaneous spread of the language, notwithstanding the formal educational system. The marketplace as an arena of linguistic spread can certainly be decisively independent of the classroom.

The spread of Kiswahili in the former Belgian Congo was also partly linked with economic changes and economic integration. It may not be entirely by accident that Kiswahili prospered best in such major mining areas of the Congo as Katanga, Upper Congo and the old Kivu.

A convergence of two historic forces favoured the spread of Kiswahili in the Congo - the movement of Swahili and Arab traders in the earlier centuries and the emigration of colonial workers in the twentieth century. Many of those workers were headed for the mines. In many cases a multi-ethnic labour force turned to Kiswahili as a lingua franca. In many homes Kiswahili became more important than the original ethnic language; Kiswahili was thus domesticated - moving from the workplace to the home.

At one level this was a case of regional integration, linguistically linking the Congo to other parts of Eastern Africa. But for a while Kiswahili seemed to reinforce the separate identity of provinces like Katanga. Indeed, the previous name Shaba (meaning "copper") was a Kiswahili word for the province. Was this provincial separatism detrimental to national integration, on the one hand, and harming the internal national integration of Congo, on the other?

Certainly in the 1970s Katanga rebelled twice against the central government of Mobutu Sese Seko. On one of those occasions the Katanga rebellion had to be put down by imported Moroccan troops, aided by the French and American logistical support. Were the Katanga rebellions detrimental to national integration or were they pro-democracy revolts?

We now know that Katanga's most famous sons of the twentieth century were Moise Tshombe, who attempted to pull the province out of the Congo in the 1960s, and Laurent Kabila, who embarked on a new effort to reunify the whole country in the 1990s. Moise Tshombe is best remembered in history as a secessionist who contributed to the murder of Patrice Lumumba, the Congo's first post-colonial prime minister. Laurent Kabila wants to be remembered as an integrationist, who completed the national and Pan-African mission of Patrice Lumumba. Katanga is the province of the birth of Tshombe and Kabila and the province of the murder of Patrice Lumumba.

In 1996 and 1997 Kabila mobilized the Swahili language as the medium of command in a multi-ethnic army of rebellion, aided and abetted by Rwanda, Uganda and Angola (Shiner, 1997).

The anti-Mobutu armed rebellion of 1996 started with the Tutsi of what was then Zaire, but escalated not only into multi-ethnic revolt but also into a multi-national movement, with Laurent Kabila as the leader. Kiswahili became increasingly important, not only because many of the fighters who were recruited already had a command of Kiswahili, but also because of the secret participation of training officers and possibly troops from Rwanda and Uganda. The Rwanda Patriotic Front as the basis of the Rwanda army is mainly Anglophone and Swahili-speaking.

In addition, according to certain Tutsi sources who prefer to remain anonymous, many of the indigenous Congolese Tutsi had for a long time increasingly emphasized the regular use of Kiswahili rather than Kinyarwanda in their own postcolonial homes precisely in order to reduce their being mistaken for Rwandan *immigrants*. Kiswahili became a kind of linguistic asylum for many Tutsi to reduce their ethnic vulnerability as speakers of "the language of Rwanda," Kinyarwanda. While they could not entirely conceal their being Tutsi, they could at least de-emphasize it in the face of ethnic prejudice (Duke and Rupert, 1997).

One of the major questions of the post-Mobutu era in Congo is whether the era would bring better economic and political relations between the Democratic Republic of Congo and her neighbours to the east and south-east. Are such regional changes already carrying linguistic consequences? The evidence would seem to suggest that there will be a decline of the Congo identification with the Francophonie community, at least as presently conceived and led by France. Second, there will be a rise of the status of English in Congo — beginning with Kabila's moves to give English a role in the new orientation of the country. Third, the status of Kiswahili in the Congo, which was officially recognized when Mobutu declared it one of the four national languages of what was then Zaire in the 1970s - the other languages being Lingala, Kikongo and Tchiluba - would now be strengthened even further. There is a chance that Kiswahili will now perform not only the subregional tasks it already performed under Mobutu's rule, but will increasingly overshadow Lingala as the language of the politico-military establishment of the new Congo.

Will Kiswahili in Congo replace Lingala as the most important indigenous language for national integration? The trend may have started but the final answer is in the womb of history. At this level economic integration links up with political integration more fully.

5. Kiswahili and Political Integration

But when a language is needed for vertical integration, especially in the sense of facilitating social communication between the rulers and the ruled, the educational system becomes once again a favored medium for dissemination. In Tanganyika under German rule, Kiswahili had among its earliest functions that of vertical integration. The Germans had opted for the language as a medium of potential administrative convenience, and proceeded in the training of second and third level indigenous administrators. The bureaucratic infrastructure was modified to suit this linguistic policy. A certain cultural and linguistic intolerance characterized the implementation of the Swahilization of Tanganyika under the Germans, but the policy was substantially effective nevertheless, and has had long-term consequences for independent Tanzania. Certainly the Swahilization of mainland Tanzania would have been far less complete today without the purposeful exercise in vertical integration pursued by German policy-makers before the first World War.

In Kenya and Uganda for at least the first quarter of this century, there was enough interest in using Kiswahili as a medium of communication between the rulers and the ruled to give the language some role in the educational system. In many schools, it had the minimal status of one of the subjects taught. In some schools, it was even used as a medium of instruction at the lower levels.

Administrators coming from England were also often required, in those days, to learn the language. Article 19 of the Regulations of the Employment of Officers, dated August 1, 1903, made Kiswahili an obligatory language. Officers appointed after that date were expected to have a fair knowledge of Kiswahili within their first year of arrival in the Uganda Protectorate, and their promotion depended in part on this linguistic skill. Certain financial incentives and bonuses were paid to administrative officers on passing the lower and higher standard examinations in Kiswahili. In Buganda, the regulation was altered in 1914, replacing Kiswahili with Luganda, but Kiswahili retained for a while a residual administrative role in the face of mounting disparagement by Luganda speakers and Christian missionaries. As the language ceased to be regarded as indispensable for vertical integration between the rulers and the ruled, its role in the educational system also shrunk.

It was not until the eve of independence that there was once again a sense of need for the language for purposes of vertical integration. The Uganda People's Congress, especially as a party with a nationwide perspective, and led primarily by non-Luganda speakers, showed an early awareness of the need for a grassroot's language of politics. At their Annual Conference on attainment of independence, the U.P.C. passed a resolution urging that Kiswahili should be taught in Uganda schools. And yet, partly because the first government was a coalition between the U.P.C. and Kabaka Yekka, there was considerable caution with regard to the implementation of this recommendation. Milton Obote's government dragged its feet, initially for reasons of amity with its Luganda-speaking partners in the first government after independence, and later for reasons more difficult to comprehend.

To a question from Mr. H.M. Luande in Parliament asking for the inclusion of Kiswahili as a language which an applicant for citizenship might offer in order to qualify, the Permanent Secretary to the Office of the Prime Minister, Mr. Alex Ojera, replied:

> Apart from the English language, which is provided in the Constitution as the official language, the only language so far prescribed under Section 22 are mother-tongues spoken by the peoples of Uganda. Swahili, though spoken widely in East Africa and elsewhere, is not a mother-tongue in Uganda. Government does not intend prescribing Swahili as a language qualification for citizenship until such time as Swahili is understood and used more extensively than it is today by the peoples of Uganda.

Mr. Luande moved a supplementary question, reminding the Minister of the resolution of the Annual Conference of the U.P.C. concerning the teaching of Kiswahili in Uganda schools. All that Mr. Ojera would say was: "The question of teaching Swahili in schools is not within my portfolio, but belongs to my Friend, the Minister of Education. Whatever the U.P.C. has passed will always be taken very seriously by the U.P.C./Kabaka

Yekka government" (Republic of Uganda, 1963).

Dr. J. Luyimbazi-Zake, who came to control the Ministry of Education until the overthrow of Obote's regime in January 1971, was later to dismiss Kiswahili as being foreign to Uganda as Gujerati. Dr. Zake himself was a native speaker of Luganda, though he was also fluent in Kiswahili. He was a member of the Uganda People's Congress, and constituted, it would seem, one of the factors which led to the linguistic drift of the Obote years in Uganda, in spite of that resolution by the Annual Conference of the U.P.C. to move towards giving Kiswahili full status in the Ugandan educational system.

The man who had answered Mr. Luande's questions in Parliament in 1963, Alex Ojera, later became Minister of Information under Obote. He and President Obote said privately to one of the authors of this book, Ali Mazrui, in 1969, that the Uganda government was on the verge of introducing Kiswahili at least on the radio. Six languages were confirmed as broadcasting languages in Uganda after independence. In February 1963, Mr. A. Lobidra asked the following question in Parliament: "As most of the people in Uganda do understand some sort of Swahili and in view of the fact that Uganda cannot afford giving every tribe a programme on Radio Uganda, would the Government examine the possibility of including up-country Swahili for Local News Broadcasts?"

The Minister of Information, Broadcasting, and Tourism, Mr. A.A. Nekyon, did not agree that most people in Uganda understood some sort of Kiswahili:

> We have already commenced broadcasts in six languages and I am quite convinced that Swahili is not one of the basic languages which is understood widely in the country... We are already broadcasting in so many languages that I do not think this is a really sound reason for adding to that number. (Republic of Uganda, 1963)

By the time Mr. Ojera and Dr. Obote were suggesting privately in 1969 that Kiswahili would be introduced on Radio Uganda, the recognized broadcasting languages were already *fourteen*. The majority of these were understood by far fewer people in the country than Kiswahili was.

The year 1969 was also the year of *The Common Man's Charter* in Uganda, and the Obote strategy of the "Move to the Left." A new sensitivity to the needs of the grassroots' level of politics emerged under the impact of the move to the left. The national service scheme in Uganda envisaged the teaching of Kiswahili, among other tasks. And Obote's electoral reforms would, in addition, have provided a further case for the rapid introduction of Kiswahili into the country's political system. Document Number 5 of the "Move to the Left" envisaged a situation whereby each member of Parliament would stand in four constituencies: one in the north, one in the south, one in the west, and one in the east of the country. That meant that each parliamentary candidate would need to woo three-quarters of his electoral support from outside his own linguistic area. He would need to campaign among peasants who did not understand his language and were equally ignorant of English. He would need a new grassroots medium for this nationwide electioneering. A Muganda campaigning in Lango could not make much progress with his native Luganda. Each parliamentary candidate would, therefore, either have to learn three African languages in addition to his own if he was to communicate effectively in all his four constituencies, or the nation as a whole would have to push systematically one *lingua franca* for the conduct of politics at the grassroots' level. The most serious candidate for such a role in the Ugandan situation seemed to be Kiswahili. The English language might have continued to be important for communication among parliamentarians themselves once they were elected, and were engaged in deliberations in Parliament, but Kiswahili would have been the connecting link between these parliamentarians on one side and the linguistically diverse constituents which each had to reach. The Uganda Parliament under such a scheme would, after a while, have had to become bilingual, with simultaneous translation between English and Kiswahili, very much as the colonial legislature of Tanganyika on the eve of independence was before Parliament in independent Tanzania moved the whole way towards Kiswahili.

Under Document 5 by A. Milton Obote, Kiswahili in Uganda seemed destined for a new and critical role in vertical integration. By the time Obote gave his first address as Chancellor of the newly autonomous Makerere University, Kampala, he was in a position to enunciate new directions in linguistic education in the years which would follow. He called for the establishment of a school for African languages at the university, and went on to declare that "the Government would endeavour to introduce the teaching of Swahili in the schools" *(Sunday Nation,* Nairobi, October 11, 1970). At long last, Governor Gower's dream about the promotion of Kiswahili in the Ugandan educational system seemed to be on the verge of fulfillment. And those delegates who had attended that historic Annual Conference of the Uganda People's Congress in 1962, and joined in voting the resolution for the introduction of Kiswahili into Ugandan schools, might have sensed at long last, the nearness of implementation. The dictates of vertical integration, as the elite sought to reach the masses, had once again proved to have more direct educational consequences than the processes of horizontal integration in the marketplace.

But the Obote regime did not remain in power long enough to fulfil its long delayed linguistic promises. On January 25, 1971, a voice on Radio Uganda — ill at ease with the English language — announced a military takeover. The voice was that of General Idi Amin Dada. A new phase in the history of Kiswahili in Uganda seemed to have started.

Partly because of his *professional background* as a soldier in the Ugandan army, partly because of his *ethnic background* as a Nilote from northern Uganda, and partly because of his *class background* as a quasi-peasant with limited schooling, Idi Amin had all the makings of a president who would be in favor of promoting Kiswahili in Uganda. And indeed on August 7, 1973, Idi Amin passed a decree declaring Kiswahili the national language of Uganda.

This decree was probably one of the few that were based on some democratic input. It was, in fact, based on a recommendation by representatives from the then twenty districts of Uganda. Under the auspices of the government, the representatives met at the International Conference Centre in Kampala with the issue of a national language for Uganda being the sole item on their agenda. After extensive deliberations, the representatives voted on the issue and the majority, twelve out of the twenty districts, voted for Kiswahili, and the rest voted for Luganda. Kiswahili then became Uganda's democratic choice for a national language.

Equally significant, however, was the division between pro-Kiswahili advocates and pro-Luganda advocates. The regions that voted for Luganda were predominantly Baganda with the support of fellow Bantu ethnic groups from the Eastern region (Bugisu, Bukedi, and Busoga) and Western region (Ankole) of Uganda. Those that voted for Kiswahili were from the predominantly Nilotic northern districts and a few from Bantu-dominated districts like Bunyoro, Kigezi, and Toro (Asaf Lulua, 1976: 12-13). Bantu speakers, then, continued to be the greatest antagonists of a Bantu language, Kiswahili, while speakers of Nilotic languages, continued being its greatest friends. A major achievement of the Amin era even before this national language decree was the inclusion of Kiswahili in the programmes of Uganda radio and television. The almost ten years of a noncommittal policy of the Obote government towards Kiswahili in Uganda's electronic media was thus overturned within three weeks of a military dictatorship. The 1973 decree, therefore, promised to consolidate Kiswahili's official status even further.

But, in fact, little came out of Idi Amin's decree on Kiswahili. There was no coherent policy on the language that was worked out and no government efforts to promote it in other domains of Ugandan society. Nonetheless, the rise of the military had undoubtedly improved the fortunes of Kiswahili in this East African country. The constant interaction between the military and the wider society, in particular, continued to foster the consolidation of Kiswahili in Uganda throughout the Idi Amin years.

For a while, the ouster of Idi Amin seemed to hold even better prospects for the future of Kiswahili in Uganda. Idi Amin was pushed out of power by a coalition of Uganda rebel groups attacking from Tanzania united under the name of Uganda National Liberation Army (UNLA), with massive support of the Tanzanian army. The thousands of Tanzanian soldiers walking the streets of Uganda, interacting with the people in Kiswahili, were seen as heroes and liberators of the Ugandan people from Idi Amin's tyranny. The national language of Tanzania, Kiswahili, suddenly acquired a new positive image in the minds of many Ugandans precisely because of the positive role that the national army of Tanzania was seen to have played in ending Amin's bloody era. The fortunes of Kiswahili seemed boundless indeed. The political climate indicated new possibilities of Tanzanian personnel, both military and otherwise, coming into Uganda on a large scale to help in the reconstruction of the country and a cultural agreement signed between the two countries included "an undertaking to develop the common African language Kiswahili" (Ireri Mbaabu, 1996:109). This move would certainly have helped in the Swahilization of Uganda.

But this positive image towards Tanzania due to its perceived role in Uganda's liberation fell just as rapidly as it rose. This is when it appeared that Tanzania's involvement in Uganda's political affairs was based less on the noble principles of freedom and liberty for the people than on a hidden agenda to return Milton Obote to power. Tanzania was now suspected of seeking to replace Idi Amin's dictatorship with Milton Obote's dictatorship. Tanzania's image as a liberator of the people of Uganda now gave way to the image of a betrayer of the democratic aspirations of the Ugandan people. The Ugandan population began to turn hostile towards Tanzania, and with this change in political opinion, Kiswahili may have lost a golden moment in its political history in Uganda.

The fall of Idi Amin in 1979, the return of civilian rule under Milton Obote, and the changed attitudes towards Tanzania, now combined to threaten the gains that Kiswahili had made under the rule of the military.

But the 1980 edition of the manifesto of Obote's political party, the Uganda People's Congress (UPC) gave advocates of Kiswahili a new glimmer of hope. According to the manifesto:

> UPC will seek to promote an African language such as Kiswahili to the status of a national, unifying language. At the same time, UPC will encourage and foster the development and teaching of various indigenous languages as proof of our heritage. English will remain the official language. *(UPC Manifesto,* 1980: 4)

While the statement by no means demonstrates a commitment on the part of UPC to promote Kiswahili, in particular, it at least left the impression that the party was seriously willing to consider that option.

By the time Obote was ousted from power in 1985, however, it was only the English part of UPC's pledge that was in effect. The English language did indeed continue to serve as the official language of Uganda. Neither Kiswahili nor any of the indigenous languages of Uganda gained from UPC's return to power. Admittedly, the new UPC government did not repeal Idi Amin's decree making Kiswahili the national language, nor did it terminate Kiswahili programmes in Uganda's radio and television. But neither did it initiate any moves to promote the language in the country.

If the Ugandan military had hitherto been regarded as a friend of Kiswahili, the ascendancy of the National Resistance Movement (NRM) in 1986 now threatened to alter this equation. Civilian governments in Uganda had proved not to be the strongest advocates of Kiswahili. Was the military, under NRM's leadership, now also going to turn against Kiswahili? This fear was partly based on the fact that NRM's army, the National Resistance Army (NRA), was to a large extent composed of some of the same ethnic groups and their Bantu allies, whose representatives voted against Kiswahili in 1973. When the Ugandan army was predominantly Nilotic in composition Kiswahili, a Bantu language, had a new lease on life in Ugandan politics. Was a predominantly Bantu army

now going to turn betrayer and end the lease on life of this Bantu language
in spite of the fact that Yoweri Museveni was himself quite articulate in
Kiswahili?

Probably one factor militated against the materialization of this fear.
And this was the fact that Kiswahili became an important medium of trans-
ethnic communication in the National Resistance Army throughout the
period of its struggle against government forces. Despite the major changes
in its ethnic composition, the military in Uganda, true to its character,
remained a loyal friend of Kiswahili. Unlike its predecessor, the Obote
government, the NRM government has been willing to take one more
step beyond Idi Amin's initiative by declaring Kiswahili as the official
language of the army.

On the other hand, the NRM government has remained manifestly
guarded in expressing its views towards the national language question.
The issue is clearly not included in NRM's *Ten Point Programme* nor in
any of its policy statements that have been made since then. Not long
after NRM came to power in 1986, both President Yoweri Museveni and
his Prime Minister, Dr. Samson Kissekka, were reported to have lamented
on separate occasions about the failure of previous governments to engage
in concerted efforts to promote a national language in Uganda. But, at the
same time, none of them indicated what the NRM government intended
to do about the issue. It was partly these statements by the president and
his prime minister that the editor of the *Weekly Topic of* Uganda reacted
to in the following terms:

> ... the NRM government should stop lamenting over the
> absence of a "local" national language. They should boldly
> take practical steps and give this country a common medium
> of communication... President Museveni and Prime Minister
> Kissekka should lead so as to translate their wishful laments
> into fruitful action. *(Weekly Topic,* Editorial, October 1, 1986)

There were modest indications, however, that the NRM government was planning to resolve the national language question through a long-term democratic process rather than through a short-term bureaucratic decision. At a 1989 function to inaugurate the Kiswahili Association of Uganda, the Minister of State in the Office of the President and NRM's National Political Commissioner, Dr. Kizza-Basigye, was reported to have said that "the subject of a national language is a constitutional matter. It must be included in the country's draft constitution and decided upon together with other matters" (Dale E.R. Mutabiirwa, 1989). And, indeed, the national language question was an aspect of Uganda's national debate since 1989 directed towards the preparation of a new draft constitution for the country. But once the process of establishing a new constitutional order was complete, the status of Kiswahili, and indeed the whole question of a national language for the country, fell, once again in total limbo without a definite policy on the linguistic future of Uganda. Will Uganda require another military coup before Kiswahili gets another boost in this East African nation?

Well after the release of its new constitution, however, Uganda continued to emit mixed signals about the future status of Kiswahili in the country. Reacting to a memorandum from the National Youth Council calling for the adoption of Kiswahili as a national language, Uganda's vice-president, Dr. Wandhira Kazibwe, said: "There is nothing wrong with Swahili. I want to assure you that whether you like it or not Swahili will win because this business of *ebyaffe, ebyeitu, ebyaife* (our things) will not lead us anywhere." *(New Vision*, July 11, 1998). But even as the vice-president was making this prediction, in a public address, about the victory of Kiswahili to the overall advantage of national and regional unity, there were murmurs of disapproval from sections of the audience. The struggle over Kiswahli continues in this East African country.

In Kenya, by the time of independence, a large section of the political elite had already become quite dependent on Kiswahili especially in their attempts to solicit the support of the people for political office. Nonetheless, the language also experienced quite a bit of opposition in the first ten years or so of independence in spite of its demonstrated role as an important medium of political integration. When a bill was tabled in parliament in 1969 proposing to make Kiswahili the official language of the country, its chief opponents attempted to discredit it by alluding to its Arabic and Islamic associations. In the words of Charles Njonjo, for example, the then powerful Attorney General of the country: "Swahili is derived from Arabic. It is a language which originated from the Arabs... Swahili is not our language, and it is not our mother-tongue: it is a foreign language just as much as English is a foreign language" (Republic of Kenya, 1969: columns 2520-2524). Another influential politician, G.G. Kariuki, had this to say: "Swahili [like English] is also a foreign language... It is an Arabic language...particularly used by Muslims. The majority of African Muslims speak very good Swahili, especially the people from the coast" (Republic of Kenya, 1969: column 2525). Some of the biased colonial attitudes towards Kiswahili, then, had now found their proponents in the post-colonial period.

It was not until July 4, 1974, after the Governing Council of the Kenya African National Union unanimously resolved to make Kiswahili the national language of Kenya and the official medium of parliament with immediate effect, that these anti-Kiswahili sentiments were silenced once and for all. President Kenyatta then decreed that the National Assembly should switch to Kiswahili, on an experimental basis, until the clause of the Constitution which made English the legislative language, was changed and until the Hansard recording facilities were modified, and other technical problems of transition solved (*The Daily Nation,* Nairobi, July 5 & 6, 1974).

The Kenya Government was at last formally recognizing Kiswahili as a potentially vital medium for vertical, as well as horizontal, integration. The fact that the adoption of Kiswahili as a national language was done on the eve of a general election raised questions about the likely composition of the next parliament. Would there be members fluent in Kiswahili, but without any competence in the English language? Would other candidates previously eligible on the strength of their English be now disqualified because they lacked Kiswahili? Would the composition of the National Assembly be significantly altered by this dramatic change in the linguistic qualifications of parliamentary candidates?

In the Kenyan situation there was a case for a transitional bilingual legislature, using both English and Kiswahili at least until the elections of 1979. Members could then speak either English or Kiswahili as they wished. The possibility of installing facilities for simultaneous translation could also have been considered for this five-year period before a final decision was made.

The case for such a bilingual transition in the Kenyan situation lay precisely in the educational lag regarding the language. Kiswahili was demoted even further in the educational system following the declaration of the Mau Mau State of Emergency in 1952. This was done in order to reduce even more political contacts between Africans across ethnic lines. This twenty-year educational lag was harmful to the quality of the language spoken up-country, and could in turn adversely affect the quality of debating in the National Assembly from 1974 onwards.

As it turned out, a bilingual legislature was precisely what President Daniel Arap Moi proceeded to establish soon after he became a substantive president toward the end of 1978. The law was accordingly changed to require that prospective candidates for the National Assembly be proficient in both Kiswahili and English. As indicated earlier, this move did not contribute to expanding the pool of elite recruitment to include those who could not speak English. Political participation in parliament was, and still is, limited to those who have some command of the English language. Nonetheless, relative to English, Kiswahili still made some modest gains because the law now excluded from parliamentary participation those whose linguistic competence was limited to English.

The Moi government took another positive step in 1985 by making Kiswahili a compulsory and examinable subject in the country's primary and secondary schools. This has given Kiswahili a momentum which is likely to improve the quality of Kiswahili debates in Kenya's future parliaments. The new linguistic policy in education is also likely to equip Kenya's future elite, both political and non-political, with the linguistic means that would enhance their interaction with the mass of the people. By all indication, then, Kiswahili's role as a medium of vertical political integration is likely to expand in Kenya in the forthcoming decades.

Combined with the changes in educational policy, are political changes in electoral laws which may again widen Kiswahili's scope to serve as a language of practical politics in Kenya. In September 1992, the Kenya parliament passed an amendment to the Kenya constitution in connection with the country's presidential elections. This new law, Section 5 (3f) of the constitution of Kenya, provides that:

> The candidate for President who is elected as member of the National Assembly and who receives a greater number of valid votes cast in the presidential election than any other candidate for President and who, in addition, receives a minimum of 25 percent of the valid votes cast in at least five of the eight provinces shall be declared to be elected as President.

As in the case of Obote's Document 5, but to a lesser extent, this new election law in Kenya now required that at least all presidential candidates are proficient enough in Kiswahili to solicit the support of a wide section of an ethnically-heterogenous public that has no knowledge of English.[16]

The status of Kiswahili in Kenya's educational system is gradually on the rise. Once again, considerations of political integration have revealed their influence on educational policy-making. And the changes in educational policy so far are bound to advance Kiswahili's role as a medium of political integration. A new phase in the history of Kiswahili in Kenya, then, might well have started.

6. Kiswahili and Cultural Nationalism

In connection with cultural nationalism, it is worth going back to the significance of Kiswahili for East African soldiers. By the time Amin captured power in Uganda, the soldiers had become, as we indicated, the residual official users of Kiswahili in Uganda. The language had, to all intents and purposes, become the language of command in the police and the armed forces. By the time of independence many Ugandan soldiers and policemen had developed a special possessiveness about Kiswahili. The psychological reasons for the popularity of Kiswahili among the soldiers are complex, and certainly include a resentment of Luganda-speakers who had been politically privileged for so long during the colonial period. The armed forces and the police had been recruiting overwhelmingly from non-Ganda areas, partly because these professions under the Baganda had declined in prestige as a result of the other advantages that the Baganda enjoyed, and partly because Britain as the imperial power preferred to recruit from some of the so-called "martial tribes" in the north of the country.

By the year 1966, when Buganda was defeated in a military confrontation with the central government, and the Baganda were for a while humiliated, it was not uncommon for soldiers from other communities to test some of their captives linguistically in order to determine their competence in Kiswahili. More often than not, the Kiswahili tests as applied to local "suspects" arrested by the armed forces were simply intended to humiliate Luganda speakers even further. But even after making allowances for the deep emotions and tensions which the Buganda question had created in the Ugandan population, there is no doubt that Kiswahili acquired a special status of loyalty among the soldiers of Uganda.

Underlying the soldiers' response was the whole phenomenon of cultural nationalism at all its four levels. These levels are ethnic (in the sense of sub-national identification), "intraracial" (in the sense of identification with the heritage of black people), territorial (in the sense of identification either with the new territorial state or with a large entity within the African continent), and fourthly, class (in the sense of identifying with the less educated, or the peasants, or the workers, or the common man).

The preference of the Ugandan soldiers for Kiswahili as against Luganda was partly a case of ethnic cultural nationalism, partially inverted. The social prestige of Luganda, and the political influence of the Baganda during the colonial period, had resulted in a certain degree of cultural defensiveness on the part of the remaining communities. To the extent that the armed forces had recruited disproportionately from these communities, Kiswahili became a symbol of their own cultural autonomy in opposition to the Baganda. This was a curious response since Kiswahili was, in fact, not the mother-tongue of any of the groups involved. The adoption of Kiswahili for purposes of asserting parity with the Baganda was, therefore, a partially inverted case of ethnic nationalism among the soldiers. They loved Kiswahili partly because it was not Luganda. They identified with it partly because it was opposed by the Baganda. The linguistic possessiveness of the Ugandan soldiers with regard to Kiswahili was therefore very much connected with one of the most central issues in Uganda's political history — the status of Buganda in national affairs.

But for as long as the educational policy of Uganda was not decided by the soldiers, and for as long as the soldiers had no say in determining the languages used for broadcasting, this semi-inverted linguistic possessiveness in the armed forces did not result in concrete policies.

There is some evidence that Kiswahili, though spoken mainly as a second language, may have briefly served as a symbol of ethno-nationalism in the Katanga/Shaba area of Congo. During the short period of Katanga's declared autonomy under Moise Tshombe (1960-1963) Kiswahili actually gained in political prestige partly because it helped define the sub-nationalism of the region. The fact that by the mid-fifties there was "a growing number of intertribal marriages, which generally entailed the use of the local variety of Swahili as the family language" (Edgar C. Polome, 1986: 390) helped to strengthen Kiswahili's role as a language of Katanga/Shaba's sub-nationalism in the Congo.

Another level of cultural nationalism aroused by Kiswahili is the racial one. This, of course, goes beyond Ugandan soldiers. It encompasses the whole movement to resurrect aspects of the cultural heritage of black people in different parts of the world and forge a new status of dignity in global cultural arrangements. Kiswahili commands this kind of symbolic attachment not only among black Africans, but also among sections of African-Americans. The language is taught in some West African countries like Nigeria and Ghana partly because it is seen as a medium that could provide a linguistic substance to black African nationalism. It has been taught in vastly differing parts of the black world as a major medium for the black cultural renaissance.[17]

In Tanzania, the language has also been promoted in part for these reasons of cultural self-reliance and self-development. One governmental area after another has been pronounced as an area in which only Kiswahili is to be used. There has definitely been a decline in the use of the English language in Tanzania and some degree of decline in general competence in that language. Law courts have increasingly used Kiswahili, and specialist committees have been appointed to work out and develop an adequate legal vocabulary. Talks in scientific education on the radio have moved in the direction of disseminating scientific knowledge through Kiswahili. The National Assembly has become uni-lingual using only Kiswahili, and many ministries have changed in a similar direction. The country's first president, Julius Nyerere, himself set an impressive example of competence and versatility in that language, ranging from dazzling oratory to the tough self-imposed assignments of translating Shakespeare's *Julius Caesar* and *Merchant of Venice*.

When Kiswahili is indeed recognized as an important expression of cultural nationalism in the racial sense, there are speedy educational consequences. Certainly the rise of the black attachment to Kiswahili in the United States soon resulted in the provision of classes in one Black Studies program after another, including programs below university level. And as the militancy of African cultural nationalism in the United States declined in the 1970s, the presence of Kiswahili in the educational system of African-America also declined. In the late 1980s and 1990s, there has been a resurgence of African-American nationalism, sometimes expressed in an *Afrocentric* ideology. This has again been accompanied by an increase in the number of Kiswahili programs in American educational institutions. In other words, in a situation like that of African-America, there is often a correlation between cultural nationalism in the racial domain, on the one side, and the introduction of a cultural symbol like Kiswahili into schools, on the other.

Thirdly, there is cultural nationalism at the territorial level, in the sense of either consolidating the identity of the particular country or in the sense of identifying with one's neighbors in a given geographical region. Again, Tanzania has utilized Kiswahili not only as an expression of the Africanness of Tanzanian people, but also as an expression of their being Tanzanian. Kiswahili in this case becomes part of Tanzania's patriotism proper, and is called upon to serve functions which would give Tanzania's national identity true expression and fulfillment.

As a result of the consolidation of Kiswahili, in fact, Tanzania's national identity came to be increasingly defined as Swahili in its cultural character. In the words of Abdulaziz Lodhi:

> The Tanzanian culture, therefore, is the sum total of all the good customs and traditions of the different language groups in Tanzania. All these regional cultures using local languages, or dialects, are now being transformed into a national culture using Swahili which is increasingly commanding the loyalty, affection, and respect of Tanzanians. (I 974: 1 1)

As Tanzanians entered the seventies the conception was already forming that a Tanzanian was, in cultural essence, an Mswahili (a Swahili person):

> Kwa hapa kwetu, Kiswahili ndiye mlezi, ametutukuza tangu
> siku za ukoloni na kutuunga pamoja hadi kufika siku za uhuru

wetu. Ni lugha inayoeleza utaratibu wetu wa maisha...
Mswahili ni Mtanzania na hapana shaka lugha ya Kiswahili ni
lugha ya Watanzania. Hivyo, inatazamiwa kwamba watu
watakubali kuitwa Waswahili na kujaribu kujenga utamaduni
mila na desturi badala ya kuthamini zaidi ukabila. (Kiango
and Sengo, 1972: 10)

Here, Swahili is our guardian; it has reared us from the colonial
era and united us to the period of our independence. It is the
language that expresses our social dynamics... An Mswahili
is a Tanzanian and there is no doubt that people will accept
being identified as Swahili and try to build values, customs
and norms [around that common identity] instead of placing
emphasis on ethnicity.

In a situation of territorial cultural nationalism, a symbol like Kiswahili
once again receives ready educational translation. The schools rise to the
occasion, minimally teaching it as one of the subjects at school, maximally
adopting it as a medium of instruction throughout the educational system.
In Tanzania, the pre-secondary educational system has been completely
Swahilized. Some degree of Swahilization has also taken place in
secondary education. English still plays a considerable role in Tanzania's
education, but there is little doubt that until recently it was constantly on
the decline.

The rising role of Kiswahili in Tanzania has inevitably resulted in a
declining role for expatriate teachers. The utilization of technical assistance
in the educational system of an African country usually presupposes the
continuing acceptance by that country of a major metropolitan language.
To the extent that Kenya, for example, uses the English language in much
of its education, or to the extent to which Senegal uses the French language,
the capacity of Kenya and Senegal to absorb technical assistance in the
educational system from Britain or France, respectively, is augmented.

The utilization of the American Peace Corps in schools in Africa inevitably depended on the ability of the host countries to utilize people trained either to teach in English or, in the case of those Americans who found their way to French-speaking Africa, equipped with a special competence in the French language.

In contrast, as Tanzania has continued to Swahilize its educational system, it has increased its own burden of producing its own teachers. Linguistic self-reliance implies educational self-reliance. The Swahilization of the educational system reduces not only the role of British and American teachers, but also of Swedish, Hungarian, and other European teachers who could more easily be expected to teach in English among Tanzanian children than to teach in Kiswahili.

There are cases of a few expatriate teachers arriving in Tanzania equipped to participate in Kiswahili in the educational system. These include Chinese teachers for physical training. But, on the whole, the era of foreign technical assistance in the educational system of Tanzania has reduced tremendously. Territorial cultural nationalism has been mobilized to serve the purposes of the Arusha Declaration as an assertion of self-reliance.

In neighboring Kenya, Kiswahili has been accorded at least a symbolic value in its quest for national identity. It seems accepted in principle that a person cannot be a *bona fide* national of Kenya without some knowledge of Kiswahili. Article 93 (e) of the Constitution of Kenya provides that any eligible person seeking to become a naturalized citizen of the country must "satisfy the Minister [of Home Affairs] that he has an adequate knowledge of the Swahili language." Implicit in this constitutional provision is the idea that there is a basic set of cultural traits that define Kenyan identity and that the set includes Kiswahili.

The first president of Kenya, Jomo Kenyatta, was desirous that Kiswahili would one day become an attribute of national identity in more than a symbolic sense. His training as an anthropologist perhaps made him particularly sensitive about the potential role of a national language in forging a national culture and, at the same time, made him wary that an imperial language would deepen the country's cultural dependence on the West. Now that Kiswahili has been made a compulsory subject in Kenya's pre-university education, Kenyatta's dream has a greater chance of fulfillment in the Kenya of the future.

Territorial cultural nationalism, with regard to Kiswahili, sometimes goes beyond the immediate country concerned. This is when Kiswahili becomes the most important cultural symbol of pan-East Africanism. The desire by East Africans to find areas of solidarity sometimes seeks stimulation from race, sometimes from the consequences of history which created shared institutions linking Kenya, Uganda, and Tanzania, and sometimes from culture. Kiswahili has particularly strong credentials in this last domain of cultural solidarity. When, at long last, Uganda under military rule adopted Kiswahili as the national language, General Amin emphasized the value of the language from a pan-African point of view. Speaking to the nation, President Idi Amin said:

> On the advice of the entire people of Uganda, it has been decided that the National Language shall be Kiswahili. As you all know, Kiswahili is the *lingua franca* of East and Central Africa, and it is a unifying factor in our quest for total unity in Africa. *(Voice of Uganda,* October 10, 1973)

Some Ugandans have been aware of the potentialities of Kiswahili not only for communication among Kenya, Uganda, and Tanzania, but also for communication with countries like Zaire and Rwanda, whose own official language is French. The adoption by different African countries of either French or English, depending on their own colonizer, has often created great barriers in communication. Among at least some sections of the population of Eastern Africa, this imperial cleavage created by the dichotomy between English and French has been mitigated by the availability of Kiswahili. Advocating the promotion of Kiswahili as Uganda's national language a Makerere University don, Dale Mutabiirwa, had this to say:

> French and English being languages of our former colonizers,
> thousands of kilometers away from our countries' borders, it
> would be nationalistic and pan-African to adopt and use
> Kiswahili already spoken in the countries next door with
> which we have inalienable evidences of blood-ties save the
> partition and the disintegration by our former colonial masters.
> We should not continue to follow the foot-steps of our former
> colonial masters even in matters which discourage and retard
> us from becoming a united nation, a united regional block,
> and a united Africa. (1989: 4)

Field Marshal Idi Amin himself, though he spoke not a single word of
French, had over the years enjoyed many a conversation with Zairean
dignitaries in Kiswahili.

But, by the time Uganda adopted Kiswahili as a national language,
the country was already short of teachers in other fields as a result of
Amin's expulsion of the Asians and his fluctuating harassment of the British.
The adoption of Kiswahili by Uganda as a national language in October
1973, required that the language be speedily introduced into schools, and
after a while made to bear much of the educational system. But the exodus
of Asian and other expatriate teachers made the Ministry of Education
circumspect about any linguistic experiment at the time. Further, the fact
that relations between Uganda and Tanzania had been uneasy since Amin's
military coup, and a number of Tanzanians had been killed in Uganda over
the period, made it very difficult for Uganda to recruit Tanzanian teachers
to teach Kiswahili in Ugandan schools. The capacity of Uganda to recruit
from Kenya had also become circumscribed by the security situation in
Uganda. On balance, therefore, the adoption of Kiswahili as a national
language of Uganda, though necessarily carrying educational implications,
did not immediately have educational consequences. President Idi Amin
saw the necessity of at least a temporary continuation of the previous

linguistic policies in education. As he said in his address to the nation:

> It must be emphasized that English shall for the time being remain the official language until Kiswahili is developed to the degree that warrants national usage. Other foreign languages shall continue to be taught in our schools. Vernacular languages shall continue to be developed. *(Voice of Uganda,* October 10, 1973)

What the military takeover fulfilled, however, was the utilization of Kiswahili on the radio and television in Uganda, and the beginnings of a more respectful atmosphere for the language even among the linguistically proud Baganda.

A sense of transnational territorial identity and nationalism fostered by Kiswahili has also been expressed in Tanzania. The spread of Kiswahili in East and Central Africa has sometimes been interpreted as a process of cultural Swahilization of the region. In attempting to give a definition of Kiswahili literature, for example, K.E.M. Senkoro states:

> Tutaamua kuwa kazi fulani ni ya fasihi ya Kiswahili au la kutokana na jinsi ilivyojitambulisha na ilivyojihusisha na utamaduni wa Kiswahili. Hapa neno Waswahili halimaanishi kabila la Waswahili kwani kabila la [namna] hiyo halipo leo. Waswahili hapa ni wananchi wa Afrika ya mashariki na kati kwa jumla na wala si wale tu wanaoishi katika pwani ya nchi hizi. (1988: 11)

We shall decide that a particular work is or is not in the realm of Swahili literature on the basis of its projection of and relationship with the culture of the Swahili people. Here the term Swahili does not mean an ethnic group of the Swahili people, for such an ethnic group does not exist today. The

> Swahili people here are citizens of East and Central Africa in general and not only those who live on the coastline ot these countries.

The Waswahili (Swahili people) themselves then are seen as having been subsumed under a more general, trans-national Swahili identity on the basis of the long-term cultural impact of Kiswahili.

As for cultural nationalism in relation to class, Kiswahili is clearly much more of a language of the common man than English. Certainly its appeal to someone like Idi Amin, himself only semi-educated and drawn from the womb of the countryside, was partially connected with the proletarian associations of the status of Kiswahili in Uganda.

In Tanzania, the fact that the language was widespread and spoken by many more people in the country than English, increased its utility as a medium for socialist egalitarianism. The recruitment of party officials, the appointment of administrators, the election of parliamentarians, the appointment of ministers, no longer required in Tanzania a competence in the English language. Political and elite recruitment in Tanzania has, therefore, been substantially democratized precisely because Kiswahili has permitted the utilization of a larger pool of talent than might have been available if the English language had remained a *sine qua non* of political office.

The educational implications of the class factor in cultural nationalism are less straightforward than in either territorial or racial nationalism. The fact that Kiswahili was a language of the masses can have no impact on the educational system unless either the policy-makers are egalitarian or socialistic, or the policy-makers are themselves semi-educated and immediately drawn from less privileged strata of society.

In Tanzania we had a president who was very highly educated himself, Julius Nyerere, but who was strongly, almost fanatically, egalitarian. In this kind of situation, the argument that Kiswahili is a language of the masses would itself be an important consideration for giving the language extra status in the educational system.

In Uganda, on the other hand, the president was someone of far more modest educational qualifications. Idi Amin was more nearly a peasant than Julius Nyerere, but Julius Nyerere was more egalitarian than Idi Amin. In the Ugandan case, the man at the top did not necessarily favor Kiswahili for the purpose of creating an egalitarian society; but he might have favored Kiswahili for the purpose of changing the distribution of power in his society and giving greater advantage to those who were once despised. This position, though superficially egalitarian, might be perfectly compatible with simply turning the previous class structure upside-down, so that the privileged of yesterday become the underprivileged of today and vice-versa. Amin's policies were not precisely that, but they were in the direction of status reversal rather than egalitarianism. Nyerere's position, on the other hand, was more clearly egalitarian. Both positions carried great potentialities for the promotion of Kiswahili in those two countries as a language with a greater role in the affairs of the nation, and a clear position in the schools. Tanzania managed to implement those policies, and Presidents Ali Hassan Mwinyi and Benjamin Mkapa basically continued to follow Nyerere's footsteps in this particular regard.

Uganda made a modest beginning under Idi Amin. Unlike Idi Amin, and more like Nyerere, but to a lesser extent, the country's new president, Yoweri Museveni, is university-educated and at some point seemed disposed to egalitarian views. What Kiswahili lost in terms of Idi Amin's common man's inclination, therefore, it might have gained in the form of Museveni's egalitarian orientation. Unfortunately, after years of civil war, the new Ugandan government has had too many pressing political and economic problems to deal with in a society that is still experiencing the divisive pull of ethnic politics. So the future of Kiswahili in Uganda may have to remain uncertain for some years to come, even though the prevailing signs in favor of the language continue to be encouraging.

In Kenya, neither Daniel arap Moi nor his predecessor, Jomo Kenyatta, has shown any tendency towards an egalitarian ideology, nor does any of them come from the ranks of the less privileged social strata. Kiswahili in Kenya, therefore, has not had the benefit of a political push based on a president's egalitarian ideology or his lower class background.

Nonetheless, both presidents have often felt the need to display a populist ideology in the form of politico-economic empathy with the interests of the common man. In a country in which the "middle class" is still relatively small, and most of the people still belong to the lower classes, the government is often under pressure at least to appear responsive to the needs of the majority. Kiswahili, then, may stand to gain, even if symbolically, from this populist pull in the country's political ideology. It is perhaps not accidental that the introduction of technical education in Kenya's pre-university education as a way of providing basic survival skills in the informal sector of the economy to the majority who would not get a chance of pursuing further studies, coincided with the introduction of Kiswahili as a compulsory subject in Kenya's primary and secondary schools. It is as if Kiswahili too has been considered an indispensable survival skill for the underprivileged who have to fend for themselves in an economically hostile world. Populist considerations may have been partly responsible for giving Kiswahili a boost in Kenya's educational system.

Whatever the case, the future of Kiswahili in the three East African countries should continue providing fascinating comparative insights into the interaction between language, ethnicity, race, territorial affinity, and social stratification.

7.   Kiswahili and East African Integration

In June 1971, one of the authors of this book, Ali Mazrui, went from Uganda to give a lecture at Bungoma Secondary School, just across the border in Kenya. At the border, a Kenya policeman asked him for a lift. They gave him a lift in the car and started a conversation. The policeman complemented him on his Kiswahili and asked how it was that he spoke it so well. He explained that he hailed originally from the Coast.

Then he asked the policeman where he was from, for his Kiswahili too was very good, though not coastal. He was a Ugandan it turned out. His uniform was that of the Kenya police. Ali Mazrui asked him how long he had been in the Kenya police, and he said eighteen years. He still regarded himself as a Ugandan, his children were at school in Uganda, and one daughter was expected to go to Makerere University before long. By a curious coincidence, Ali Mazrui's lecture at Bungoma Secondary School was going to be precisely on issues of East African integration, at the request of the school itself. And there was this policeman in the car with them, a living embodiment of the historic connections between the security forces and East African integration.

Nor should we forget the saga of "Field Marshal" John Okello, the man who spearheaded the Zanzibar revolution. Okello had served once in the Zanzibar police during the days of the Sultanate. Here was a Ugandan, from Lango, who had migrated to the islands as part of the general flow of population in East Africa. He still regarded himself as a Ugandan, and yet there he was spearheading a momentous revolution on an island state far from home. What was even more remarkable was that he had a following on that island, and that for at least a couple of weeks or so the limelight of the world was on him as the initiator of that revolution. "Field Marshal" John Okello was a living embodiment of East African integration in relation to the general mobility of the people.

What is the place of language in this whole phenomenon? Precisely because recruitment into the King's African Rifles was region-wide, a trans-ethnic language of command was necessary. Before long Kiswahili asserted its credentials as the most trans-ethnic as well as the most inter-territorial of all the indigenous languages of East Africa. Kiswahili became the language of both the army and the police, and this role in the security forces was its last remaining official function in Uganda after independence. Kiswahili had, after all, been squeezed out of Ugandan schools way back in the colonial period, partly in response to the negative lobbying of Luganda speakers. By the time of independence, Kiswahili did not even have five minutes on Radio Uganda, or one single book in Uganda's educational system, but it retained an official role within the police and the army.

Milton Obote was a genuine believer in the value of Kiswahili. He intended to introduce it on Radio Uganda and as one of the compulsory languages to be learned in his proposed National Service, and announced at Makerere University in October 1970 his intention to promote its teaching in the schools of Uganda. But he never got around to fulfilling these promises of a new language policy in the educational system of Uganda. He never even fulfilled the promise to introduce Kiswahili on Radio Uganda, which he had considered doing for many years.

And then, on January 25, 1971 as we have noted, the military coup took place in Uganda. Within less than three weeks of the coup, Kiswahili was on Radio Uganda and on Uganda television. Indeed, on Radio Uganda Kiswahili has acquired almost the status of a national language. It is the only news bulletin in an African language to be read simultaneously on both channels of Radio Uganda. The old attachment to Kiswahili which the armed forces had shown, and which was a residual symbol of the connection between military service and East African integration, had now found yet another manifestation. On taking over power in Uganda, the soldiers decided that one of their first policies was indeed to introduce Kiswahili in the mass media of the country.

Again it was fitting for a soldier-President like Amin to be so influenced by a realization of the importance of language. Shortly after taking over control, Field Marshal Amin announced a pet project of his own — a dream of his to see established in Uganda, a university especially committed to the study of language. His idea did not preclude the study of other subjects, but the focus on language was dictated by the geographical situation of Uganda itself.[18] The three most widespread languages in Africa as a whole are, in fact, English, French, and Arabic. Uganda shares a border with one predominantly Arabic-speaking country, the Sudan; with two predominantly French-speaking countries, Congo and Rwanda; and with two predominantly English-speaking countries, Kenya and Tanzania.

Among indigenous languages in Africa, Kiswahili may well be the most widely spread in terms of crossing national boundaries and serving central functions in a variety of countries. In four of the five countries that Uganda shares a border with — Kenya, Tanzania, Rwanda, and Congo—Kiswahili is spoken. This special situation of Uganda in regard to the four languages of English, French, Arabic, and Kiswahili imposes upon Uganda the necessity of being particularly conscious of the connection between language and regional integration.

In terms of the functions of language regionally, there are three levels of integration relevant here. Upper horizontal integration means greater contact, communication, and interaction among elite groups. On a regional scale, upper horizontal linguistic integration came about when leaders of Uganda, Tanzania, and Kenya could sit together and conduct serious business in a *lingua franca* which was shared only by members of the elite. When the Mulungushi Club met in the late 1960s, Presidents Nyerere, Kaunda, and Obote illustrated in their discussions a case of upper horizontal integration at a regional level. In Eastern Africa it is the imported European language or languages which have managed to serve such a function.

Lower horizontal integration concerns the degree to which the masses are in contact with each other and are able to establish a linguistic basis for sustained interaction. In East Africa the most important language for lower horizontal integration has, of course, been Kiswahili. Its spread through the region was facilitated at one time by labor migration as East African men left their homes to seek their fortunes in distant urban or mining centers. While the majority of those who spoke English had to be relatively well educated, the majority of those who spoke Kiswahili were among the illiterate or semi-literate masses. Both English and Kiswahili were primarily second languages to the majority of their speakers in East Africa; but while English was often the second language of the elite, Kiswahili was the most important second language among the masses. The English language consolidated important links between the educated elite of Kenya, Uganda, and Tanzania; Kiswahili, on the other hand, promoted greater communication at the lower horizontal level.

As for vertical linguistic integration, this concerns the language by which the rulers communicate with the ruled and vice-versa. Vertical integration in this sense is the process by which the elite successfully penetrates the masses and the masses have adequate access to the elite.

For as long as English was the official language of the three partner states, it was at least formally designed to be the medium of vertical linguistic integration. In many cases, English could not work directly as the medium through which instructions from the elite were transmitted downwards to the villages, or demands and requests from the villages were transmitted to the elite. What really happened was that English carried political messages from the top echelons to the middle range elite. The latter then translated these messages in multiple languages as they communicated with villagers in different parts of the country. Similarly, the villagers transmitted their own hopes, fears, and demands in their own languages through the middle elite, who then transmitted them in the official language upwards.

Kiswahili became increasingly important in Tanzania and Kenya, as it was often a third language operating in the vertical process of elite penetration and mass access. Demands from the masses were transmitted upwards either in so-called "vernacular" languages or in Kiswahili; and at some stage, these demands were translated into the official currency of the English language.

By the middle of the nineteen-sixties, Tanzania had embarked on a more systematic policy to increase the role of Kiswahili in the process of vertical linkage between the elite and the masses, as well as to promote it further among the masses themselves.

In Kenya too Kiswahili has assumed a role in vertical integration, partly as a result of the policies pursued by the colonial powers in the last years of its rule, and partly because the language became important for African nationalism and nationalistic activity after World War II. It was in

1974 that President Kenyatta at last made Kiswahili the language of Parliament. It had for so long already been the language of parliamentary campaigns before elections. And since Kiswahili became a compulsory subject in Kenya's pre-university education, its potential for vertical integration has been substantially increased.

Throughout the three states, as we have already noted, Kiswahili had also been the language of the security forces for several decades. Both the army and the police in each country had long utilized Kiswahili. In Uganda its role within the security forces was virtually the last official function it served until Idi Amin Dada captured power and started the process of elevating the status of Kiswahili in national affairs in Uganda.

From the point of view of facilitating future cultural conversion, two important processes should perhaps be simultaneously undertaken. One is the continued elaboration of Kiswahili to enable it to cope with new areas of modern life, ranging from constitutional law to technology. Secondly, it is also important to initiate the process of the *East Africanisation* of English, enabling the language to cope more efficiently with the nuances of East African culture, and to evolve a distinctively regional character of its own without compromising its universal currency.

In Kenya Kiswahili has indeed become the language of politics, as we observed before, though the acts of Parliament, as contributions to the total body of law in Kenya, are still primarily in English--though the debate about those acts has been conducted in both English and Kiswahili.

Next to any address by the President himself, the most important speech of the year in Parliament has been the budget speech. That too has been given in English, though a summary in Kiswahili has sometimes been delivered for the sake of the wider public.

What all this means is that even in the recognized area of using Kiswahili as a language of political communication there is a marked dichotomy between the informal areas of politics and the technical areas of politics. Kiswahili has increasingly been allowed a role in the informal areas, but has yet to be proficient in Kenya for such technicalities of the political process as legislation, budgeting, and the judicial process.

In this task of the elaboration of Kiswahili more effective consultations and cooperation among the partner states of East Africa is needed. There is little point in duplicating technical terminology from one discipline to another, with Kenyan specialists inventing one collection of words in constitutional law or chemistry, and Tanzania specialists working on an alternative set of words, with Uganda torn between the two terminological traditions. Tanzania has already embarked on a number of projects which seek to increase Kiswahili's capacity to deal with important new areas of modern life. Instead of letting such enterprises be primarily national, as they tend to be at the moment, they should increasingly fall under one international umbrella and provide one of the bases of linguistic cooperation in the region.

The localization of the English language has been taking place independently of any policy, but East Africa still lags behind West Africa in this respect. There is not as yet an East African English in the way in which there is a West African one. But that is mainly because English in East Africa is still much more of an elite language than it is in West Africa. A foreign language gets localized when it begins to be at least in some respects a language of the marketplace as well as the classroom, a language of the person in the street as well as of the bureaucrat in an office. There is evidence that the English language has started percolating downwards into the mass sector of East Africa's population, especially in Kenya. The English language is beginning to bear the marks of popular democratization, of usage by those who are not purists, of the influence of those who are not completely at home with the Queen's English. The localization of the English language in East Africa would be in part its democratization, as it serves the needs of common people and gets "distorted" in the mill of mass experience. The localization of the English language must, therefore, be also a medium for the increasing cultural interaction which is underway in East Africa.

But before we can fully understand the importance of language for

East African integration, we must assess the significance of culture as a whole for regional unification.

For a number of years Kenya, Tanzania, and Uganda pursued the principles of economic cooperation and common market under the umbrella of the East African community. This cooperative endeavor, however, started experiencing tensions not too long after its formation partly because of the pull of national self-interest in a climate of deteriorating economic conditions. These tensions were later exacerbated by an increasing deterioration of political relations between Idi Amin's Uganda and Julius Nyerere's Tanzania. The community finally collapsed in 1977 after Tanzania took the dramatic decision to close its border with Kenya, complaining that capitalist Kenya was reaping more benefits. But, in fact, it is possible that the community's instability and its final break-up had much deeper cultural roots.

In terms of what is happening within East Africa, it is worth interpreting the experience of Western European countries in a comparative perspective, and deriving from that experience four stages in the sequence of integration. These are, first, imposed hegemony, which in Europe's case ranged from the Roman Empire to the more diffuse Holy Roman Empire and into Hitler's attempts to create a new German hegemony in the continent.

Partly out of imposed hegemony and general interaction among European peoples, cultural convergence took place resulting in a broadly shared western civilization. Cultural integration in Europe's case was, therefore, the second major stage towards general continental unification. It was out of that cultural convergence that Europeans regarded themselves as European and sought to give expression to their collective identity in a new modern economic community.

With the Treaty of Rome came the third stage of integration, consisting of the ambition to create a shared economic identity. The insistence on a shared political culture as a precondition of membership of the community resulted in the dictum that Spain could not be a member until Western democracy was established; and Portugal could not be a member for as long as it was either under fascism or under the threat of a communist takeover. The freezing of relations with Greece was also a case of the community's insistence on a shared liberal political culture before a European country could apply for membership.

For the more ambitious of the members of the community there is a fourth stage, still deeply controversial. Following cultural, and then economic integration, there should ultimately be political integration resulting in a supra-national structure of authority in Europe and a truly powerful European Parliament. What has been in the way is a residual isolationism implicit in the process of maturation of national consciousness. The earlier stages of national consciousness see the nation state in excessively isolationist terms; the mature stages result in a readiness to reconcile more effectively the needs for national distinctiveness with the requirements of international interdependency.

Did the East African community experience its tensions, and sustained increasing weakness of its economic institutions, mainly because there was not as yet an adequate congruence between the level of cultural integration achieved in East Africa and the level of economic integration which has been attempted?

Some commentators saw the difficulties of the East African community in terms of an absence of political integration. Mwalimu Julius Nyerere's own thesis that East African federation was a necessary precondition for genuine economic integration was itself based on the assumption that political integration had to come before economic integration.

Our thesis here is to the effect that there had been inadequate cultural unification, in the sense of a shared universe of values and predispositions, a shared approach to the definition of interests, a shared book of rules of the game, and the limits of competition. The East African community started with a bigger structure of economic unification than the cultural foundation could support. But a process of cultural convergence has been underway regardless of the collapse of the community. The maturing of national consciousness implies a greater similarity of outlook in spite of differences in ideological rhetoric. Kenyanism, Ugandanism, and Tanzanian nationalism are much more real forces from the point of view of East African integration than the official ideologies which each of those countries seeks to pursue.

But national consciousness has two stages, the stage of inner-orientation with an obsession for protecting narrow national interests, and the stage of outer-orientation when national interests are defined partly in international terms. East Africa may be approaching the end of the first stage. When we get over the hump and achieve a new level of national self-awareness East African integration will fare better.

But even more explicitly unifying has been linguistic integration at both the elite level and the mass level among the partner states. Both English and Kiswahili have played a part in this convergence.

But the balance as between English and Kiswahili is beginning to shift. Tanzania's attempts at Swahilizing parts of its educational system are to some extent at the expense of English. Kenya's adoption of Kiswahili as the parliamentary language and as a compulsory school subject is to some extent at the expense of English. When Uganda's adoption of Kiswahili is truly accompanied by its promotion in the educational system, it will to some extent be at the cost of the English language also.

And yet it would be untrue to say that English is on the way out in East Africa. On a ten-point scale its regional status may have come down from .9 near the top to .7 or .6. The region is approaching greater parity of esteem between its two *linguae francae,* but English continues to have an important edge in Kenya and Uganda.

The speakers of the two languages are both increasing. There are many more speakers of the English language in Tanzania today than there were on Independence Day in 1961. This is partly because the number of educated Tanzanians has increased considerably, and certain levels of education still carry with them some degree of competence in the English language.

The number of speakers of Kiswahili in all three countries is much greater today than it was in the colonial period and seems to be rising all the time. But while there are fewer speakers of English than there are of Kiswahili, both languages are still expanding in terms of people who acquire competence in them.

Cultural convergence is also aided by journalism, literature, and broadcasting. Whenever Kenyan newspapers are permitted to enter Uganda they are in great demand. Today virtually all Kenyan newspapers and magazines—from *The Standard* to *The Daily Nation* and its sister paper in Kiswahili *Taifa Leo,* from *The Weekly Review* to *Economic Review*—find their way to Uganda on a regular basis. Likewise, Uganda's *New Vision* has become a common, though by no means, a regular item on some newspaper stalls in Kenya. Therefore both Kenyans and Ugandans at certain levels are exposed to similar journalistic influences with important consequences for cultural convergence.

At one time Tanzanian newspapers were very popular in Kenya. There were occasions when a Tanzanian newspaper would sell in the streets of Nairobi or Mombasa at several times its normal price. A scramble for *The Daily News* outside, say, the New Stanley Hotel was not an unusual sight. Today there continues to be a regular exchange of English newspapers between these two East African countries with a host of Kiswahili newspapers from Tanzania appearing regularly in some stalls in Nairobi and Mombasa. What this means is that a section of Kenyans and a section of Tanzanians are to some extent exposed to the same journalistic world.

One reason for the popularity of East African newspapers across their own boundaries concerned the limits of censorship within each of the partner states. There were occasions when the most candid news about Kenya could only be read in a Tanzanian newspaper. And there were certainly occasions when the most candid news about Uganda could best be obtained in Kenyan newspapers. In a sense then, there was a kind of decentralized press freedom in East Africa, provided newspapers of partner states were given general free circulation. Once again, the relatively open discussion of fundamental issues across territorial frontiers are a healthy element in the general process of convergence. The exposure of newspaper readers to a shared world of journalism is also an important feature of the slow process of intellectual and cultural unification.

Today the demand for newspapers and magazines from across the borders has a lot to do with an increase in human traffic, trade, and commerce. As relations between the three countries keep improving there is a growing exchange of people, goods, and services which depend on the knowledge of English at the top horizontal level and Kiswahili at the bottom horizontal level. As Uganda seeks to stimulate the recovery of its economy it has sometimes attempted to attract investors from its neighbors. Kenyan entrepreneurs are increasingly discovering that Uganda may have a lot to offer for their investments. There is also a thriving border trade in places like Busia, Migori, and Taita-Taveta which uses Kiswahili as the main medium of linguistic exchange. Kenyan women traders have also been flocking the markets of Kampala (*Sunday Nation*, October 4, 1992) initiating a tradition of long-distance trading among East Africa's "market women." All this international activity promotes an interest in what the newspapers from the various nations have to say about events in their own countries as well as in the region as a whole. Trade and journalism, therefore, have combined in East Africa to foster cultural convergence with both Kiswahili and English as the prime linguistic facilitators of the process.

Of particular significance in this promotion of convergence of values are mass media projects with a regional focus, with *The East African*, owned by the nation group of newspapers, having attained spectacular success in this new initiative. With the contribution of some of the most noted journalists from Kenya, Uganda and Tanzania, *The East African* has given prominence to topical issues with trans-national ramifications touching on broader political, economic and cultural processes in the region.

In the meantime, while Radio Tanzania's Kiswahili service has long been accessable (and even popular) in Kenya and Uganda, more integrated regional experiments in the electronic media may be under way. A new television service, Direct to Broadcaster Programming (DTB), has recently been launched to broadcast into Kenya and Uganda among other countries, even though its mandate is limited to sports and entertainment. In liason with Media Plus Sports, DTB will offer advertisers an opportunity to target a regional market from a single office (*Daily Nation*; July 1, 1998). What we are witnessing, then, are expanding horizons for the mass media to serve as facititators of cultural convergence in the region.

The gradual increase in trade and traffic between the three East African countries, however, is itself partly a product of convergence at the level of political culture. With the end of the Cold War, and due to local pressures of deteriorating economies and international pressures of the IMF and the World Bank especially, the polarization between Tanzania's economic nationalism and Kenya's mixed-economism, for example, is gradually capitulating to the dictates of economic liberalism. And after years of a civil war that put its economy in disarray, Uganda is even more strongly inclined towards a liberal economy. The spirit of free enterprise, private investment, and economic competition seems to be increasingly taking root in the political culture of all the East African countries, for better or for worse.

In terms of party policies, too, there is some convergence towards greater liberalism. A tradition of political pluralism seems to be re-establishing itself in both Kenya and Tanzania. And while Uganda has yet to take the road towards multi-party politics the fact that there is a ban only on party politics, but not on political parties, demonstrates that forces in favor of political pluralism are fairly strong. In addition, as political pluralism re-consolidates itself, the region is unlikely to experience the kind of ideological polarization in party politics that once existed between, say, the capitalist-leaning Kenya African National Union (KANU) and the socialist-leaning Kenya People's Union (KPU) in Kenya, or between the conservative Democratic Party (DP) and the radical Uganda Peoples Congress (UPC) in Uganda, after the latter's "Move to the Left." Virtually all the political parties registered in Kenya and Tanzania have tended to revolve around the "political center" in terms of their ideological orientation.

East African nations, therefore, have been experiencing increasing convergence in their economic and political values. And this convergence has, in turn, widened the political space for economic exchange, both formal and informal, that is likely to lead to even further cultural convergence.

Given then that one of the main ways of strengthening East African integration in the decades ahead is the facilitation of this general convergence in culture and ideas, it is important that the East African countries should pay more attention to cultural and intellectual institutions than it has done in the past. Culture here is broadly defined to include the promotion of shared political values, the facilitation of shared languages of communication, the promotion of educational consultation and cooperation, the encouragement of scientific collaboration, the promotion of general mass participation in regional institutions, and the reaffirmation of a free circulation of books, newspapers, and other publications throughout the region without governmental interference.

After many years of discussions and uncertainties, the East African countries have finally moved to establish the East African Co-Operation with its secreteriat in Arusha, Tanzania. In addition to harmonizing trade tariffs and monetary regulations, there have been pledges to rehabilitate the East African Road Network and plans to set-up an East African Legislative Assembly and an East African Military Liason Office to increase defense cooperation (*The East African*, June 15-21, 1998). As these initiatives are in progress, however, there may be need to experiment with regional institutions that can expedite the process of cultural convergence. The list of such institutions may include:

(a) An *East African Educational Council.* For the time being there seems to be no effort at studying educational experiments going on in one's neighboring country. Greater consultations on educational reforms and experiments should yield a larger pool of innovative ideas. A regional approach to syllabuses and examinations has unfortunately disintegrated with the collapse of the East African community. But an educational council can now look at how to balance nationally-defined educational goals against the needs for facilitating the growth of a genuine East African civilization, defined in regional dimensions. If at all possible, the regions should revert to a system whereby children in all the three East African countries followed comparable, if not identical, systems, curricula, and syllabi allowing for certain national variations, but maintaining a regional approach. A common regional examination in at least some fields of study would also be in order. Periodic meetings of educators, curricula builders, and general educational policy-makers, should also help to deepen a sense of shared intellectual direction.

(b)   An *East African Language Council.* This would build on the old interterritorial languages committee and promote more systematic cooperation. A major task under the council would be constant cooperation in the elaboration of Kiswahili discussing new words in scientific, legal, economic, political, and popular domains, and seeking agreement on a variety of proposals. The Language Council would need to be also in close touch with the Education Council about the implications of the use of Kiswahili and English in the three partner states. Recruitment for language teachers across territorial boundaries could also be facilitated in part by this council. There may be a need for considerable recruitment of Kiswahili teachers from Tanzania for Ugandan schools. The East African Language Council could help in this.

(c) *An East African Press Council* should be set up. This should consist primarily of journalists themselves. The council should start from the principle—to be agreed on by all three governments—that there was to be absolutely free circulation of all East African newspapers throughout the region as a whole. Complaints from one of the partner states either through its government or through any private aggrieved party against a newspaper in another partner state should be submitted to the East African Press Council. The Press Council would have mainly powers of censure and of non-cooperation with a recurrently offensive newspaper, but the council would not have the power to directly censor any of the newspapers in the three partner states. A major precondition of intellectual convergence is substantial freedom of communication in the two *linguae francae*. Freedom for the newspapers of each partner state is to some extent controlled and circumscribed by the government of that state. The ban of *Finance*, *The Star*, *Kenya Confidential* and *Post on Sunday* in Kenya and of *Kasheshe*, *Chombeza* and *Anisha Leo* in Tanzania in mid-1998 is a continuing demonstration of the threat to the press posed by the respective governments in the region (*Daily Nation*, July 15, 1998).What we are proposing here is that the government of each partner state should not—in addition to censoring its own newspapers—impose a ban on the entry of other newspapers from neighboring countries, of whatever language.

In 1996 some thirteen countries launched the East African Media Institute (EAMI). Its main objective, according to its constitution, is to promote "media development, freedom and diversity in Eastern Africa with emphasis on training to meet

specific needs of the market. It will take steps to safeguard
freedoms where such freedoms are violated and seek to
remove obstacles and barriers to the free flow of information."
This is an initiative that is likely to be a major contribution to
cultural convergence in the region once it becomes fully
operational.

(d) *An East African Literature Bureau.* This should be re-
established and considerably strengthened with additional
resources to promote writing by East Africans on East African
affairs and topics of East African importance, and to facilitate
distribution of the publications in Kiswahili and English all
over the region. The Bureau would have to be in conjunction
with some of the other councils, including those of education
and language.

But just as East Africa must embrace the principle of bilingualism, it
must also embrace the principle of bi-nationality or dual citizenship. The
three sister countries have already launched an East African passport and
set-up clearance desks for East African nationals at their airports (*Foreign
Affairs Bulletin,* Nairobi, June 1998). This is definitely a major step
towards East African integration; but it is not sufficient. An East African
who was born in or acquired the citizenship of one partner state, and is
now fully resident in another partner state, should be eligible to acquire the
citizenship of his country of residence without relinquishing his original
citizenship. Thus, Ugandans or Tanzanians who have lived in Kenya for
three years and already have regular jobs should be eligible to apply for
Kenyan citizenship without giving up their Ugandan or Tanzanian passports.
Other countries abroad with far less in common than Kenya, Uganda, and
Tanzania have been able to bear the anomalies. There is no reason why
East Africa could not accept a similar principle. It would be in keeping
with certain areas of traditional collective hospitality of indigenous East

African societies. It would also give a greater sense of security and of belonging to those East Africans who sometimes feel like emigres in neighboring partner states. For these citizens there should be a requirement that they be fully competent in either Kiswahili or English, but preferably both.

One solution that has been proposed to the bloody conflicts in Rwanda and Burundi is a federation with Tanzania so that Hutus and Tutsis stop having *de facto* ethnic armies of their own, but have those soldiers retrained as part of the federal army of the Republic of Tanzania. The fact that Hutus and Tutsis have themselves been getting partially Swahilized should facilitate this extension of the process of East African integration to Rwanda and Burundi inspite of the divergent colonial experiences.

As East Africans seek to promote greater economic cooperation, then, they should realize that a greater consolidation of cultural convergence is a necessary, but not a sufficient, condition for the long-term viability of a genuine regional community. Since it is impossible to gauge how much cultural integration is necessary for what degree of economic integration, East Africans should struggle to consolidate what they can in the cultural sphere. In both endeavors the importance of communication cannot be overestimated. The capacity to feel linguistically at ease with each other is sometimes a necessary—though not a sufficient—condition for readiness to compromise on fundamental issues.

8.   Kiswahili International

Much of the recent debate as to whether it is wise to make Kiswahili the official language of a country like Kenya or Uganda has rightly pointed out that Kiswahili is much less of an international language than English. What has been overlooked is the simple fact that when all is said and done, Kiswahili is still the most international of all the indigenous languages of the African continent or of the black people as a whole. Should Kiswahili be underestimated because it is less international than English?

Or does it deserve to be developed further because it is the most internationally promising of all the native-born languages of Africa?

We define an indigenous African language quite simply as one whose origin lies in the African continent and whose structure is derived from or bears affinity to one or more other languages associated with Africa. Kiswahili belongs of course to the Bantu family of African languages. In terms of distribution and functional potential, Kiswahili has now become the most important of the Bantu languages.

We started by describing Kiswahili as the most international of Africa's own languages. But it is possible to go further and describe it as the *only* truly international language which the African continent has produced for itself.

First, we should distinguish between four types of languages—communal, national, regional, and world languages. A communal language in our sense is one which is indigenous to only a section of a particular country or countries and has not been adopted as an official language. An official language is here defined as a medium used in conducting the affairs, wholly or in part, of one or more departments of the government. Examples of communal languages would include Luganda, Provencal, Kikamba, and Welsh.

A national language in this narrow sense is *uni-national*—confined primarily to one country and may or may not have been adopted as an official language for that country alone. Examples include Japanese, Persian, Turkish, Czech, and Somali.

A regional language in our sense is one which is widely spoken by both natives and non-natives of a particular geographically contiguous region and has been adopted as a national language by at least two of the countries of that region. Examples of regional languages include Arabic, German, and Kiswahili.

A world language is one which has spread beyond its own continent of birth, is widely understood in at least two continents, and is the official language of several states in those continents.

Of these four types of languages (communal, national, regional, and world), only the last two types are truly international. Of all the continents of the world, only Europe has produced world languages—English and French being widely recognized as such.

But although English and French are spoken in more countries than any other language, it is Chinese which is spoken by more people than any other medium. The over eight hundred million speakers of Chinese are virtually the equivalent of all the speakers of English and French in the whole world added together. But to all intents and purposes, Chinese is at best a regional language.

While Europe produced world languages and Asia massive regional languages, Africa was in danger of being a continent of only communal languages—spoken by small groups, with no official status as languages even in their own countries. Only the Horn of Africa (Ethiopia and Somalia) and a couple of other countries seemed destined to have home-born national languages of their own.

But as independence approached, the full potentialities of Kiswahili began to emerge. Like Hausa in West Africa, Kiswahili had spread to more than half a dozen countries, but *unlike* Hausa, Kiswahili stood a realistic chance of being adopted as a state language by one or more countries. That chance has now been realized. The language has been accorded an official status in one or more institutions of the states of Tanzania, Uganda, and Kenya. In none of the three countries has the language fully consolidated its official role, but the status of Kiswahili as Africa's most international language is now irreversible.

How did this language spread? How did it become international? How is it faring in Tanzania, Uganda, Kenya, Rwanda, Burundi, the Democratic Republic of Congo and elsewhere?

In a world broadcast delivered on the radio on February 9, 1941, Winston Churchill, then wartime leader of Britain, had occasion to say: "In wartime there is a lot to be said for the motto: 'Deeds, not words.'"

And yet in that very exercise of broadcasting to the world in wartime,

Winston Churchill was belying his own words. Indeed, in that very broadcast, Churchill cited lines from Longfellow towards the conclusion of his speech. The verse from Longfellow had been written out by President Roosevelt in his own handwriting in a note addressed to Churchill, and the lines were intended to be a tribute to England in the throes of war with Hitler's Germany.

> ... Sail on, 0 Ship of State!
> Sail on, 0 Union strong and great!
> Humanity with all its fears,
> With all the hopes of future years,
> Is hanging breathless on thy fate!

Churchill was using Roosevelt's tribute brilliantly as he continued to seek greater American support in the war. In that same speech in which he approved of the motto, "Deeds, not words," Churchill uttered some of his most famous words. He asked the American people to give the British people their faith and their blessing. What Churchill meant was that he wanted the American people to give the British people more equipment with which to wage the war. And he assured the American people in this concluding paragraph to his broadcast: "We shall not fail or falter; we shall not weaken or tire. Neither the sudden shock of battle, nor the long-drawn trials of vigilance and exertion will wear us down. Give us the tools, and we will finish the job" (1959: 90).

General Eisenhower was later to complement Winston Churchill for having "mobilized the English language to the battlefield." At a time when the danger of low morale was ever present among his people, and the strength of Germany and its victories dominated the scene, Churchill's oratory sought to reassure his countrymen, as well as a demoralized Europe.

What we have here then is the *inspirational* function of language in wartime. Language is utilized to capture certain ideas and manipulate the emotions in the direction of psychological stamina.

But, concurrently with Winston Churchill's utilization of English for inspirational purposes was the initiation of a new phase for Kiswahili in East Africa for organizational purposes in the armed forces, as we indicated earlier. Kiswahili acquired influential friends in the barracks--friends whose power for future policy-making was at the time not fully apprehended, but who later came to assume positions of critical significance in their countries.

And yet, at that time, in Uganda the utility of Kiswahili was still basically organizational rather than inspirational. Along the coast in the nineteenth century, poets had used Kiswahili as a source of military morale. But in the hinterland of East Africa it was still true to say, as Wilfred Whitely once put it, "Gone are the stirring phrases with which Muyaka sought to stiffen Mazrui resistance against the invaders from Zanzibar" (1969:58).

Language for organizational purposes may be relatively simple, and yet still effective; language for inspirational purposes needs greater depths of meaning. Kiswahili in Uganda has not as yet acquired the sophistication necessary for effective inspirational utilization. The missing factor concerns the educational system.

As we indicated, Kiswahili disappeared from school syllabuses in Uganda following the controversies of language in the inter-war years. Obote though, as we noted earlier, was in favor of expanding Kiswahili in Uganda, but never succeeded in doing so. But the partiality of his successors for Kiswahili does give reason to expect moves towards resurrecting Kiswahili at least as a school subject in Uganda in the years ahead.[19]

It is only when Kiswahili acquires sophistication and depth as a result of its resurrection in the schools in Uganda that the language will at last find inspirational functions, as well as organizational ones. In Kenya, Mzee Kenyatta, with his impressive mastery of the language, went a long way towards giving it an inspirational role even in *political* mobilization. His very concept of *'Harambee'* has remained a throbbing slogan in the political vocabulary of Kenya. Self-help schemes ranging from water supplies to community schools have invoked the slogan of *Harambee* as a clarion call for national endeavor.

But it is plainly in Tanzania that Kiswahili has attained its most elaborate forms of inspirational usage. The language has been called upon to fight the battles of cultural nationalism and demonstrate Kiswahili's capacity to bear the weight of social phenomena ranging from the law to the plays of William Shakespeare. Kiswahili has been called upon to bear the burdens of national integration and give Tanzanians a sense of belonging to one national entity in spite of varieties of ethnic and linguistic origin. Finally, Kiswahili in Tanzania has been called upon to serve the inspirational aims of socialism itself, ranging from the very word *Ujamaa*, denoting kinship solidarity and fellowship on a national scale, to the slogan of *Kujitegemea*, the spirit of self-reliance. The ghost of the Maji Maji Rebellion smiles in satisfied vindication at the turn of linguistic history in Tanzania. To quote M.H.Abdulaziz, once again:

> The Maji Maji war of 1905-7 against German colonial rule drew its support from different mother-tongue speakers who already possessed a rallying force in Swahili...All movements of national focus [in Tanzania] have used Swahili as an instrument for achieving inter-tribal unity and integration.(1971:164)

With the use of language for socialistic inspiration in Tanzania, the concept of *war* itself has become demilitarized, and both inspiration and organization as served by language are now directed towards new targets of national effort.

The impact of the *French* language on Kiswahili might need to be examined in Burundi, the Democratic Republic of Congo(DRC), and Rwanda. Rwanda and Burundi— to the extent to which they are linguistically homogenous—need Kiswahili less for either vertical or horizontal integration. Kinyarwanda-Kirundi serves both roles well, supported by the French language in some matters. But in DRC, Kiswahili has been important already in horizontal integration across ethnic groups. As indicated earlier President Mobutu declared Kiswahili, alongside Lingala,

Kikongo and Tchiluba, as one of the national languages of Congo. The language now stands the chance of getting further consolidated since President Laurent Kabila's Alliance of Democratic Forces for the Liberation of Congo (AFDL) came to power. In the meantime, DRC's policy-makers on the language front might continue to study Switzerland and India as countries which adopted more than two languages to cope with cultural pluralism and cultural nationalism in their own national situations.

At the ethnic and class levels cultural nationalism has a rather unsure effect on educational policy-makers. But where cultural nationalism becomes necessary for territorial or racial identification, its translation into concrete educational policies can be speedy and wide-ranging. In relation to Kiswahili these have ranged from its role in black studies in the United States, as we noted earlier, to its propagation as a legal language in Tanzania.

The church, for the time being, seems to have declined as a major factor in the fortunes of Kiswahili. New gods now command African loyalties, in addition to those that came with the church. These new gods include the quest for greater cultural dignity, the pursuit of racial fulfillment, the forging of territorial identities, the revision of class and status in societies, and the construction of a new Eastern African civilization.

Chapter III

Kiswahili, Dependency and Decolonization

In this book we have paid particular attention to Kiswahili's role in expanding the horizons of knowledge and social relations, and in integration. The language has accelerated detribalization, induced new class-formations, promoted secularization, facilitated greater political participation, and enhanced scientific and technological ability.

But would this process not have been even faster if, instead of promoting Kiswahili, greater efforts were devoted to the task of making more and more East Africans learn English or French? Kiswahili may have been a greater force than ethnic languages in broadening the social, scientific, and technological world of East Africans. But is not Kiswahili a poorer agency in this regard as compared with either English or French? The European languages in Africa have had a great potential for speeding up "detribalization," fostering new class-formations, promoting greater secularization, and enhancing scientific and technological know-how in Eastern Africa. Some would say that only in expanding popular participation can Kiswahili indisputably be shown to have been more effective than either English or French in their respective areas.

If the ultimate ambition of Eastern African societies then is rapid expansion of their social, scientific, and technological horizons, why bother with Kiswahili? Why not devote more energy and investment in promoting the more effective European languages?

In reality, African countries have been aiming at two related processes, one that has sometimes been called "modernization," and the other "development."

"Modernization" has been seen as a process of change in the direction of narrowing the technical, scientific, and normative "gap" between industrialized western countries and the Third World. Partly because the industrial revolution first took place in the West, western civilization as a whole became the criteria for assessing and measuring "modernity." Western technology, culture, and life-style became the conscious or unconscious reference point not only for public policy-making, but also for individual private behavior over most of the world. "Modernization," then, has largely been equated with westernization, in spite of rhetorical assertions to the contrary.

Because "modernization" has connoted a constant struggle to narrow the technical, scientific, and normative gap between westerners and others, "development" has often been seen as a sub-section of "modernization." Most economists in the West and in the Third World itself have seen economic development in terms of narrowing the economic gap between those two parts of the world both in output and in methods of production. Most political scientists have seen political development as a process of acquiring western skills of government, western restraints in political behavior, and western-derived institutions of conflict-resolution.

If both "modernization" and "development" are seen as a struggle to "catch up with the West," the twin processes carry considerable risks of imitation and dependency for the Third World. Developing countries become excessively preoccupied with attempting to emulate western methods of production, western techniques of analysis, western approaches to organization, and western styles of behavior. In that very imitative complex lies vulnerability to continuing manipulation by western economic and political interests.

Language in Africa has to be seen in this wider context. Is utilizing English or French in African countries enhancing their capacity for development? Is it facilitating the advancement of management, planning, analysis, and administrative skills? Or is Africa adopting instead languages which are inappropriate to its current needs, culturally expensive in relation to other priorities, detrimental to social equity, and vulnerable to external exploitation?

Because of these questions in the background, language policy in

Africa has to be examined in relation to those wider processes of "modernization," "development," and alien penetration. But these, in turn, have to be reconceptualized if the Third World is not to be trapped into the dark cells of cultural bondage.

Capacity building, or what has sometimes been called "modernization" in the Third World, must be accompanied by serious attempts to reduce dependency. Some of the gaps between the West and the Third World have indeed to be narrowed — *but this narrowing must include the gap in sheer power*. To narrow the gap in, say, per capita income in a manner which widens the gap in power is to pursue affluence at the expense of autonomy. To narrow the gap in the effective utilization of English and French, while increasing western cultural control over the Third World, is to prefer emulation to independence. Somehow then each African society would need to strike a balance between the pursuit of capacity building, of expanding its social and intellectual horizons, and the pursuit of self-reliance.

But let us return to the role of Kiswahili in broadening social relations and scientific and technological capacity before we examine the language as an instrument of decolonization. Change in the direction that is compatible with the present state of knowledge and which does justice to the potentialities of the human person includes the process of detribalization and the emergence of new class relationships. In these processes the English language (in Kenya, Uganda, and Tanzania) and French (in the Democratic Republic of Congo, Rwanda, and Burundi) have played at least as important a role as any African language. It follows that Kiswahili cannot be examined in isolation, but has to be related to the impact of its European rivals. Language policy has to be placed in the context of the total linguistic situation.

1. Detribalization and Class-Formation

The critical goals of language policy in relation to "detribalization" and new class-formation are the goals of, firstly, national integration and, secondly, social integration. For our purposes in this essay, national integration is a process of merging sub-group identities into a shared sense of national consciousness. In Africa the creation of a supra-ethnic loyalty to a national homeland is the goal of the integrative process in this national sense.

Social integration, on the other hand, is not the merger of ethnic group with ethnic group, but is the process by which the gaps between the elite and the masses, the town and the countryside, the privileged and the underprivileged, are gradually narrowed or evened out. Social integration is not necessarily a process by which the difference in income between the richest man and the poorest man in the country is minimized. That absolute difference might remain the same, or even be increased, without implying that there has been no integration. But if the distance between the top and the bottom of the curve of income differences remains the same, the slope of the curve should be gradual and not steep. In a country where there are only very rich people and very poor people and no one in between, social integration has a long way to go. But if between the pauper and the millionaire there are a lot of people with intermediate rates of income in a gradual gradation, the social integrative process has indeed made progress. We can indeed have a well-integrated "traditional" society in this social sense of "integration," as we can have a well-integrated "modern" society, but the prerequisites are different in each case. A well-integrated "traditional" society has to be largely egalitarian, with no major difference in income between the richest and the poorest. A well-integrated "modern" society need not be egalitarian, but the process of differentiation of structures and specialization of functions must be sufficiently advanced to have created an even or gradual slope of incomes from the top to the bottom.

Can a society move from "traditional" social integration to "modern" social integration without passing through the agonies of major gaps of incomes and life-styles between the new elite and the masses, the town and the countryside? Can it move from social equality to social differentiation without passing through a stage of convulsive disparities? This is one of the most agonizing dilemmas of contemporary Africa.

Language policy in East Africa is linked to the problems of both national integration and social integration. And the place of the relevant European language is critical in both. A case can be made for the proposition that in relation to national integration in Uganda or Kenya, the English language is functional; whereas in relation to social integration, the English language is dysfunctional. We shall examine these two parts of the proposition in the course of the analysis.

A Survey of Language Use and Language Teaching in Eastern Africa was started in 1967, committed to compiling language data for Uganda, Kenya, Ethiopia, Zambia, and Tanzania. The Uganda Survey was completed in 1970 under the directorship of Professor Peter Ladefoged. The Kenya Survey, under the directorship of Professor Wilfred Whitely, was published by Oxford University Press in 1974. The Tanzania Survey was published in 1980 under the editorship of Edgar Polome and C.P. Hill. The Ethiopian and Zambian Surveys also got underway, but these would take us outside Swahililand. A special grant of the Ford Foundation enabled such a survey to be undertaken. And a regional Language Survey Council, with academic and political representation from all the countries concerned, was entrusted with policy-making issues within the terms of the Ford Foundation grant.

Information about who speaks which languages in East Africa, who is bilingual or trilingual, how widely is this or that language spoken, is the primary output of these language surveys. Uganda, as we indicated, was the first to be surveyed, and the report appeared in 1970. From the point of view of cultural engineering there is particular interest in the figures about the spread of Luganda and Kiswahili in the country as a whole.

Kiswahili is more widely understood in Uganda than was previously assumed, though it is on balance a language of men rather than women in that country. In other words, partly because of the phenomenon of men's mobility in relation to work and the whole phenomenon of the rural-urban continuum, significantly more Uganda men than women have been exposed to Kiswahili and learned to use it for specialized purposes.

But although Kiswahili is better understood than previously assumed, and although its political respectability has risen as a result of the decline of Buganda's influence, Kiswahili was not regarded by Obote's government as a serious candidate for adoption as a national language for Uganda. Dr. Luyimbazi Zake, then Minister of Education, was speaking more like a Muganda nationalist than a social scientist when he said in a debate in parliament on the new constitution in 1967 that Kiswahili was as foreign to Uganda as Gujerati. But the new constitution had "no alternative" but to adopt English as the national language of the country. This was the role English was intended to fill in the process of national integration.

The decision to make English the national language in no way implied that it was the most widely understood language in the country. Luganda and Lunyoro are spoken by the greatest number of people. But the whole problem of fair political representation and ethnic balance in political recruitment would be dangerously aggravated if these languages were adopted instead of English. As President Obote put it:

> ...immediately we adopted [either Luganda or Lunyoro] as the official language for administrative purposes or legislation, some of us will have to go out of Government. I, for instance, would not be able to speak in Parliament in Luganda, neither could I do so in Lunyoro, and I think more than half the present National Assembly members would have to quit. The areas we now represent would not like to have just any person who speaks Luganda to represent them. They would feel unrepresented. So, there again, we find no alternative to

English. (1964: 4)

Fairness in political representation and balance of recruitment sometimes dictates that a language which is uniformly lesser known throughout the country should have priority over a language which is very well known by only one section of the community and not known at all by others. Hindi has suffered from the same disability as a projected national language of India. It was felt by its opponents that native-speakers of Hindi would have too big an advantage over others in important sections of recruitment. But English, by being foreign to everyone, was a shared handicap. In situations of this kind, distributive justice itself becomes a question of distributive disability. A uniformly distributed linguistic handicap throughout the country becomes an important condition of political stability and a possible basis of closer integration.

The Baganda, even on the basis of how many of them speak good English, might still have a disproportionate share of the fruit of political recruitment. Certainly in absolute terms, and possibly in relative terms too, the Baganda are better educated than most of their compatriots. But disparities of advantage would be worse compounded if Luganda itself became the national language of Uganda.

But although English has become so very convenient for the whole task of national integration in Uganda, it ought not to be overlooked that the lack of a grassroot language for such a purpose continues to put Uganda at a disadvantage when compared with either Tanzania or Kenya. After all, national integration is not simply a case of fair distribution of advantages and disadvantages among ethnic groups, although this itself might be a critical *sine qua non*. National integration also presupposes the growth of a high socio-economic intercourse between the different ethnic groups, a high degree of authoritative penetration from the center to the periphery, and access from the periphery of the society to the center. These variables of socio-economic intercourse between groups and political intercourse between the populace and those in authority all demand or actually mean greater *communication*. English is for the time being limited in its capacity to provide this kind of intercommunication involving the grassroots.

Socio-economic intercourse between groups by way of trade, marketing, and cooperative and labor organization, is served more effectively by Luganda and Kiswahili than by English. This is one area where the success of English in national integration and its failure in social integration becomes indistinguishable. English as an inter-ethnic language between the educated is clearly integrative; but for inter-ethnic communication at the grassroots, English is intrinsically and hopelessly ill-equipped to meet the challenge.

We have already indicated that Tanzania was concerned about the gulf between the elite and the masses. It introduced a National Service, compulsory for university graduates and products of other major education institutions, and designed in part to expose this presumptive educated elite to the rigors of manual self-reliance. The exercise was also intended to sensitize the educated to the needs of the masses, and narrow the gulf of incomprehension between the city and the countryside. Tanzania sought to achieve social integration through social equality (as in the case of integrated "traditional" societies) rather than through social differentiation (as in the case of "developed" states). Tanzania now seems to have concluded that the whole approach was based on an error, but at least there was here a commitment to a specific direction of national change. The availability of Kiswahili as a language of the masses was fortunate from the point of view of Tanzania's egalitarian bias.

For all practical purposes Tanzania has now abandoned its socialist experiment and is less committed to egalitarian ideals than it was once. The quest for social equality is now giving way to a new reality of social differentiation. The extent of social integration that will emerge from this transition will depend on how steep or how gradual the curve of social stratification will turn out to be. If the economic disparities between the elite and the masses, between the urban and the rural, are very prominent with little gradation in-between, then Tanzania is unlikely to achieve much social integration under its new economic order.

Kiswahili may again come to Tanzania's aid in promoting an integrated pattern of social differentiation. English, a language which is spoken by a relatively small proportion of East Africans, is less indispensable as an instrument of elite formation in Tanzania than it is in Kenya and Uganda. By enabling a much wider section of the population to have potential access to the corridors of political and economic power, Kiswahili in Tanzania may help in fostering a less sharply differentiated and, therefore, a more fully integrated social structure than has been so far achieved in either Kenya or Uganda.

Kenya, on the other hand, seems to have been seeking social integration by increasing social differentiation and functional diversification among the African populace. The Government embarked on the deliberate creation of an African entrepreneurial class. The whole controversy about the Africanization of capitalism in Kenya, the gradual displacement of Asians and Europeans in some critical economic functions, was part of Kenya's commitment to the concept of diversifying the African man's economic experience. The African had known what it was like to be a peasant, what it was like to be a teacher, what it was like to be a railway porter, and what it was like to be a Cabinet Minister. But that was not enough. What about the experience of knowing what it was like to be an investor and shareholder? What about the experience of running a successful modern shop on Kenyatta Avenue in Nairobi? Kenya decided to give the full potential of the African as an economically creative being a chance to fulfill itself.

Kenya, for the time being, is therefore not interested in trying to prevent the emergence of new economic classes in the country. As far as Kenya is concerned, the expansion of its resource capacity lies through rapid functional diversification and not through desperate preservation of a presumed pre-existent African social equality. The promotion of Kiswahili in Kenya is not — as it was in Tanzania — inspired by egalitarian imperatives, but more purely by considerations of national integration.

The gap which English might continue to create between the elite and the masses is, therefore, compatible with a policy of promoting Kiswahili as a medium of political penetration and socio-economic intercourse at the grassroots level.

Uganda is, in this as in so many other issues, holding an intermediate position between Kenya and Tanzania. Like Kenya, Uganda is indeed committed to a policy of creating an African entrepreneurial class. The Ten Point Programme of Yoweri Museveni's NRM government is committed to a dual economy, part government and part private, even though by all indication the private sector seems to be increasingly assuming greater prominence. The NRM government has even been encouraging private investments from Ugandans who have been living in exile. The need for economic reconstruction has also led the NRM government to seek the return of Asian businessmen who were expelled from the country by Idi Amin in his bid to create new opportunities for the formation of a class of African entrepreneurs. Conscious of the wide economic gap that may develop between the elite and the masses, however, the NRM government has instituted political education schools to be attended by all civil servants and designed to sensitize the elite to the needs, problems, and plight of the masses and decrease the "communication gap" between them. To that extent Uganda does appear to be seeking to achieve social integration through functional diversification, rather than through the quest for an egalitarian society.

Obote's government once announced plans to start a National Service for the newly graduated, partly inspired by a desire to ensure that the educated were not too distant from the needs of the masses. Amin's government experimented with a Commission on Land, partly to ensure greater social justice in land-ownership. Uganda's situation continues to be ambivalent. Traditional society in the kingdoms, for example, was not egalitarian. But status was more often ascriptive than based on criteria of personal achievement. On the other hand, Museveni's policy of trying to create a modern African business class, though still incompatible with egalitarianism, is at least a quest for replacing criteria of birth with criteria of achievement as a basis of social success. Successive Uganda governments have tried to attack traditional so-called "feudalism" by promoting a trans-ethnic modern "commercialism." Like Kenya, and unlike Tanzania, Uganda is not trying to prevent the emergence of new economic classes, but has actually promoted them. The only difference between Kenya and Uganda in this particular regard is that Uganda has sometimes been so ambivalent that it has appeared a little guilty about this quest for new classes. Even on the issue of promoting English, Obote's government was aware that the policy emphasized a gulf between the elite and the masses. There was a sense of guilt about it all, but also a sense of inevitability. In the words of President Obote:

> ...our policy to teach more English could in the long run just develop more power in the hands of those who speak English, and better economic status for those who know English. We say this because we do not see any possibility of our being able to get English known by half the population of Uganda within the next fifteen years... Some of our people can use it to improve their economic status...[and] those amongst us in Uganda...who have obtained important positions because of the power of the English language are liable to be regarded by a section of our society as perpetrators of colonialism and imperialism; or at least as potential imperialists. (1964: 4)

Yet President Obote once again went on to say sadly: "We find no alternative to English". Perhaps that captures the great dilemma of the English language for a country like Uganda. It lends itself well, though not perfectly, to the task of national integration; but for the time being, it still remains all too often dysfunctional to the process of social integration. The military era did not change this in Uganda.

This is where Kiswahili once again presents itself as a potential alternative. This is also the context within which national and social integration have to be seen in relation to the expanding popular participation in public affairs. It is to this theme that we must now turn.

2. Expanding Popular Participation

President A. Milton Obote once described English as "the political language" of Uganda. In his day no person could be a member of Parliament if he were unable to speak English. Why was English necessary for Parliamentary life? In order to ensure that members of Parliament from different linguistic groups could be mutually intelligible to each other as they discussed national issues.

But each backbencher in Parliament before Amin's coup had at least two basic audiences. One audience consisted of his fellow Parliamentarians, and the other audience of his constituents. For as long as the Parliamentarian had only one constituency, he could rely on one local language in addressing his constituents while retaining English for his fellow MPs.

But if parliamentary life is now returning to Uganda, should there be rethinking as regards a language policy for politics in Uganda? English is a trans-regional language in Uganda, but primarily at the level of the educated elite. At the grassroots level inter-ethnic communication is served better by Luganda and Kiswahili than it is served by English.

But can Luganda be elevated to the status of one of the official political languages of Uganda? We have referred to the danger of provoking competing claims from other major linguistic areas of Uganda. The political sensitivities surrounding the adoption of Luganda as an official political language of Uganda may not be quite as acute as those which have beset India in her policy of fostering Hindi as an official language. But Luganda does pose problems comparable in kind, if not in magnitude, to the communal passions surrounding the issue of Hindi in India.

In addition to provoking competing claims from other language groups, the adoption of Luganda in addition to English as a language of politics would give Luganda speakers undue advantage. Uganda in the future should try harder than ever to reduce the effects of ethnic rivalry. Promoting Luganda would make that task more difficult.

A third argument against the adoption of Luganda as an official political language concerns the risk of "linguistic isolation" for Uganda as a whole. Again, Milton Obote once drew attention to this risk. Addressing a seminar on Mass Media and Linguistic Communications in East Africa, held at Makerere in 1967, President Obote said:

> ...the adoption of any one of our present languages in Uganda may just go to endorse our isolation; we cannot afford isolation... It is possible today for the people of Uganda to communicate with the people in the neighboring countries in broken Swahili, but it is not possible for the people of Uganda to communicate with the neighboring countries in broken Luganda today, how much more difficult would it be to try to communicate in first class Luganda? (1967)

More or less similar sentiments were expressed in an editorial of Uganda's *Weekly Topic* of October 1, 1986:

> There is a lot of nonsense that is usually urged against Swahili in this country. But if we attach any significance to regional unity and cooperation, leave alone our national unity, then we should not choose to remain a chaotic island of English and "tribal" languages surrounded by neighbors who opted for Swahili.

And yet the need for the grassroots language of politics is indeed there in the future arrangements of Uganda. Future politicians should be encouraged to seek support outside their ethnic areas. A Muganda parliamentary candidate going to campaign in West Nile or Acholi may indeed use an interpreter, as he himself uses English. But if the candidate can only communicate with his new non-ethnic constituents through an interpreter, the candidate may become not only unknown among those new political supporters, but also *unknowable*.

Again, few political commentators have put the linguistic predicament in more poignant language than Obote himself once did. He lamented how every time he moved around the country he had to speak in English.

> Obviously I have no alternative, but I lose a lot especially as far as the Party is concerned. The Uganda Peoples' Congress welcomes everybody and some of the greatest and most dedicated workers are those who do not speak English. And yet the Party leader cannot call his great dedicated worker alone and say "Thank you" in a language the man will understand. It has to be translated. There must always be a third party — and that is why it is said there are no secrets in Africa. (1967)

And yet the party leader and president of the country, even if he were to use only English, has a lot of other ways of getting to be known by the people. He is the center of the political life of the country, and much of the political discussion and political activity revolve around him. The mass media give due publicity to every major speech of his, in every major language of the country. The handicap which the president suffers from by addressing the nation only in English is reduced in its consequences by the exceptional exposure to the people of his political life as a whole.

But the ordinary member of Parliament has to try and reach his multi-ethnic constituents directly and personally or he may never reach them at all. In the case of the backbencher, the handicap of reaching his constituents only through an interpreter carries a serious risk of political alienation.

What all this analysis indicates is a need for re-thinking about the language policy of Uganda now that civilian rule and civilized political standards are being restored. The soldiers may have helped to bring

Kiswahili closer to the center of national politics, but the next creative phase for Kiswahili in Uganda needs the stability and compassion of a democratic civilian government.

Now that there is a new democratic dawn in Uganda there may be a case for adopting one of two possible policy recommendations affecting the language of politics in Uganda:

> (a) A requirement that each candidate for the National Resistance Council or Parliament should be able to speak *both* English and Kiswahili; or

> (b) A requirement that each candidate should be able to speak *either* English *or* Kiswahili.

The latter recommendation would necessitate the installation of a system of simultaneous translation in the National Assembly. There is a precedent for this in Tanganyika on the eve of independence, when both Kiswahili and English were full-fledged official parliamentary languages. The great advantage of policy (b) is that it would greatly widen the sector of the population from which parliamentarians could be drawn. There must be a sizable number of Ugandans who are politically astute and fluent in Kiswahili, but know no English. Thus, from the purely democratic point of view, this policy, requiring *either* English *or* Kiswahili, would be preferable. It would result in extending the boundaries of political recruitment. More Ugandans would be qualified to be active in national politics than was the case before.

The policy requiring *both* English and Kiswahili (policy a) would narrow the boundaries of political recruitment — since fewer Ugandans would be qualified for Parliament than were qualified at independence. But policy (a) would raise the linguistic needs of the common man to a parity of status with the needs of the educated Uganda.

The advantage of policy (a) [both English and Kiswahili] over policy

(b) [either English or Kiswahili] would be technical rather than democratic. A member of Parliament who spoke both English and Kiswahili would be likely to be technically better equipped to deal with parliamentary bills and perhaps politically more sophisticated than a person who was at home only with Kiswahili.

But the first point to be grasped is a simple one — that Uganda in the future cannot innovate on a large scale in its political institutions without reconsidering its language policy. If there were attempts to *nationalize* electoral campaigns for each parliamentary candidate, the country would once again have to face the issue of a national language. The case for the retention of the English language is still strong. But it need not be incompatible with a systematic promotion of Kiswahili as a second national language for politics at the grassroots.

If the either/or policy were to be adopted, both in requirements for parliamentary candidature and in the amount of time allowed for Kiswahili in education, on radio and television in Uganda, the impact on the future political culture of Uganda may be even more comprehensive and far-reaching than people's most ambitious expectations. The role of Kiswahili in expanding political participation and modernizing the class structure of Uganda may well become increasingly significant.

Finally, there is the role of personality in the politics of participation. Indeed, a major difference between politics in Africa and politics in more developed political systems is the simple fact that in Africa personalities count for more. And a pre-eminence of personalities is a pre-eminence of individual leadership. It is true that Africa's experience in the last ten years has demonstrated how ineffectual individuals can be in the face of certain types of problems. But even after we have made allowances for that, it remains true that in Africa major changes in political arrangements or administrative machinery can be made by the simple decision of a couple of individuals at the top, civilian or military. That such a decision can as easily be negated not long afterwards by the counter-intervention of another two leaders is itself further proof of how easily change can be brought about by individual personalities. If small elites are therefore of such importance in African conditions, a discussion of language and leadership is more than just pertinent.

A factor which needs to be immediately grasped is that there are times when a national language is necessary precisely in order to make national leadership possible. If Jomo Kenyatta had been a man who spoke no other language than Kikuyu, there is no doubt that his national stature would have suffered. Ordinary members of other ethnic groups would have found it difficult to identify fully with him as their own leader. Julius Nyerere would also have had a reduced authority among the populace if the only speeches he could make were in the language of the Wazanaki. And Kwame Nkrumah would hardly have aroused widespread national enthusiasm at home for so long if every state utterance he made was in the Nzima language, intelligible to most other Ghanaians only after some interpreter had translated it.

In short, effective national leadership in Africa demands the command of a trans-ethnic language. And Kiswahili is the best candidate available in Eastern Africa.

The extent to which East African presidents *need* a command of Kiswahili may, of course, vary from country to country. In none of the three East African countries is proficiency in Kiswahili *alone* a sufficient linguistic qualification for the presidency. Kenya, for instance, has now reached a situation in which a president has to be *trilingual*. A Kenyan president has to be competent in English, in Kiswahili, and in a language of ethnic constituency (like Kikuyu, Kalenjin, or Luo). A trilingual president in Kenya is a *de facto* requirement.

In Tanzania a president need only be bilingual in Kiswahili and English. An ethnic language is not a political necessity in Tanzania. Julius Nyerere has such an ethno-language of his own, but it was not a political asset. Indeed, it was sometimes a political liability. For Ali Hassan Mwinyi, the succeeding president, who was a native speaker of Kiswahili, an ethnic-bound language was quite irrelevant in any case. Nor has Benjamin

Mkapa, the current president of the Republic of Tanzania, attempted to resort to his native tongue in his political life.

In Uganda the imperial language, English, has been the undisputed qualification for the presidency, even though it is claimed that president Yoweri Museveni's public addresses are sometimes in Kiswahili (Ireri Mbaabu, 1996:110). The ethnic language has been a political risk in this deeply divided society. On the other hand, Kiswahili has been more popular among the Northerners and the military than among the more numerous Southern Bantu. Theoretically, a Ugandan president could be *unilingual* - simply competent or at best brilliant in the English language.

Theoretically, Ugandan presidents could survive by being only unilingual in the imperial language just as President Hastings Banda in Malawi originally was when he first captured power in his country. Ugandan presidents need to belong to a local ethnic group, but not necessarily to command a local ethnic language. They may need ethnic support, but not necessarily ethno-linguistic proficiency. That was precisely Hastings Banda's trade-off. He had lost his ethnic language in exile, but still retained his ethnic identity. That political equation could also work in Uganda. But it cannot work in Tanzania where a bilingual executive is needed, or in Kenya where a trilingual presidency is required.

3. Secularization

As for the process of secularization in the history of Kiswahili, this has to be related to the influence of both Islam and Christianity. From Islam's point of view, it is worth remembering that there is a Swahili *culture* as well as a Swahili language. The culture is getting secularized much more slowly than the language.

Kenya offers a particularly interesting example. It is sometimes taken a little too readily for granted that to adopt the Swahili language is to adopt the Swahili culture. Swahili culture does, of course, include the Swahili language, but it is possible to adopt the language without the other aspects of culture.

   We can best grasp this distinction by looking at the broadcasting policy. The more common broadcasting problems in Africa are those arising from the presence of many languages in the same country. Yet the problem could sometimes be one of having one language, but different sub-cultures. In the 1950s in Kenya there were indeed radio programmes in the Swahili language, but there were hardly any programmes to cater for the Swahili culture of the Coast. Swahili culture is neo-Islamic in almost the same sense in which French as a culture is neo-Christian. This does not mean that one cannot speak French without being a Christian. On the contrary, a large proportion of the French people themselves are no longer believers. But it does mean that the French culture has, in the course of the centuries, acquired a wealth of intellectual and idiomatic associations which bear the influence of Christianity.

   The Swahili culture of the Coast of Kenya is neo-Islamic in almost the same sense. Swahili as a culture or sub-culture is the way of life of those groups along the Coast of Kenya and Tanzania who speak Kiswahili as a mother-tongue. Only a minority of Kenyans speak Kiswahili as a mother-tongue. Yet it was precisely this minority which was not catered for in the broadcasting policy sometime prior to Kenya's independence. It was perhaps taken for granted that because those Coastal people spoke Kiswahili, the national programmes from Nairobi would meet their needs. Yet these were a people with distinct Swahili musical forms of their own, distinct Swahili poetry, distinct religious interests, and, of course, highly sophisticated Swahili dialects of their own. The Nairobi programmes at that time, though many were indeed in Kiswahili, were directed mainly at non-native speakers of the language in the interior of the country. The language was the same, but the cultural universe was different. And so Kenyans of the Coast often tuned in to the Voice of Zanzibar or the Voice of Dar es Salaam whose programmes were culturally more akin to the interests of coastal Kenyans than the Nairobi programmes in those days ever managed to be.

It was in the face of this broadcasting anomaly that a number of Coastal Kenyans themselves took the initiative in founding the *Sauti Ya Mvita* broadcasting programme from Mombasa. The authorities encouraged them in this venture by first making available the basic broadcasting equipment itself at Cable and Wireless coastal headquarters, and later by other kinds of help and facilities. But essentially, the *Sauti Ya Mvita* started as a volunteer project by coastal Kenyans who felt culturally starved on the radio in spite of the fact that their own language was used on national radio programmes. These people shared a language with fellow Kenyans without necessarily sharing a common culture.

This brings us to the fundamental anomaly of the Kenya aesthetic situation. It is Kenya, and not Zanzibar or Tanganyika, that is the home of Swahili aesthetic genius at its richest. Most of the classical masterpieces of Swahili poetry came from the Kenya coast — from Lamu and its sister islands, from Mombasa and further south. Tanzania's contribution to Swahili literature has much more recent origins — attaining a new height of achievement with Shaaban Robert this century. But the home of the older poetic traditions of Kiswahili, and the source of most of the great epics, was the Kenya coast.

And yet, in terms of general dissemination, Swahili culture is more widespread in Tanzania than in the Kenya nation as a whole. Kenya has a narrow geographical area of concentrated aesthetic achievement in Kiswahili, but elsewhere in the country it is the Swahili language as a neutral medium of communication rather than the Swahili culture as a rich vessel of heritage which has spread.

This situation may, of course, be only transient. Before long, Kenya might more systematically "nationalize" the aesthetic achievements of Lamu. Countries build up a shared cultural heritage precisely by nationalizing some of the cumulative local accomplishments of individual regions. As Kiswahili becomes more established in the rest of Kenya, some of the coastal classics of the eighteenth and nineteenth centuries would almost certainly be accorded a national cultural status. But that is a matter for the

future to confirm. For the time being, the basic aesthetic anomaly remains—
the country which has produced some of the greatest achievements of
Swahili culture in one of its parts has only a simplified version of the Swahili
language elsewhere. It is, in addition, in the throes of a cultural reappraisal
of potentially long-term implications.

What should be borne in mind are the Islamic origins of those cultural
achievements of the Waswahili. Much of pre-twentieth century Swahili
literature is full of didactic religious epics calling upon members of Swahili
society to live within the framework of Islam. Many of the epics were
couched in religious terms, often derived from a wider Islamic tradition,
but there was that old magnetic synthesis in imagery and idiom. Much of
the earliest written Swahili literature was Islamic both because of the
subjects it treated and because of the influence of the wider Muslim culture
on canons of composition in East Africa.

What Thomas Hodgkin said of Ghana's Islamic literary tradition
was also true of the earlier stages of much of written classical Swahili
literature: "It is a literature which can be properly called "Islamic" in the
sense that its authors were Muslims, trained in the Islamic sciences,
conscious of their relationship with the Islamic past, and regarding literature
as a vehicle for the expression of Islamic values" (1966: 442).

Significant also is the fact that much of the poetry was composed,
as we indicated elsewhere, by *Ulamaa* scholars versed in Islamic theology
and jurisprudence. Some were descended from a line of scholars, all with
a high sensitivity to the metaphysical relationship. In poetry one of the
most prominent of them all has now become Sayyid Abdalla bin Nasir. A
descendant of a long line of Swahili scholars, he composed the epic
Al-Inkishafi (A Soul's Awakening) around 1800. In the poem, the poet
draws inspiration from the historical ruins of Pate and draws the analogy
of death from them. By reflecting on the once accomplished and splendid
achievements of the Swahili people of Pate, the beautiful architectural
relics, the hedonist rulers, the intellectual life at the time, the poet castigates
his own heart and urges it to take its cue from the fallen ruins and ephemeral

nature of life. By verbal dexterity and touching imagery of pythons in hell fire, solitude amidst the ruins, he urges his heart not to take this world seriously, and almost begs it to repent its past sins and pray for the eternal peace and happiness that can only be found in the life after death.

The nineteenth century saw the rise of a written poetic tradition posturing towards the *secular*. Everyday issues of social and political importance were captured in verse and preserved for posterity by the Arabic-Swahili alphabet. The leading spirit behind the popularization of the more secular poetic tradition was the inimitable Muyaka bin Mwinyi Haji, who lived and composed in Mombasa between 1776 and 1840. In the hands of *Muyaka*, the quatrain was restored to its rightful place as an important genre in the Swahili poetic diction. Muyaka produced poems with an unmatched mastery on the topical issues of his period. He wrote on love and infidelity, prosperity and drought, the sex-exploits of key figures of his time and the calamities of the Mombasans. Above all, Muyaka became the celebrated poet of the Mazrui reign of Mombasa in the first half of the nineteenth century. To read Muyaka's poems is to delve into the past. His poetry, during the rivalry between the Mazruis of Mombasa and the Sultanate of Zanzibar, played a significant role in inspiring the Mazrui faction during military combats. Scholars of his poetry liken him to the court-poets of Europe.

Muyaka's genius lay partly in his linking the social relationship with the relationship of the ego. The poetry of the private self is more limited in Afro-Islamic literature than in Afro-European literature. But poets like Muyaka helped to build bridges between individual privacy and public concern. Modern Swahili poets like *Abdilatif Abdalla* and *Ahmed Nassir Bhallo*, working within the traditional prosodic framework, have been significantly influenced by the classical Swahili tradition. Muyaka's poetic influence in terms of theme, style, and tone has had a direct impact on these two young poets. Their poetry is replete with archaisms drawn from the generation of poets who were contemporaries of Muyaka, going backwards. To fully assimilate, appreciate, and evaluate the poetry of

Abdilatif and Ahmed Nassir requires a grounding in classical poetry. Swahili culture is so vital a component of their poetry that it is difficult to dig into the nuances without some familiarity with the various registers of the language. Abdilatif's poetry is at once intellectual and committed, dissident and diffident. What sets him apart from his contemporaries is his virtual mastery of poetic diction and idiom in a way that few of them can match. His poetry is classical, inventive, and creative without being stilted.

The public concerns of Abdilatif are not only primarily secular, they are also partly political. Radical in his politics, he was imprisoned for supporting the opposition party in Kenya. After a five-year term in jail for sedition and libel, he compiled an anthology of his prison poems which span his whole experience in Kenyan jails. His poems are militant and unrepentent in tone. The sense of isolation and the effects of solitary confinement are vividly recaptured in the imagery he uses. The anthology is reminiscent of the poems of Muyaka in which he castigated the treasonable behavior of some of his compatriots. Equally striking is his nationalism. In one poem, reflecting on whether to embark on a self-imposed political exile by a finer flight of imagination, he puts himself in a position not unlike that of a crab: "Where else can a crab run to, save in its own shell?" (1973: 77).

Unlike many of the African poets writing in European languages, the poets writing in Kiswahili are seldom groping for an identity. There is a conspicuous absence of poems obsessed with cultural alienation, or with the cultural conflict with Europe, or even poetry of the surrealist type. The only genre that comes near "alienation" are those poems composed to condemn the evils of neo-colonialism in its political sense and poems that recount the virtues of African socialism or *Ujamaa*. These have collectively come to be known as "the poetry of political combat." The very fact that Abdilatif and poets like him have continued to compose on a variety of themes that are of direct relevance to the realities of modern Africa, have vindicated the assumption that modern themes and issues are capable of being versified within the traditional poetic diction. Among those who have defended the classical tradition has been a former Tanzanian Justice Minister, the late K. Amri Abedi, himself a poet of note.

These poets were trained in the classical Islamic education system and, in most cases, suffered a minimum of cultural alienation. While the traditional Islamic system of education accommodated aspects of traditional African culture, the Western system of education alienated and sometimes suppressed traditional value-systems. The recipients of traditional Islamic education came out equipped with both the Arabic alphabet and the Roman alphabet and tended to use the two interchangeably. They became conscious of the existence of the legacy of Swahili literature before being initiated into the heritage of literature in European languages. They accepted the legacy of the *ulamaa*, the priestly poets of old, and at the same time groped for a new idiom of *ujamaa* as a modern worldview.

Tanzania, among African countries, has the least number of creative writers writing in *English*. The largest output in both prose and poetry is in Kiswahili. The literature in general is a reflection of the nationalistic nature of Tanzanian society. Once the most radical nation in East Africa, it managed to decolonize the various aspects of life there, ranging from an emphasis on Kiswahili for legislative deliberations to the politicization of the masses. Finding themselves in a radically tempestuous political climate, the poets and novelists also preoccupied themselves with the problems of development. Poets composed long political epics extolling the virtues of socialism and the pitfalls of too excessive a dependence on external economic and cultural models. Day after day, the predominant Swahili newspapers were inundated with poems urging for greater reliance on the land as the backbone of the Tanzanian economy and the beauty of the Swahili language, customs, and political culture.

But it is not merely with products of the creative imagination that language has a relation of intimacy. It is also with works of the reasoning intellect. In translating Shakespeare's *Julius Caesar*, Nyerere was involved in a work of the creative imagination. But in writing his piece of political theory entitled *Democracy and the Party System* Nyerere was involved in a work of the reasoning intellect. It is to the latter kind of activity and its relationship to language that we must now turn.

In the controversies in the Kenya Press, one question which arose once was whether "African socialism would be more accepted if it had been propagated in Swahili." The statement was originally attributed to Mr. Peter Temu, a Tanzanian lecturer at the University College, Nairobi. Later, discussions in the Press raised doubts as to whether Mr. Temu had, indeed, made that remark. And the *East African Standard* said in an editorial that such an assertion could be "successfully challenged" (*East African Standard* Editorial, February 23, 1967). Yet the *Standard* left it at that, without demonstrating *how* the claim could be so challenged.

In point of fact, the question as to which language should be nationally promoted cannot be regarded as irrelevant to the consolidation of socialism. The relevance lies in two broad areas. It lies in the necessary link which exists between words and ideas at large; and it also lies in considerations of class-formation in African countries.

The whole movement to evolve a distinctively African socialism, is in fact, a quest for ideological uniqueness. In general, ideological distinctiveness is more difficult to attain through an international language than through a local one. Ideas have to be expressed in words. And the word "socialism" in the English language, for example, carries so many European connotations that it is difficult to make it appear distinctive in African conditions if the same English medium is used. But call "socialism" *Ujamaa* and a whole new world of subtle associations and connotations is suddenly revealed. Nothing could have given Nyerere's socialism a more striking African ring than the simple Swahili label *Ujamaa* that he gave it. Nyerere was using an old Swahili word, but in a new context. All the subtle associations of bonds of kinship, ethnic hospitality, and the welfare obligations of the extended family, were compressed within that single Swahili expression. African socialism in Tanzania acquired an extra Africanness by the simple device of bearing an African name. No English word could possibly have achieved the same result. Nyerere, in his pamphlet on *Ujamaa*, added to the Africanness of his socialism by the further device of using an African proverb. The ethic of hard work and of opposition to parasitism in Tanzania's ideology was again given an African identity by a new way of utilizing an old Swahili adage. *"Mgeni siku mbili, siku ya tatu mpe jembe,"* Nyerere quoted ancestral wisdom. ("Treat your guest as a guest for two days; on the third day, give him/her a hoe.") The Tanzanian leader was, in fact, using one Swahili concept to qualify the implications of another. After all, the concept of *Ujamaa*, with its suggestion of the obligations of kinship and the extended family, could be used to legitimize living on one's relatives. A person might go to his kinsman and exploit his hospitality indefinitely. And so Nyerere qualifies this notion of kinship with the notion of requiring your guest to help in the field on the third day after his arrival. Kinship hospitality must be qualified by an anti-parasitic ethic. And so, "Treat your guest as a guest for two days; on the third day, give him/her a hoe."

If Tanzanians continue to utilize Swahili concepts in sophisticated political theorizing, it is to Tanzania then that we should ultimately look for Africa's most distinctive ideological formulations. Such formulations need not be the most original in the policies they propagate. But they might well be the most African in their idiom of rationalization.

If then African socialism was indeed a quest for ideological nativeness, Kiswahili was a better medium for it than English. The old religious language of the Muslim *ulamaa* had indeed become the new secular language of *ujamaa*.

As for the role of Christianity in the secularization of Kiswahili, it lies especially in the impact of the churches and missionaries on East African societies. The role of Western missionaries was paradoxical all along. On the one hand, they were carriers of a new religion, messengers of the Gospel of Jesus Christ. On the other hand, Western missionaries were also carriers of the new secular civilization of the Western world. They built schools which disseminated both Christianity and Western science, both the Gospel and the new rationalism of Europe. To that extent the impact of these churches on Africa was both Christianizing and secularizing.

Kiswahili felt both influences. In Tanzania, parts of Kenya, and parts of the Democratic Republic of Congo, Kiswahili became a major language of the new evangelical crusade, the medium of spreading the Christian Gospel. On the other hand, Kiswahili also began to absorb the new vocabulary of Western technical civilization. It also facilitated the spread of that civilization.

The universe of Kiswahili continued to expand — from the Qur'an to the crucifix, from the crucifix to the computer.

4. Western Science and African Dependency

In the acquisition of modern science and technology Africa has shown clear signs of dependency on the West. In this book we have been interested in change, not only in a direction which is compatible with the present stage of human knowledge, but also which does justice to the potentialities of the human person both as a social creature and as an *innovative being*. Excessive dependency is, by definition, a denial of innovation.

Science and technology are part of the Western package of "modernity." But that package has also come to Africa with many cultural strings. In this connection it may once again be worth our while to contrast Africa with the Japanese experience.

Japan's original attempts at capacity building involved considerable selectivity on the part of the Japanese themselves. The whole purpose of selective Japanese westernization was to protect Japan against the West, rather than merely to submit to western cultural attractions. The emphasis in Japan was, therefore, on the technical and technological techniques of the West, rather than on literary and verbal culture. The Japanese slogan of "western technique, Japanese spirit" at the time captured this ambition to borrow technology from the West while deliberately protecting a substantial part of Japanese culture. In a sense, Japan's technological westernization was designed to reduce the danger of other forms of cultural dependency.

The nature of westernization in Africa has been very different. Far from emphasizing western productive technology and containing western life-styles and verbal culture, Africa has reversed the Japanese order of emphasis. Among the factors which have facilitated this reversal has been the role of the African university.

One primary function of culture is to provide a universe of perception and cognition, a societal paradigm, a world view. Thomas Kuhn's work on the structure of scientific revolutions has provided new insights about the process through which scientific paradigms shift, and new alternative systems of explaining phenomena that come to dominate scientific thought.

But what about shifts in cultural paradigms? And how are these related to shifts in scientific ones?

Religion is often a cultural paradigm in its own right. Copernicus and Galileo between them, by helping to transform scientific thought on planetary movements, in time also helped to change the Christian paradigm of the universe.

Charles Darwin, by helping to initiate a revolution in the biological sciences, also started the process of transforming the Christian concept of "creation." These are cases in which paradigmatic changes in the sciences have led to paradigmatic changes in religion. Historically there have also been cases where religious revolutions have resulted in scientific shifts. The rise of Islam gave the Arabs for a while scientific leadership in the northern hemisphere. Puritanism and non-conformity in Britain in the eighteenth century was part of the background of both a scientific and an industrial revolution in that country.

But paradigmatic changes are caused not merely by great minds like those of Copernicus, Newton, Darwin, and Einstein, nor only by great social movements like Islam and the protestant revolution, but also by acculturation and normative diffusion.

It is in this sense that colonialism constituted a major shift in the cultural paradigm of one African society after another. Traditional ideas about how rain is caused, how crops are grown, how diseases are cured, and how babies are conceived, have had to be re-examined in the face of the new scientific culture of the West.

If African universities had borrowed a leaf from the Japanese book, and initially concentrated on what is indisputably the West's real area of leadership and marginal advantage (science and technology), the resultant African dependency might have been of a different kind. But the initial problem lay precisely in the model of the university itself — the paradigm of academia, with its distrust of direct problem-solving in the wider society:

> There is much in our education system [in Britain] which makes it easier to define problems in terms of narrowly scientific objectives. The existing relationship between universities (with the unidirectional flow of "experts" and advisors, the flow of overseas students to this country, etc.) have tended to transfer the same standards and expectations to the LDCs... Technologies for the satisfaction of basic needs and for rural development have received little attention... curricula, textbooks, and teaching methods are too closely imitative of practice in industrialized countries. This has spilled over from teaching into research expectations. Universities have aimed to achieve international standards in defining the criteria for staff recognition and promotion; in practice this means using the international scientific and engineering literature as the touchstone. However, applied work directed at the solution of local problems...can rarely be associated by publication in "respectable" journals: a far better test is the local one of success or failure of the particular project in the LDC environment. (L. Pyle, 1978: 2-3)

The one paradigmatic change which was necessary for the imported universities did not in fact occur. The missing factor was a change in the conception of the university itself and what its purposes were.

But the "lack of change" in the conception of the transplanted university caused a lot of changes in the attitudes, values, and worldview of its products. Since the university was so uncompromisingly foreign in an African context, and was transplanted with few concessions to African cultures, its impact was more culturally alienating than it need have been. A whole generation of African graduates grew up despising their own ancestry and scrambling to imitate others. It was not the traditional African that resembled the ape; it was more the westernized one, fascinated by the West's cultural mirror. A disproportionate number of these cultural "apes" were, and continue to be, products of universities.

Those African graduates who have later become university teachers themselves have on the whole remained intellectual imitators and disciples of the West. African *historians* have begun to innovate methodologically as they have grappled with oral traditions, but most of the other disciplines are still condemned to paradigmatic dependency.

This includes those African scholars that discovered Karl Marx. The genius of Marx did indeed initiate a major international paradigmatic shift in social analysis. But Marx's theories were basically Eurocentric, and his legacy constitutes the radical stream of the western heritage. Those African scholars that have substituted a western liberal paradigm with a western radical paradigm may have experienced a palace coup in their own minds or a changing of the guards within the brain. But they have not yet experienced an intellectual revolution in this paradigmatic sense. The ghost of intellectual dependency still continues to haunt the whole gamut of Africa's academia.

An important source of this intellectual dependency is the language in which African graduates and scholars are taught. For the time being, it is impossible for an African to be even moderately familiar with the works of Marx or Ricardo without the help of a European language. *Das Kapital* is not yet available in Hausa or Kiswahili, let alone in Kidigo or Lutoro. In short, major intellectual paradigms of the West are likely to remain unavailable even in a single African language unless there is a genuine *educational* revolution involving widespread adoption of African languages as media of instruction.

As matters now stand, an African who has a good command of a European language has probably assimilated other aspects of western culture as well. This is because the process of acquiring a European language in Africa has tended to be overwhelmingly through a formal system of western-style education. It is because of this that the concept of an African Marxist who is not also westernized is at the present time a socio-linguistic impossibility.

This need not apply to a Chinese or Japanese Marxist, where it is possible to undergo an ideological conversion at a sophisticated level without the explicit mediation of a foreign language. Japan especially has tamed its language to cope with a wide range of intellectual discourse.

Of course the Japanese range goes beyond ideological and political literature. But today, in black Africa, a modern surgeon who does not speak a European language is virtually a socio-linguistic impossibility. So is a modern physicist, a zoologist, an economist.

Nor is this simply a case of the surgeon, or physicist, or economist acquiring an additional skill called a "European language" which he is capable of discarding when he discusses surgery or physics with fellow professionals in his own society. Professional Japanese scientists or social scientists can organize a conference or convention and discuss professional matters almost entirely in Japanese. But a conference of African scientists, devoted to scientific matters, and conducted primarily in an African language is not yet possible.

Almost all black African intellectuals conduct their most sophisticated conversations in European languages. Their most complicated thinking has also to be done in some European language or another. It is because of this that intellectual and scientific dependency in Africa is inseparable from linguistic dependency.

And since a major function of culture lies, as we indicated, in providing media of communication, the choice of European languages as media of instruction in African universities has had profound cultural consequences for the societies which are served by those universities.

5. Towards Decolonization

How, then, can the Third World achieve that elusive goal of capacity building without the chains of dependency? How can the contradictions of premature technological change be resolved? And in what way does Kiswahili illustrate these wider issues?

In our view, the process of decolonization involves the following five processes — indigenization, domestication, diversification, horizontal inter-penetration, and vertical counter-penetration. What do all these five strategies mean?

First, there is the strategy of *indigenization*. This involves increasing the utilization of indigenous resources, ranging from native personnel to aspects of traditional local technology. But in applying this to language policy we have to relate it to the second strategy as well.

The second strategy is that of *domestication*. This is the other side of the coin of indigenization. While indigenization in our sense means using local resources and making them more relevant to the modern age, domestication involves making imported resources more relevant to the local society. For example, the English language in East Africa is of course an alien medium. To domesticate it is to make it respond to local imagery, figures of speech, sound patterns, and to the general cultural milieu of the region. On the other hand, the promotion of Kiswahili as against English in Tanzania is a process of indigenization. It involves promoting a local linguistic resource, rather than making an alien resource more locally relevant.

With regard to western institutions in Africa, domestication is the process by which they are in part Africanized or traditionalized in local terms. But with local institutions, the task is partly to make them compatible with the present state of knowledge. Thus, English in East Africa needs to be Africanized, while Kiswahili needs to be elaborated in the sense of enabling it to cope with life and knowledge in our age.

Clearly the two strategies of domestication and indigenization are closely related and are sometimes impossible to disentangle. This is particularly so when we apply these strategies of decolonization to educational institutions.

The Western school in Africa is, of course, more like the English language in Africa than like Kiswahili. The school is a piece of alien culture. Can it be domesticated?

We believe it can, but the introduction or expansion of this institution in an East African country must be much more carefully planned than has so far been the case. The domestication of the school would first and foremost require increased indigenization of personnel. This would require, first, greater commitment by African governments to promote relevant training at different levels for Africans; second, readiness on the part of both governments and employers to create a structure of incentives which would attract Africans of the right caliber; third, greater political pressure on educational officials and headmasters to develop Africa-related curricula; fourth, stricter "domestication" of the foreign component in the syllabus in a bid to make it more relevant to the local context; and fifth, a gradual introduction of Kiswahili as a medium of instruction, moving upwards slowly from lower to higher grades.

The cultural and political milieu of the new reforms should affect and perhaps modify problem-definition. This Africanization of the local school should also facilitate in time the Africanization of scholarship and science. What should be borne in mind is that the efficient indigenization and domestication of the school does require a *gradualist* and *planned* approach. It also requires careful linguistic preparation, including resources for developing Kiswahili further.

The third strategy of decolonization is *diversification*. At the broader level of the society, this means the diversification of ways of perception, sources of expertise, techniques of analysis, types of goods produced, markets for these products, general trading partners, aid-donors, and other benefactors.

This approach — though sometimes inefficient — should help an African country diversify those upon whom it is dependent. Excessive reliance on only one alien culture is more dangerous for a weak state than reliance on half a dozen other cultures. Reliance on only the West is more risky than diversified dependency on both East and West.

Kiswahili should respond to the stimulus of a range of civilizations than merely to the West. Julius Nyerere translated Shakespeare, his compatriot Mushi translated Voltaire, and the Christian missionaries long ago translated the four Gospels. Then the field expanded and Karl Marx, V.I. Lenin, and Frantz Fanon have now also appeared in Kiswahili on a modest scale.

But when will the Indian poet Tagore and the Chinese philosopher Confucius be available in Kiswahili? The Qur'an is available in Kiswahili and so are the Arabian Nights. But what about more recent classics of the culture of Islam?

In short, a language cannot be developed merely by appointing a special commission with the task of coining new words. A language has to develop through facing new challenges, confronting new ideas which need to be expressed.

If Kiswahili now abandons Arabic and borrows only from English and French, it may indeed become "modernized" — but also excessively westernized. If it limits itself to only Europe and Arab civilization, Kiswahili would deny itself the potential enrichment which can only come from more diverse stimulation.

The fourth strategy of decolonization is *horizontal inter-penetration* among African societies themselves. In the field of trade this could mean promoting greater exchange among, say, African countries themselves. In the field of investment it could, for example, mean allowing Libyan money to compete with Western and Japanese money in establishing new industries or promoting new projects in Africa. In the field of aid it must also mean that oil-rich African countries should increase their contribution towards the economic and social development of their resource-poor sister countries. In the field of technical assistance it would have to mean that African countries with an apparent excess of skilled manpower in relation to their absorption capacity should not only be prepared, but also encouraged to facilitate temporary or permanent migration to other African countries. This last process is what might be called the horizontal brain drain — the transfer of skilled manpower from, say, Egypt to the Sudan , or from Nigeria to Zambia.

In the field of education, horizontal skill-transfers among African countries are particularly promising in the short run as part of the process of decolonization. If an African country wants a computer it has now to buy it from Europe, North America, or, theoretically, Japan. Almost by definition, these sophisticated machines are products of highly industrialized economies.

But an African country does *not* have to import highly-skilled computer personnel from those same industrialized states. As part of horizontal inter-penetration, Third World countries generally must learn to poach on each other's skilled humanpower, at least as a short-term strategy. President Idi Amin of Uganda learned after a while to distinguish between Indians with strong economic and historic roots in Uganda and Indians on contract for a specified period. He expelled almost all of those who had strong local roots, and then went to the Indian sub-continent to recruit skilled professional teachers, engineers, and doctors on contract terms.

The wholesale expulsion of Asians with roots was basically an irrational act. But the recruitment of skilled Indians on contract was sound. Kenya too should turn increasingly to the Indian sub-continent instead of Western Europe for some of its temporary skill needs, including the need for computer personnel pending adequate indigenization. The present pervasive African distrust of people of Indian extraction may be incompatible with the quest for a New International Economic Order.

What is even less rational is the reluctance of African countries to give permanent residence to skilled Africans from other lands. African universities also do not welcome African national corporations.

Even the Southern capacity to impose clear political conditions on Northern firms is a case of *vertical counter-penetration*. The Arab's success in forcing many Western firms to stop trading with Israel (if they wished to retain their Arab markets) was a clear illustration of a Southern market dictating certain conditions to Northern transnational corporations instead of the older reverse flow of power.

Yet another element in the strategy of counter-penetration is the northward brain drain itself. On the whole Third World countries cannot afford to lose their skilled human resources. But it would be a mistake to assume that the northward brain drain is totally to the disadvantage of the South. Indian doctors in British hospitals are indeed recruited to some extent at the expense of the sick in India. But those emigre Indian doctors are becoming an important sub-lobby in British society to increase British responsiveness to the health and nutritional needs of India itself.

The American Jews that are not prepared to go to settle in Israel are not merely a case of depriving Israel of skills and possessions which they would have taken there. They also constitute a counter-influence on the American system to balance the influence of the United States on the Israeli system.

The presence of Irish Americans in the United States is indeed partly a case of agonizing economic disadvantage for the Irish Republic. But Irish Americans are also conversely an existing economic and political resource for the benefit of the Irish Republic.

This is also true of Greek Americans, Polish Canadians, and Algerians in France. Migration from one country to another is never purely a blessing nor purely a curse to either the donor country or the receiving country. The costs and benefits vary from case to case.

As more and more Africans become highly skilled in technology and usage, some of them will migrate to Western states. As matters now stand, the costs of this kind of brain drain are for the time being weightier than the benefits for African countries. What should constantly be borne in mind is that the intellectual penetration of the South by Northern industrial states must one day be balanced with reverse intellectual penetration by the South of the Think Tanks of the North. Given the realities of an increasingly interdependent world, decolonization will never be complete unless penetration is reciprocal and more balanced.

From Kiswahili's point of view, *counter-penetration* would include making more and more Swahili masterpieces available in translation in dominant world languages. The great poem *Al-Inkishafi* is already available in more than one English version. It seems to be also available in German and French. Several other classical pieces of Swahili poetry, in particular, also exist in English translation. Lovers of Swahili culture should maintain and even intensify the effort to translate great Swahili works for possible use not only in educational courses in Europe and the Americas, but also in those parts of Africa where Kiswahili is not spoken.

A course on African literature in Nigeria may include Ngugi wa Thiong'o but is unlikely to include either Shaaban Robert or Muyaka. This state of affairs is surely not necessary. There is a definite market for Swahili culture in West Africa — provided it is translated into English or French. There is also a market in Europe and North America provided the effort to exploit that market is sophisticated and sustained. The governments and societies of Eastern Africa should try to share their cultural riches with the rest of the world. That is indeed part of development. It is certainly part of the process of adding an African component to global civilization.

As for enriching world languages with Swahili words and phrases, it is time to go beyond *jambo, kwa heri*, and *safari*. The measure of the influence of a language is partly the extent to which it is not merely a borrower of loan words, but also a donor. Tanzania has managed to internationalize the word *ujamaa*. The word is now used among Australian Aborigines and African Americans, and from London to Papua, New Guinea. There are *ujamaa* dinners in Detroit and *ujamaa* dances in Port

Moresby.

Kiswahili has begun to affect the lives of other black people in distant lands. It may one day affect the texture of world culture itself as Africa increases its contribution to the total heritage of humanity.

6. Conclusion

We have attempted in this book to place Kiswahili in the context of the much wider issues raised by it. The language is now a piece of African culture in a technological age. Its functions in society have identifiable consequences in expanding the horizons of knowledge, science, technology, and social interaction. Kiswahili has helped to secularize the science of explanation, to transform the class structure, and to promote a capacity for transcending parochialism and broadening allegiance.

While European languages in Africa probably help to promote this direction of change, they also aggravate Africa's technological and intellectual dependency on Western Europe and North America. English, when used efficiently, would greatly aid the process of African "advancement." But its consequences are negative in such tasks as reducing dependency, expanding innovation, reducing disparities between town and country, and broadening popular participation.

Africa cannot escape the technological age indefinitely. It cannot completely avoid adopting the science and technology from the West. But in its quest to expand its scientific and technological capacity can it escape the factor of dependency? Can it decolonize as it seeks to develop?

We enumerated the five strategies of decolonization. The new science and the new technology have to respond to the imperatives of indigenization, domestication, diversification, horizontal inter-penetration among Third World countries, and vertical counter-penetration from the South into the citadels of technological and economic power in the North. Kiswahili can be given a larger role in these processes of decolonization.

But in the final analysis language is merely a symbol of much wider forces, ranging from technology to kinship, from the impact of transnational corporations to the process of class formation, from ethnic relations to problems of authority and power.

When adequately strengthened and promoted, Kiswahili in Eastern Africa could become a mediator between the ancestral world of collective wisdom and personal intuition on the one side, and the new world of quantified data and scientific analysis on the other. The sociology of knowledge is undergoing a change in Eastern Africa. And Kiswahili is part of that process of change. The psychology of living together is also undergoing a change — and Kiswahili is part of the new East African mind in communion with the modern world.

Appendix I

Social Engineering and Lauguage Policy in East Africa[20]

Ali A. Mazrui

The critical goals of language policy in relation to social engineering in East Africa are the goals of, firstly, national integration and secondly, social integration. For our purposes in this paper, national integration is a process of merging sub-group identities into a shared sense of national consciousness. In Africa the creation of a supra-tribal or supra-ethnic loyalty to a national homeland is the goal of the integrative process in this national sense.

Social integration, on the other hand, is not the merger of tribe with tribe, but is the process by which the gaps between the elite and the masses, the town and the countryside, the privileged and the underprivileged, are gradually narrowed or evened out. Social integration is not necessarily a process by which the difference in income between the richest man and the poorest man in the country is minimized. That absolute difference might remain the same, or be even increased, without implying that there has been no integration. But if the distance between the top and the bottom of the curve of income differences remains the same, the slope of the curve should be gradual and not steep. In a country where there are only very rich people and very poor people and no one in between, social integration has a long way to go. But if between the pauper and the millionaire there are a lot of people with intermediate rates of income in a gradual gradation, the social integrative process has indeed made progress. We can indeed have a well-integrated *traditional* society in this social sense of "integration," as we can have a well-integrated *modern* society, but the prerequisites are different in each case. A well-integrated traditional society has to be largely egalitarian, with no major difference in income between the richest and the poorest. A well-integrated modern society need not be egalitarian, but the process of differentiation of structures and specialization of functions must be sufficiently advanced to have created an even or gradual slope of incomes from the top to the bottom.

Can a society move from traditional social integration to modern social integration without passing through the agonies of major gaps of incomes and life-styles between the new elite and the masses, the town and the countryside? Can it move from social equality (the basis of traditional integration) to social differentiation (the basis of modern integration) without passing through a stage of convulsive disparities? This is one of the most agonizing dilemmas of contemporary Africa.

Language policy in East Africa is linked to the problems of both national integration and social integration. And the place of the English language is critical in both. A case can be made for the proposition that in relation to national integration in Uganda or Kenya the English language is functional, whereas in relation to social integration the English language is dysfunctional. We shall examine these two parts of the proposition in the course of the analysis.

A Survey of Language Use and Language Teaching in Eastern Africa was started in 1967, committed to compiling language data for Uganda, Kenya, Ethiopia, Zambia, and Tanzania. The Uganda Survey was completed recently under the directorship of Professor Peter Ladefoged. The Kenya Survey is well underway under the directorship of Professor Wilfred Whitely, and the Tanzania Survey is scheduled to start later this year (1969). The Ethiopian Survey is also well underway with Professor Charles Ferguson as Country Director. The Zambian Survey is yet to come. A special grant of the Ford Foundation has enabled such a survey to be undertaken. And a regional Language Survey Council, with academic and political representation from all the countries concerned, was entrusted with policy-making issues within the terms of the Ford Foundation grant.

Information about who speaks which languages in East Africa, who is bilingual or trilingual, how widely is this or that language spoken, is expected to emerge from the language survey of each of these five African countries. Uganda, as we indicated, was the first to be surveyed, and the report should be out within the coming months. From the point of view of cultural engineering particular interest has already been aroused in the figures about the spread of Luganda and Swahili in the country as a whole. Preliminary indications are that Swahili may be more widely understood in Uganda than previously assumed, though it is on balance a language of men rather than women in that country. In other words, partly because of the phenomenon of men's mobility in relation to work and the whole phenomenon of the rural/urban continuum, significantly more Uganda men than women have been exposed to Swahili and learned to use it for specialized purposes.

But although Swahili is better understood than previously assumed, and although its political respectability has risen as a result of the decline of Buganda's influence, Swahili is not for the time being a serious candidate as a national language for Uganda. Dr. Luyimbazi Zake, the Minister of Education, was speaking more like a Muganda nationalist than a social scientist when he said in a debate in Parliament on the new constitution in 1967 that Swahili was as foreign to Uganda as Gujerati. But the new constitution had no alternative but to adopt English as the national language of the country. This is the role English is intended to fill in the process of national integration.

The decision to make English the national language in no way implies that it is the most widely understood language in the country. Luganda and Lunyoro are spoken by the greatest number of people. But the whole problem of fair political representation and ethnic balance in political recruitment would be dangerously aggravated if these languages were adopted instead of English. As President Obote put it:

> ..immediately we adopted [either Luganda or Lunyoro] as
> the official language for administrative purposes or legislation,

some of us will have to go out of Government. I, for instance, would not be able to speak in Parliament in Luganda, neither could I do so in Lunyoro, and I think more than half the present National Assembly members would have to quit. The areas we now represent would not like to have just any person who speaks Luganda to represent them. They would feel unrepresented. So, there again, we find no alternative to English. (1964: 4)

Fairness in political representation and balance of recruitment sometimes dictates that a language which is uniformly lesser known throughout the country should have priority over a language which is very well known by only one section of the community and not known at all by others. Hindi has suffered from the same disability as a projected national language of India. It was felt by its opponents that native speakers of Hindi would have too big an advantage over others in important sections of recruitment. But English, by being foreign to everyone, was a shared handicap. In situations of this kind, distributive justice itself becomes a question of distributive disability. A uniformly distributed linguistic handicap throughout the country becomes an important condition of political stability and a possible basis of closer integration.

The Baganda, even on the basis of how many of them speak good English, might still have a disproportionate share of the fruit of political recruitment. Certainly in absolute terms, and possibly in relative terms too, the Baganda are better educated than most of their compatriots. But disparities of advantage would be worse compounded if Luganda itself became the national language of Uganda.

But although English has become so very convenient for the whole task of national integration in Uganda, it ought not to be overlooked that the lack of a grassroot language for such a purpose puts Uganda at a disadvantage when compared with either Tanzania or Kenya. After all, national integration is not simply a case of fair distribution of advantages and disadvantages among ethnic groups, although this itself might be a critical *sine qua non*. National integration also presupposes the growth of a high socio-economic intercourse between the different ethnic groups, a high degree of authoritative penetration from the center to the periphery, and access from periphery of the society to the center. These variables of socio-economic intercourse between groups and political intercourse between the populace and those in authority all demand or actually mean greater *communication*. English is for the time being limited in its capacity to provide this kind of inter-communication involving the grassroots.

Socio-economic intercourse between groups by way of trade, marketing, and cooperative and labor organization, is served more effectively by Luganda and Swahili than by English. This is one area where the success of English in national integration and its failure in social integration become indistinguishable. English as an inter-tribal language between the educated is clearly nationally integrative, but for inter-tribal communication at the grassroots, English is intrinsically and hopelessly ill-equipped to meet the challenge.

Then there is the question of political penetration and political access between the center and the periphery also to be examined. Language is, of course, an important factor in determining the degree of political penetration which a Government can achieve. How effectively and in what comparable terms can the news media, for example, reach different parts of the countryside? The national programme on Radio Tanzania is in Swahili. This ensures a shared exposure to radio programmes by different audiences in different areas of the country. The national programme on Radio Uganda is in the English language. This also is heard (not always well) in different parts of Uganda, but is it listened to in different parts of Uganda? Outside the towns, a high proportion of those who listen to Radio Uganda's National programme may, in fact, be the Government's own servants. Since the national programme requires a certain standard of education in the English language, and since a high proportion of those who have attained such a standard go into Government and related services, political penetration by national programmes on the radio is to a disproportionate degree *intra*-governmental. It is broadcast by Government employees under the Ministry of Information for the inadvertent benefit of other Government employees under the Ministries of Education, Labor, Regional Administration, and others. There is, of course, an element of exaggeration in putting it in these terms. But the point which needs to be grasped is that a national programme in the English language in an African country may indeed have a mixed audience in the towns. But outside the towns a disproportionate number of the consumers are either foreigners (like European hotel managers and Asian dukawallas) or people already connected with Government. In Uganda the European managers may in any case prefer to listen to the BBC and Asian dukawallas may have a greater partiality for All-India Radio than for the National Programme of Radio Uganda. The remaining rural audiences of Uganda's national radio programme might, therefore, basically be administrators and civil leaders, educated enough to understand in comfort programmes in the English language, and isolated enough to feel starved of Kampala news and of sophisticated radio discussions.

The Uganda government is aware of the limited utility of the national programme as an instrument of political penetration. The result is that the number of programmes in vernacular languages in Uganda has increased since independence from five (English, Luganda, Runyoro/Rutoro, Ateso, and Luso) to fourteen. This certainly enables the Government to reach different audiences quite effectively in at least some matters. But there are two costs. One cost is that the period of time devoted to each programme is necessarily limited — a couple of hours a day for this or that language. For programmes with such a specialized linguistic audience, often restricted to one part of the country, it does not pay to employ a full-time staff to keep programmes in that language going all day long. There would also be complications in having over a dozen wavelengths in use all the time from Kampala. Instead, Radio Uganda limits itself to two channels — the Red and the Blue channels — which are shared by over a dozen languages, including English, over a period of about thirty-six hours of combined broadcasting time from both channels.

Another cost in having a large number of vernacular programmes instead of one national one is that the programmes themselves become less national in perspective. The medium may not be the message, but it certainly affects the message profoundly (Marshall McLuhan, 1964). That part of cultural engineering which is concerned with nationalizing what is sectional becomes difficult in a situation of such sectionalized media. A news bulletin which is in a language understood all over the country dictates a different bias from a news bulletin for a localized linguistic group, especially if the group is in a remote and less sophisticated part of the country. Even a bulletin which is consciously intended to be on "national news" has often got regionalized in perspective over Radio Uganda when the bulletin is given in a regional language. Radio Uganda is not committed to a policy of having exactly the same bulletin translated in all the fourteen odd languages in exactly the same order of news emphasis. The news translators and news readers are often journalistic artists of a kind catering for a particular taste. Moreover, members of Parliament and Ministers from a particular region have a way of inviting the interest of the Ministry of Information in their activities for transmission to their own areas. The same parliamentary debate might receive a different emphasis in a Lugbara news bulletin from what it receives in Luganda. The most important speech for one region may be different from the most important for another region. The speech of the Member of Parliament from a Lugbara constituency may receive a mention in the Lugbara bulletin, but not merit such a mention in the Luganda bulletin.

If these are the difficulties encountered with news — which is in many ways the most easily nationalized — one can imagine how much more difficult it is to keep the other radio features from becoming relatively localized in interest. Special talks on the radio, and cultural features, often become narrowly restricted in interest to the lingo-cultural group to whom they are addressed.

Even in promoting local cultural activity, Radio Uganda as now constituted poses problems for cultural engineering as an attempt to nationalize the aesthetics of sectionalism. As President Milton Obote put it:

> Since the Radio began broadcasting these various languages, there has been a new spirit in Uganda, simple composition of songs, dance teams, and various competitions around the countryside. Every village is eager to surpass the other in its cultural activities with a view that one day Radio Uganda recording vans will pass around the village and record the songs and the poems of a particular group. We find this useful although we are creating a problem of how to coordinate these activities in the future. (1967: 6)

A case can, of course, be made for the desirability of catering to local biases and local tastes in their own right. But in such situations the radio is handicapped as an instrument for the promotion of a national perspective on the different events affecting the country. This is an important handicap in countries where there are relatively few alternative media for such a task. The written word is not as yet widely disseminated, or even capable of being widely read, in the rural areas. Newspapers in the English language are a phenomenon of the sizable city and a luxury to be enjoyed mainly by the intelligentsia and the sub-intelligentsia. The radio could be the most important medium of political penetration, and often is. But its role in nationalizing what is sectional in political outlooks is circumscribed by its reliance on local vernaculars and by the resultant catering for local biases in taste and perspective.

Kenya's experience illustrated different aspects of the relationship between cultural engineering and the mass media. As we have observed, the more common broadcasting problems in Africa are those arising from the presence of many languages in the same country. Yet the problem could sometimes be one of having one language, but different sub-cultures.

About twenty years ago in Kenya there were already radio programmes in the Swahili language, but there were hardly any programmes to cater for the Swahili sub-culture of the Coast. Only a minority of Kenyans spoke Swahili as a mother-tongue — and these were and are concentrated at the Coast. Yet it was precisely this minority which was not catered for in broadcasting policy two decades ago. It was perhaps taken for granted that because these Coastal peoples spoke Swahili, the national programmes from Nairobi would meet their needs. Yet the Coastal people were a people with distinct musical forms of their own, distinct Swahili poetry, distinct religious interests (often Islamic), and, of course, a highly sophisticated Swahili dialect of their own. The Nairobi programmes at that time were mainly directed at non-native speakers of the language in the interior of the country. The language was the same, but the cultural universe was different. And so, Kenyans of the Coast often tuned in to the Voice of Zanzibar or the Voice of Dar es Salaam whose programmes were culturally more akin to the interests of coastal Kenyans than the Nairobi programmes in those days ever managed to be.

It was in the face of this broadcasting anomaly that a number of coastal Kenyans themselves took the initiative in founding the *Sauti Ya Mvita* broadcasting programmes from Mombasa. The authorities encouraged them in this venture by first making available the basic broadcasting equipment at Cable and Wireless coastal headquarters, and later by other kinds of help and facilities. But essentially the *Sauti Ya Mvita* started as a volunteer project by coastal Kenyans who felt culturally starved on the radio in spite of the fact that their own language was used on national radio programmes. These people shared a language with fellow Kenyans without necessarily sharing a common culture. I happen to have been one of those who volunteered to run the *Sauti Ya Mvita* in those initial days. Apart from taking part in discussion programmes, I also used to have a regular half-hour feature to myself reading out fictional stories which I had written myself, to the accompaniment of music from my own record library at home. Indeed, the "Listeners' Choice" as a record programme also relied quite heavily on my own disc collection.[21]

The programme as a strictly regional enterprise became a complete success, and was then adopted by the Government as a regional programme with its own studios and equipment at the Coast. But as independence approached, the issue of centralization of the broadcasting medium invited renewed attention. Should all the broadcasting in Kenya be coming from Nairobi? If so, would not this be a return to the old days when Nairobi, while broadcasting in Swahili, did so only for those who spoke it as a second language — while the native speakers of Swahili tuned in to Dar es Salaam?

The Ministry of Information in independent Kenya has substantially averted this danger by a compromise between the demands of centralization and the demands of regional tastes and biases. *Sauti Ya Mvita* is indeed now dead, and there are no autonomous broadcasting facilities at the Coast or at any other region. But within the National Swahili Service, different Swahili tastes are catered for. They range from the drums of Kwale to a political biography of Mzee Kenyatta, from Christian sermons to Arabic tunes imitating Cairo's Farid el Atrash, from Swahili pop songs of the Nairobi dancing halls to classical poetry from Lamu. The language is the same, but the tastes are diverse. Yet the integration of the different tastes into one programme is one approach towards effective political penetration on a nationwide scale. It is, of course, also an approach towards the gradual standardization of Swahili in Kenya. This, in turn, over a longer period of time, might be part of the homogenization of culture. And this last is directly related to the broader goal of national integration. The making of a nation involves processes within processes in a multi-dimensional enterprise.

But the centralization of broadcasting in Kenya has not taken merely the form of concentrating the planning and mechanics at Nairobi and merging the Swahili sub-programmes. The centralization has also taken the form of reducing the number of broadcasting languages in the country radically since self-government. Tanzania has gone further and limited itself to Swahili and English. Of the three countries, Uganda is the only one which has felt the need to multiply its vernacular programmes since independence instead of reducing them. As President Obote once explained:

> I am in Government and I have to take political feelings of the people into account in formulating policies. I would not say that all fourteen languages on the Radio are necessary...but we would find it exceedingly difficult to inform the Karamajong in Luganda or any other language except their own... We want to inform the people of Uganda... so we have Karamajong broadcast on the Radio. (1964: 6)

The handicap of having to rely on district languages manifests itself also in the fortunes of that other news medium, the newspaper. Among the tasks facing the countries of East Africa is not simply the elimination of illiteracy, but also the prevention of a relapse into illiteracy after a person has acquired the skill to read and write. The skill to read and write, if it is minimal, can all too easily be lost if it is not utilized. It is not just shorthand which gets hazy and then disappears, if it is not put into use; longhand also can suffer the same fate if it is not consolidated with sustained utilization. The simple ability to make out the words and read a passage can also disappear if the newly-literate gets nothing to practice his reading on.

A newspaper is one answer to the problem, though it should not be too sophisticated. UNESCO was interested in a project of rural newspapers for Uganda, partly to arrest the process of relapse for the newly literate and partly to provide the villager with news and information relevant to his needs and interests. In this case catering for local biases was precisely the object of the exercise, but deriving added justification from the ambition to maintain a literate countryside. A UNESCO specialist did come to Uganda, and the Makerere Institute of Social Research set up a research consultative committee to help in assessing feasibility for the projected rural newspapers. The idea was not to provide official Government handouts, but to attempt to produce simple news-sheets which were relevant, entertaining as well as informative. What was needed was the kind of product which would compel local interest as a matter of course — and make the literate read.

Ideally, the newspapers were to be under private initiative, sensitized to local interests and local needs. But one of the problems continues to be the limited size of readership in most of the local languages in Uganda. It becomes questionable whether it is economical either financially or in terms of effort to have a newspaper in Ateso or even Runyoro/Rutoro for any length of time. The lack of an inter-tribal lingua franca in Uganda capable of being used for a simple newspaper with a wide rural readership was one of the stumbling blocks in the way of experiments like the one envisaged by the UNESCO project. Uganda has no national paper in an African language of the kind one finds in Kenya and Tanzania. Swahili in Kenya and Tanzania, partly through newspapers like *Baraza*, *Taifa Leo*, and *Ulimwengu*, is a partial safeguard for some newly literate against the risk of a relapse into illiteracy. In Uganda, on the other hand, the only African languages which are journalistically viable happen also to be sectional, and sometimes politically sensitive. The arrest of illiteracy through a local language newspaper is possible for Luganda speakers, but for few others in Uganda except in terms of brief experimental news-sheets from time to time.

The problem of illiteracy takes us back to the whole issue of social integration and the narrowing of the gap between the elite and the masses, the town and the countryside. If the newly literate remains literate, that is itself a modest contribution towards narrowing that gap. But if the newly literate has a relapse, the yawn which was beginning to close opens up again.

However, the ability to understand even spoken English, let alone written English, presupposes in East Africa a degree of exposure to formal education. The situation is not one in which one can easily pick up English casually by the ear. It may one day become so if the language becomes sufficiently widespread, and its uses sufficiently diversified, for it to be picked up down the alleyways and playgrounds, and not merely from a classroom. But for the time being acquisition of the English language lies in the universe of the *literate* culture.

The Governments of both Uganda and Tanzania seem sensitive to the risks of this gap between an English-speaking elite and the rest of the populace. The Government of Tanzania has an answer to the problem. The answer is to reduce the need for English in one area of national life after another. A combination of cultural nationalism and socialistic egalitarianism was thrusting Swahili forward in Tanzania as a strong rival to English in the business of the nation. Cultural nationalism embraces Swahili in romantic terms of loyalty to African culture; socialistic egalitarianism is thankful to Swahili for widening the area of elite recruitment. The first Vice President of Tanzania, Mr. Abeid Karume of Zanzibar, has hardly any knowledge of English. By relying increasingly on Swahili rather than English, Tanzania has given itself a much wider pool from which to choose its civic leaders and functionaries up and down the country. Even before independence Swahili in Tanganyika was being allowed by the colonial authorities a role which it could not be permitted in colonial Kenya even if it were as well established. A pre-eminent example was the acceptance of Swahili as the second official language of the Legislative Council in Dar es Salaam in the 1950s. African Members of LegCo no longer needed to have a command of English in order to serve as such members; Swahili was now a viable legislative language as an alternative.

In Kenya during the same period, demands by Dr. Gikonyo Kiano for greater recognition of Swahili were received with derision. After all, settler Kenya enquired, could Dr. Kiano have taught his students at the Royal Technical College Keyne's theory of unemployment by using Swahili? It was not until the Lancaster House conference of 1960 that Sir Michael Blundell, as a leading European participant, sensed that the wind had roughly changed. And more as a gesture than in earnest, he proposed that the constitutional conference in London which was discussing the possibility of self-government under African majority rule in Kenya should in fact conduct its business in what Blundell possessively called "our language, Swahili." Ian Macleod, representing the British Government, was hardly likely to enthuse over the proposal. And although Tom Mboya himself had a very good command of Swahili, not all the other African delegates at the conference were as well-endowed linguistically.[22]

Since independence Kenya has still not been able to give Swahili equal standing with English, though Swahili has now greater standing in education and broadcasting than it had during the colonial period.

But once again Uganda seems even more handicapped by comparison. Mzee Kenyatta gives most of his major speeches outside the capital in Swahili, certainly those which are delivered at popular rallies. Kenyatta's Swahili is superb. As an instrument of oratory, it is better than his English. And he can, of course, chat with the ordinary people outside Kikuyuland in Swahili. But Dr. Obote of Uganda is in a different predicament. In this respect, Obote's position is more typical of African heads of government elsewhere south of the Sahara than either Nyerere's or Kenyatta's. To that extent the pathos is the more striking. In a moving statement Obote once said:

> When I move out of Kampala to talk to the people, I have to talk in English...I lose a lot especially as far as the Party is concerned. The Party welcomes everybody, and some of the greatest and most dedicated workers are those who do not speak English; and yet the Party Leader cannot call this great dedicated worker alone and say "Thank you" in a language the man will understand. It has to be translated. There must always be a third party, and that is why it is said there are no secrets in Africa. (1967: 6)

Party functionaries of this kind can only be used in their home areas as a rule. The idea of inter-regional mixing of certain kinds of officials is not easily accomplished; and the transfer of a promising unilingual functionary from his district to the center in the capital again poses problems if his one language is not trans-tribal.

As for that heart of law-making, Parliament, ability to speak English is inevitably a qualification for membership. The pool of talent from which Parliamentarians are chosen in Uganda must of necessity be more circumscribed than it is in Tanzania.

We have already indicated that both Uganda and Tanzania are worried about the gulf between the elite and the masses. Tanzania has already introduced a National Service, compulsory for university graduates and products of other major educational institutions, and designed in part to expose this presumptive educated elite to the rigors of manual self-reliance. The exercise is also intended to sensitize the educated to the needs of the masses, and narrow the gulf of incomprehension between the city and the countryside. Tanzania seeks to achieve social integration through social equality (as in the case of integrated traditional societies) rather than through social differentiation (as in the case of modern developed states). Tanzania's whole approach may be based on an error, but at least there is here a commitment to a specific direction of national change. The availability of Swahili as a language of the masses has been fortunate from the point of view of Tanzania's egalitarian bias.

Kenya, on the other hand, seems to be seeking social integration by increasing social differentiation and functional diversification among the African populace. The Government is embarked on a deliberate creation of an African entrepreneurial class. The whole controversy about the Africanization of commerce in Kenya, the gradual displacement of Asians in some critical economic functions, is part of Kenya's commitment to the concept of diversifying the African man's economic experience. The African has known what it is like to be a peasant, and what it is like to be a teacher; what it is like to be a railway porter, and what it is like to be a Cabinet Minister. But that is not enough. What about the experience of knowing what it is like to be an investor and shareholder? What about the experience of running a successful modern shop on Kenyatta Avenue in Nairobi? The full potential of the African man as an economically creative being ought to be given a chance to fulfill itself. Kenya for the time being is, therefore, not interested in trying to prevent the emergence of new economic classes in the country. As far as Kenya is concerned, real modernization lies through rapid functional diversification and not through desperate preservation of a presumed pre-existent African social inequality. The promotion of Swahili in Kenya is not — as it might be in Tanzania — inspired by egalitarian imperatives, but more purely by considerations of national integration. The gap which English might continue to create between the elite and the masses is, therefore, compatible with a policy of promoting Swahili as a medium of political penetration and socio-economic intercourse at the grassroots level.

Uganda is, in this as in so many other issues, holding an intermediate position between Kenya and Tanzania. Like Kenya, Uganda is indeed committed to a policy of creating an African entrepreneurial class and replacing Asians in some economic functions. To that extent she does appear to be seeking to achieve social integration through functional diversification, rather than through a quest for an egalitarian society. On the other hand, the Government has announced plans to start a National Service for the newly graduated, partly inspired by a desire to ensure that the educated are not too distant from the needs of the masses. The Government has also set up a Commission on Land, partly to ensure greater social justice in land-ownership. Uganda's situation is clearly ambivalent. Traditional society in the kingdoms, for example, was egalitarian. But status was more often ascriptive rather than through criteria of personal achievement. On the other hand, Obote's policy of trying to create a modern African business class, though still incompatible with egalitarianism, is at least a quest for replacing criteria of birth with criteria of achievement as a basis of social success. To some extent the Uganda Government is trying to attack traditional so-called "feudalism" by promoting a trans-tribal modern "commercialism." Like Kenya, and unlike Tanzania, Uganda is not trying to prevent the emergence of new economic classes but is actually promoting them. But the only difference between Kenya and Uganda in this particular regard is that the Uganda Government is so ambivalent that it sometimes feels a little guilty about this quest for new classes. Even on the issue of promoting English, the Uganda Government is aware that the policy emphasizes a gulf between the elite and the masses. There is a sense of guilt about it all, but also a sense of inevitability. In the words of President Obote:

> ...our policy to teach more English could in the long run just develop more power in the hands of those who speak English, and better economic status for those who know English. We say this because we do not see any possibility of our being able to get English known by half the population of Uganda within the next fifteen years... Some of our people can use it to improve their economic status...[and] those amongst us in Uganda...who have obtained important positions because of the power of the English language are liable to be regarded by a section of our society as perpetrators of colonialism and imperialism or at least as potential imperialists. (1967: 4)

Yet President Obote once again went on to say sadly: "We find no alternative to English."

Perhaps that captures the great dilemma of the English language for a country like Uganda. It lends itself well, though not perfectly, to the task of national integration; but for the time being, it also remains all too often dysfunctional to the process of social integration.

But need its dysfunctionality to the process of social integration be anything more than a temporary aberration? It depends upon whether the integration is intended to be egalitarian or by differentiation. In a provocative article in *Transition*, Pierre van den Berghe has drawn attention not only to the tendency towards elite-formation inherent in the role of English in Africa, but also to the tendency towards elite-*closure*. He argued that the class structure in African countries was in a process of rapid consolidation. Knowledge in depth of a European language and culture conferred prestige and status, and the privileged class which possessed the knowledge passed it on to the children. Van den Berghe called the whole process "the crystallization of the Black mandarinate." He observed:

> Indications are that this process of crystallization of a mandarinate will take no more than a single generation. Already members of the elite are frantically scrambling to get their progeny into African Etons. Concern for getting one's children into the "proper" schools (which often means formerly European ones) even begins at the Kindergarten level. (1968: 20)

And yet monopolizing the English language and monopolizing the African Etons are two distinct forms of elite closure, and van den Berghe seems to confuse the two. Those African Governments which have adopted English as the national language make no attempt whatsoever to restrict the dissemination of this linguistic skill only to their children. On the contrary, there is an energetic attempt to build schools and spread education. And the school curricula are often so humanistic and British-inspired that emphasis on English is still an important part of the prevalent educational philosophy. In Uganda, Government policy since independence has tended towards increasing, rather than reducing, the proportion of a child's education devoted to learning the English language. If elite closure in this instance is supposed to imply an attempt by those already in power to monopolize the linguistic skill which helped in putting them into positions of power, there is no evidence whatsoever of such an attempt by the reigning elites of East Africa. On the contrary, all the evidence runs counter to this particular suggestion in van den Berghe's article.

But van den Berghe's point about elite monopoly of elite schools is much more defensible — and it really does start at the kindergarten. In Uganda the most prestigious primary school is Nakasero. The admission procedures of this school are not only discriminatory in favor of W.A.S.P.S.! And the legitimating rationale for the discrimination is indeed competence in the English language.

I know of an East African professor [then at Makerere] who submitted an application to Nakasero Primary School on behalf of his child. The application was submitted in February for admission the following January. Admission to the school was supposedly by interview, and the purpose of the interview is mainly to test competence in the English language. The East African professor's child had one British and one American playmate who happened to be applying for admission to Nakasero in the same year. The parents of these playmates heard from the school within a few weeks granting the children admission — and without the need for an interview. The East African professor waited to know his son's fate.[23]

As it happened, the first language of the East African professor's son was indeed English. And the level of vocabulary and discourse that the boy heard at home put him above one or both of his Anglo-Saxon mates in command of the language. In addition, the boy's mother was a W.A.S.P. anyhow. Yet the nationality of the boy as given on the application form was an East African nationality. An interview, therefore, was necessary. The boy had first to wait to be called for an interview at all, and then wait for a verdict after that interview — while his British and American playmates had their admission confirmed well before the East African was even invited for a look-over.

The racialistic connotations of these procedures partly arise out of this readiness by the school to grant admission to Anglo-American children before the East African children are even interviewed. It is almost as if the East African children are given a residual quota. The system might have looked fairer if everyone was interviewed before anyone was admitted. But even if Anglo-Americans were automatically exempted from the interview, at least they should not be admitted until all the others had been interviewed and a joint selection of the candidates is made from the two groups together.

But even if these other niceties of fairness were fulfilled by Nakasero school, the criterion of prior command of the English language biased the admission procedures too heavily in favor of those from English-speaking homes — be those homes Anglo-Saxon or Afro-Saxon. The elite in Uganda are not monopolizing the English language; but they are perhaps using their prior command of the English language as a method of monopolizing the best schools. In England itself one criterion of elite status is not command of the language, but the accent with which one speaks it. And the elite accent is often derived from elite schools. In Uganda for the time being accents when an African speaks English are not associated with schools or social classes, but with the original native language of the speaker. But should public school accents evolve in East Africa, superimposed over the tribal accent, and a Munyoro from Nakasero and Budo be differentiated by mode of English from a Munyoro educated elsewhere, a new form of elite closure might have come into being. If there are intermediate accents between the most upperclass at the top and the most proletarian at the bottom, by a linguistic curve which is gradual rather than steep, we might at last be able to say that the English language in East Africa has indeed been functional to social integration — but decidedly through a process of social diversification rather than social equality. And the interplay between cultural engineering and language policy in East Africa would by then have entered yet another exciting phase.

Appendix II

African Languages in the African American Experience[24]

Alamin M. Mazrui

African societies, including those of Arab origin in the northern part of the continent, are known to have concepts of ethnic identity that are quite liberal and assimilative. "Purity of the bloodline," for instance, is a notion that is relatively alien to the relational universe of African peoples. To be a member of any European ethnic group, both parents would normally have to be European. But maternal or paternal parentage alone in the case of most African peoples, would normally be sufficient to qualify the offspring for membership of a particular African ethnic group. Ali Mazrui dramatizes this difference between Afro-Arab and European conceptions of identity in the following hypothetical terms:

> If the white citizens of the United States had, in fact, been Arab, most of the colored citizens would have become Arab too. It has been estimated that over seventy percent of the Negro population in the United States has some "white" blood. And the "white" blood was much more often than not derived from a white *father*. Now given the principle that if the father is Arab the child is Arab, most of the Negroes of the United States would have been Arab had the white people of the United States been Arab too. But the white Americans are Caucasian and the dominant culture is Germanic. And so if either of the parents is non-Germanic, the offspring cannot be Germanic either. (1964: 22)

But the liberalism and assimilative nature of the "Afro-Arab" concept of identity are by no means limited to the area of genetics. It also extends to the sphere of culture, and, more relevant to our present discussion, to the phenomenon of language. Anyone who speaks Hausa as a first language, for example, would, under normal circumstances, be regarded as ethnically Hausa. The same can be said of virtually all other African languages. This stands in marked contrast to European languages which do not admit into their ethnic fold people who are not *genetically* European. European languages may be acquired by all and sundry; but when it comes to linguistic definitions of European ethnicity, European languages have failed to neutralize genetic boundaries. African languages, on the other hand, defy genetic boundaries in their contribution to ethnic identities.

Making another hypothetical projection, then, had the American *lingua franca* been Swahili, for example, instead of English, the entire African American population which, for generations, has been speaking English as a first and often only language, would probably have been ethnically Swahili. Likewise, if the mother-tongue of African peoples throughout the world were Swahili, then the entire African diaspora would again have been Swahili.

It is perhaps in view of this assimilative tendency of Swahili and other African languages that Julius Nyerere, the first president of Tanzania, sometimes used the term "Swahili" to refer to any person of African origin. Nyerere thus made Swahili, in the collective consciousness of the Tanzanian people, a local equivalent of a trans-continental, pan-African identity. It was as if Nyerere was anticipating the development of Swahili into a language of global Africa. Inadvertently, Nyerere was also pitting the liberal humanist boundaries of African languages against the narrower racial boundaries of the European languages at the stadium of international politics of human relations.

The restricted genetic (or "racial") boundaries of the English language, a phenomenon that may have emerged with the rise of imperial capitalism in the northern hemisphere,[25] have made it impossible for African Americans to become fully a part of the American "mainstream." It was natural, therefore, that language too would become a factor in the struggles for equality in the civil rights movement of the sixties. But if the system ultimately capitulated, to some degree, in the politico-economic sphere, it was not about ready to do the same in the arena of linguistics. No matter how extensively "assimilated" African Americans were, in cultural and linguistic terms, the system ensured that they would remain "black," that they would remain American with qualification. At the frontier of linguistics of identity, therefore, the English language simply failed to forge a nation that is truly one.

Apart from its segregative ethno-linguistic "nature," however, the English language has sometimes been regarded as inherently racialist. With words that evoke all sorts of negative images the English language is supposed to have served as an instrument of racism against people of color. It is in this regard that Ossie Davis once declared that the English language was his enemy and indicted it "as one of the prime carriers of racism from one person to another in our society" (1973: 72).

In an instructional manual on racism in the English language, Robert Moore (1976) outlines some of the ways in which the English language has contributed to conditioning racial attitudes in American society. These range from the association of blackness with evil, ignorance, and death, to the employment of passive constructions to blame African victims of racial prejudice. And, in conclusion, Moore calls for what amounts to a deracialization of the English language, arguing that "while we may not be able to change the language, we can definitely change our usage of the language" (1976: 14).

The ethnic exclusiveness and racial invocativeness of the English language naturally led to a quest for alternative sources of ethnolinguistic identity. But for African Americans this search was not without its problems. African Americans remain the only minority group in the USA whose linguistic roots have been completely obliterated by centuries of slavery and oppression. From which source, therefore, could they derive a sense of independent ethnolinguistic identity? The growing consciousness of themselves as an African people in the particular racialist setting of the USA, and of their heritage in a continent that was engaged in a major struggle for liberation in a more global political context, ultimately prompted a bi-focal approach to the question of ethno-linguistic identity.

The first dimension of this approach was one of reaffirming the autonomy and uniqueness of African American English, or "Black English" as it has often been called. If "Black English" had hitherto been considered a mere corruption of the "European brand" of English, a corruption that is unworthy of any dignified status in American civil society, it now became a cherished symbol of African American identity. Even the term "Black English" now became racially suspect and new names like *PALWH*, an acronym for Pan-American Language in the Western Hemisphere (Twiggs, 1973), and *Ebonics* (Williams, 1975) were coined to refer to the African American tongue.

The attempts to reappraise the status of "Black English" were not merely symbolic. Scholars trained in linguistics took the initiative to demonstrate that "Black English" was not a corruption of any pre-existing linguistic norm but an autonomous, internally logical and coherent linguistic organism, with a strong continental African linguistic heritage that the Middle Passage was unable to destroy. "Africanisms" now became a point of emphasis in some linguistic descriptions of "Black English". Thus, in the words of LeRoi Jones (or Imamu Amiri Baraka as he came to be called), "It is absurd to assume, as has been the tendency, among a great many Western anthropologists and sociologists, that all traces of Africa were erased from the Negro's mind because he learned English. The very nature of the English the Negro spoke and still speaks drops the lie on that idea" (1963: 9).

Perhaps the most extensive studies of linguistic Africanisms is that of Lorenzo Turner (1949) in which he gives a comprehensive list of words from the so-called Gullah dialect which he traces to an African linguistic origin. And in a prefatory note to the 1969 reprint, Turner indicates that the decision to reproduce the study was essentially prompted by the desire to make it more generally accessible in the wake of growing African American interest in their African heritage.

Following Turner's line of inquiry, J.L. Dillard argues that there "is hardly any reason to assume that any of the Africanisms listed by Turner were limited to the Gullah area in the eighteenth and nineteenth century" (1972: 117). Dillard admits that the African linguistic contribution to American English may seem proportionately small, but he regards it as being no smaller than that of Native American words if place names are excluded. "When it is considered that American Indians survived an essentially monolingual tribal group while Africans in the New World did not, the 'contribution' to American English by Africans begins to seem impressively large" (1972: 119). In fact, in Dillard's opinion, a much larger proportion of Africanisms could probably be discovered in (African) American English if the academic establishment was not unduly hostile to this kind of research (1972: 123).

Expanding the scope of this inquiry, Molefi Asante has argued that the most enduring evidence of the African essence in African American speech can be obtained, not from the lexical domain as Turner and others have tried to demonstrate, but from the domain of linguistic pragmatics. "Retention of lexical items constitutes one part of this linguistic continuity with Africa, but the major burden," argues Asante, "has been carried by communicative processes (i.e., African American manners of expression) supported in the main by verb serialization and the unique use of tense and aspect" (1990: 250).

Both symbolically and substantively, therefore, "Black English" and its "inherent" Africanity came to be markers of a new kind of consciousness among sections of the African American population. To some extent this situation can be compared with that of the Irish. As Deane explains with regard to Irish nationalism:

At its most powerful, colonialism is a process of radical dispossession. A colonized people is without a specific history

and even, as in Ireland and other cases, without a specific
language. The recovery from the lost Irish language has taken
the form of an almost vengeful virtuosity in the English language,
an attempt to make Irish English a language in its own right
rather than an adjunct to English itself. (1990: 10)

This linguistic exercise among African Americans, the Irish, the Kurds,
and the other "colonized" people can be seen as one modest attempt
among many to repossess their histories.

The second dimension in the bi-focal quest for ethnolinguistic identity
among African Americans was the attempt to relink, in a more direct
manner, with continental African languages. The demand for civil rights,
therefore, sometimes came to include the right of access to the African
linguistic heritage in the corridors of American academia. The existence of
several African languages in American educational institutions that we now
seem to take so much for granted, then, is one of the products of those
major battles for civil rights which were fought on American campuses in
the 1960s.

Today African languages are taught widely in American universities
and in some high schools, with Swahili being by far the most popular.[26]
The *right* of African Americans to pursue the study of African languages
is now widely accepted in the USA. It is, in fact, explicitly recognized in
the National Language Policy of the USA which describes one of its
objectives as: To foster the teaching of languages other than English so
that native speakers of English can rediscover the *language of their
heritage* or learn a second language.[27]

The African American quest for an alternative ethnolinguistic symbol
of identity rooted in the African continent, however, has not been without
its detractors. In my experience, teaching Swahili in the USA since 1969,
I have often been confronted with two arguments seemingly intended to
deride the African American ideological motives for studying African
languages. It is argued, first, that if the African American interest in African

languages has been prompted by the instrumental quality of English as a language of racism and slavery, then African languages themselves have not been completely innocent of a similar charge. It is suggested that African "middlemen" used African languages as the media of communication with their African brethren when pursuing or mobilizing captives for the trans-continental slave trade. How, then, it is asked, can such African languages be considered any more liberating than European languages inherited from the slave tradition?

There are two fundamental problems with this argument. First, it unjustifiably puts the African middlemen in the slave trade at par with the European owners of African slaves in the "New World" and elsewhere. Coming from a more humane tradition of indigenous "slavery"[28] these middlemen did not even have a sense of the multifarious horrors of the trans-Atlantic slavery system. They were no more than peripheral and transient "entrepreneurs" in this new human commodity whose contact with other African peoples, except in very few instances, did not lead to linguistic dislocations of any magnitude. In essence, it is the linguistic experience in the Americas, and not the contact with African middlemen, that led to the African Americans' loss of a continental African ethnolinguistic identity. And it is against the backdrop of this particular experience that African Americans now seek to establish a linguistic reconnection with the African continent.

The second problem with this argument is its historical staticity which renders it superfluous and even void. Language is not a mass of lifeless molecules. It is, in a sense, a living organism that responds dynamically to changing politico-economic stimuli. Thus, the language of Russian tsardom also became the language of Bolshevik socialism; the language of English feudalism also became the language of its liberal capitalism. So, if Swahili or Yoruba, for example, were used in the slave trade at some point in history, they "moved on" to become important media of struggle against, and opposition to, European imperialism.

On the other hand, even after the abolition of slavery, the English language in the USA has continued to be the language of a racialist, oppressive class that continues to articulate its legitimating ideology through this particular linguistic medium. There continues to be a cultural dimension to the legacy of slavery, which has included African Americans' experience with the English language, which has sometimes induced a re-emphasis on cultural continuities, and a re-establishment of cultural links, with continental Africa.

The second argument against the African American quest for a linguistic "return to the source" has tended to be targeted specifically against Swahili. By the 1960s Swahili was second only to Arabic as the most widely spoken African language on the continent. It was already spoken across several national boundaries. In Kenya, Tanzania, and Uganda it was beginning to acquire some national and official status. It had demonstrated its ability to serve as a common medium of communication among African people of diverse ethnic origins in their struggle against European colonial rule in eastern Africa. Later, it was increasingly to be heard on radio broadcasts throughout the world. In Tanzania, Swahili was also beginning to acquire a reputation as a counter-idiom to class oppression, as a linguistic medium of an African-based socialism or *Ujamaa*. It was also in the heartland of Swahili political culture, that trans-continental pan-Africanism found its "resurgence" with the convening in Tanzania of the Sixth Pan-African Congress. And it is the combination of these and other political reasons that rendered Swahili the most popular language among African Americans.

But as the momentum for the study of Swahili was growing, opinions reminiscent of the divide-and-rule policies of the colonial era in Africa began to emerge in the USA. Swahili, it has sometimes been pointed out, is an eastern African language, while Africans in the Americas originated from West Africa. It is suggested, then, that their search for an ethnolinguistic identification with Africa should draw from West African languages like Yoruba and Wolof, and not from an East African language like Swahili. After decades of attempts to divide peoples of continental Africa along ethnolinguistic lines, a similar rationalizing equation was now brought into play at the level of global Africa.

First, it is not completely true that East Africa did not feature in the slave trade across the Atlantic Ocean. There were Portuguese, Spanish, and French connections in eastern Africa which contributed in no small measure to the translocation of Africans. The Portuguese are known to have procured slaves from the East African coast from the very beginning of their encounter with the region in the fifteenth century. At first the Portuguese also supplied slaves to the French. But as a result of recurrent Swahili struggles against the Portuguese, the French turned their attention to the East African port of Kilwa and made their own arrangements for procuring slaves. The Spanish are also known to have taken thousands of slaves from the Swahili coast round the Cape to South America (Nicholls, 1971: 200). Furthermore, slave raids from West Africa sometimes went deep into the Congo where Bantu languages akin to Swahili were spoken. All in all, then, the Swahili speaking region of Africa was not altogether excluded as a source of European slavery.

But to attempt to justify the promotion of Swahili or any other African language in the United States of America on the basis of these demographic features of the European slave trade is to succumb to a Eurocentric vision. It is a line of reasoning that completely misconceptualizes the nature of African Americans' consciousness of their Africanity. The ethnolinguistic divisions in continental Africa that Eurocentric scholarship is wont to highlight do not exist, nor need they exist, in the African American collective imagination. African consciousness in the Americas has always placed emphasis on the continent's *unifying qualities* and not on its *divisive attributes*; and it is perhaps for this reason that trans-continental pan-Africanism, though inspired by the "motherland," was born in the African diaspora first before it established roots in the African continent. There is some sense of shared destiny among peoples of the African diaspora that seeks a common political expression which may, of course, vary in degree and form. In the process Africa has become fused and homogenized to a point where any of its languages could serve as a shared source of inspiration and symbolic expression of a new consciousness among African Americans. And for reasons mentioned earlier, Swahili turned out to be the natural choice for this purpose.

At another level this particular African American linguistic initiative can be seen as an extension of the growing pro-Swahili sentiments within continental Africa itself. Swahili is offered as a university subject not only in East Africa, but also in some West African universities, in places like Nigeria and Ghana. It is also the declared continental language by the Organization of African Unity (OAU). And distinguished creative writers from East Africa (like Ngugi wa Thiong'o) and West Africa (like Wole Soyinka) have, at different times, campaigned for its establishment as a pan-African language of the continent. There is a sense, then, in which African Americans are inadvertently responding to the silent throbbings of a continental African quest for unity whose linguistic manifestation has tended to revolve mainly around the Swahili language.

I have so far discussed the question of African languages in the African American experience at a macro-linguistic political level. What, then, are some of its micro-linguistic political manifestations? There is no doubt that the micro-dimension of this issue is bound to vary a great deal from place to place, from experience to experience, from individual to individual. It is nonetheless possible to make at least two generalizations.

The first generalization has to do with naming. The demise of European colonial rule in Africa brought with it an entire naming "revolution". This was part and parcel of the wider African consciousness movements variously called "African nationalism" in some places, "Negritude" in others, "Authenticity" in places like the former Zaire and so forth. In clusters of domino-effect people began to drop their Euro-Christian names and "return" to more indigenous naming systems abounding in various African languages. And since these naming systems are founded on a deep-rooted gnosis that defines human relations with people, history, or the environment, their re-adoption has been, in effect, a wider cultural embrace between

Africa and its sons and daughters.

The naming revolution that has been going on in Africa, however, has also found expression among African Americans. Since the 1960s and 1970s many African Americans have looked upon African languages as a source of symbolic affirmation of their African identity as an increasing number came to discard their baptismal names — many of which had their roots in the slave experience — and acquire African names. In the words of Molefi Asante:

> During the 1960s and 1970s, we came to terms with our collective name and chose to be either "African," "Afro American," or "black" rather than "Negro" or "colored." We must certainly sooner or later make the same observation on a personal level that we have made on a collective level. In the future there is no question that this will be undertaken on many occasions. It is not only logical, it is practical and we have always responded to logic and pragmatism. The practical value of changing our names is in identification of names with people. We are an African people and it is logical for us to possess African names. Already we are on the verge of a breakthrough, young black parents are seeking African names for their children in an attempt to assign meaning to their identity. (1988: 27-28)

Euro-Christian names, however, have been seen not only as a method of negating the Africanity of African Americans, but also of inflicting racial blows against them. As George Livingston pointed out:

> Names have been used not only to identify a human being, but also to vilify, depersonalize, and dehumanize. Sam and Sambo, which Dr. Puckett identified as common slave names of the seventeenth century, became racist slurs in the twentieth century when black men were commonly summoned by these names. (1975: v)

These racial politics of naming, in fact, came to inspire Puckett (1975) to undertake an extensive study of the origins and usage of different names in the African American experience, tracing some to the American slave context and many others to African languages from various parts of the continent.

Unlike their compatriots in the African continent, however, many African Americans who opt for African names do not select them in accordance with any specific African *ethnic* tradition. Often times, names have been selected for their symbolic and semantic content even if they are at variance with the ethnic naming systems from which they are derived. First and last African names among African Americans have sometimes come from different ethnic groups and even different countries, for example, Kwame Toure (a Ghanaian first name and Guinean last name). What we are witnessing among African Americans, then, is the pan-Africanization of Africa's naming systems as a result of the particular political circumstances of their space and time, circumstances which have forged an African consciousness that transcends the narrower continental ethnic lines of Yorubaness, Zuluness, Amharaness, and the like. The African naming system among African Americans, then, is yet another example of how political-economy can be the mother of culture.

But "what is in a name?" one might ask. Slavery and racialism in the United States of America have generally reduced African Americans to a rootless state with skin pigmentation as the essence of their being. Their identity became "black" and their personal names became a reminder of their ruthless severance from their roots. The struggle for civil rights, therefore, had to include an affirmation of their Africanity, of the historicity of their being; and this new sense of African identity had to be raised to the realm of public knowledge.

Like material objects, however, identities do not become "public knowledge" until they are named. Without a label to capture our conception of them, they have little social relevance because there is no awareness of their existence in the first place. The emergence of a new label, therefore, carries with it the elevation of a new sense of identity to the domain of "public knowledge." It is this important function of bringing their historical Africanity and political pan-Africanity to the public sphere that names from African languages came to serve in the African American experience.

The second generalization on the impact of African languages in the African American experience has to do with the area of ceremony. People generally have a very strong attachment to ceremonial activities especially of a religious nature. Such activities are important symbolic expressions of valued ideas, events, institutions, struggles, and sometimes the entire ideological orientation of a people. As a result ceremonial activities can be very important in enhancing a sense of collective identity and their demise may not augur well with the collective consciousness of a people. There is also a sense in which the infusion of "foreign" ceremonial symbols undermines some of the binding elements of an independent identity of a particular society and signals its cultural capitulation to the "other". And it is against this backdrop that we must understand the emergence of the *Kwanza* ceremony among African Americans.

The legacies of slavery and colonialism have been some of the most important factors in the spread of Christianity and in rendering Christmas and the New Year supreme ceremonial symbols of Euro-Christian preeminence among large sections of global Africans. But the growing African consciousness among African Americans ultimately led to the birth of *Kwanza* as a direct antithesis to Christmas/New Year. Inspired by African harvest ceremonies as markers of new temporal cycles, an entire idiom,[29] drawn mainly from Swahili, came into existence to designate *Kwanza* principles, practices, and artifacts.

The *Kwanza* ceremony is, of course, itself rooted in a wider ideology of nationhood propounded by Ron Karenga (1978). This ideology, *Kawaida*, with its various concepts and principles, is again based on an idiom that is entirely Swahili and seeks to unfold a creative motif for African American identity. Once again, therefore, African languages came to serve as a source of counter-symbols to European predominance in American society, as a source of symbols of African American counter-consciousness that positively affirms their Africanity.

Karenga's initiative of projecting the *Kawaida* ideology in an African idiom has also served to introduce an important issue into the Afrocentric agenda: Is Afrocentric discourse possible in a non-African language? Need not the articulation of the present state of African consciousness be liberated from the prison-house of European idiom? Is it possible to unlearn the Eurocentricity that we have internalized without rejecting the languages through which our conceptual disorientation was accomplished in the first place?

As this debate continues, however, the Center for African Studies at Howard University has already mobilized its resources to experiment with Afrocentric discourse in an African language. Plans are at an advanced stage to use Swahili as a medium of instruction in, at least, one section of the center's introductory course on the African World. Whatever the results of this bold initiative in the history of African American education, it is obvious that we are experiencing a functional diversification of African languages in the African American experience.

Conclusion

We have seen, then, how the racial circumstances that led to the cultural disAfricanization of African Americans may also have been responsible for the emergence of a new African consciousness. This naturally led to a quest for counter-philosophies, counter-ideologies, and counter-symbols, often inspired by Africa, to give substance to this new consciousness. In this search African languages too came to play an important role. Linguistic Africanisms in certain African American dialects of English, the use of aspects of African languages for naming and ceremonial purposes, all came to serve as contributing features to a neoAfricanity in the African diaspora. But precisely because Eurocentricity always attempts to universalize its paradigms, it regards any counter-insurgency as necessarily provincial, subjecting it to attack and derision. This is an ideological offensive that Africans must simply resist. "Afrocentricity," "Negritude," "Africanity," and so forth can be regarded as manifestations of a nationalism whose essence is rooted in metaphysics and utopianism. On the other hand, nationalism must also be seen as an indispensable dialectical social stage towards liberation. There has been a tendency among (both European and African) Marxists, in particular, to diminutize the importance of this kind of African nationalism in favor of the class struggle. But as Terry Eagleton notes:

> Nationalism...is in a sense like class. To have it, and to feel it, is the only way to end it. If you fail to claim it or give it up too soon, you will merely be cheated, by other classes and other nations. Nationalism, like class, would thus seem to involve an impossible irony. It is sometimes forgotten that social class, for Karl Marx at least, is itself a form of alienation, canceling the particularity of an individual life into collective anonymity. Where Marx differs from the commonplace liberal view of such matters is in his belief that to undo this alienation you had to go, not around class, but somehow all the way through it and out the other side. To wish class or nation away, to seek to live sheer irreducible difference *now* in the manner of some contemporary post-structuralist theory, is to play straight into the hands of the oppressor. (1990: 23)

Africans, therefore, must continue to strive to set their own terms of definition and discourse on the global arena, and the attempts to deride their efforts in this regard must be seen as an ideological offensive that needs to be resisted.

But African Americans must not be seen merely as *recipients* in their cultural and linguistic relationship with Africa. They have also been and may continue to be *donors*. African Americans have made important philosophical and political contributions to the formation of movements like Negritude, pan-Africanism, and the African personality. Their African heritage led to the emergence of a distinctive type of music which has, in turn, been feeding back to Africa. Even hair styles like "Afro," though arguable that they originated in the United States of America, became popularized in Africa partly through the African American link. In other words, the global children of Africa have long had a give-and-take relationship with their mother continent.

What, then, are some of the language-related contributions that African Americans can make to Africa? One important contribution may be in the area of *national* languages. Many African countries are still grappling with the problem of choosing appropriate national languages from their indigenous languages. There is usually a felt need that the European languages inherited from the colonial tradition should be replaced with local languages at the national and official levels of operation. But the internal politics of ethnic pluralism have not always made it easy for African policy makers to "elevate" one language to national and official status over other languages. In many instances, there has been the concern that the choice of one ethnic language over others may generate fears of ethnic dominance that may propel the countries towards political instability.

The African American quest for a linguistic link with Africa, however, may help internationalize certain African languages from individual African countries. If the trend to study African languages like Hausa, Lingala, Wolof, Zulu, and so forth continues to become more firmly established, the languages may acquire an international image that may help reduce their ethnic "essence." In this way they may eventually be found more acceptable as national languages by speakers of other African languages in their respective countries. Likewise, the popularization of a language like Swahili among African Americans, may increase its chances of becoming a pan-African language.

The other language-based contribution to Africa is connected with the *Kwanza* ceremony. As indicated earlier, this is a ceremony that has been articulated and brought into the sphere of public knowledge through an African language, Swahili. In Africa there is today a quest for a cultural pan-Africanism, and it has sometimes been suggested that different cultural practices could be adopted from different parts of Africa: Swahili from eastern Africa, a mode of dress from West Africa, a cuisine from north Africa, music from Zaire, and the diaspora and so forth.[30] Is it possible that *Kwanza*, with its African idiom, will one day become a spiritual component of this potential cultural pan-Africanism? Perhaps. It is yet too early to tell. But let us not forget that great achievements often have humble beginnings.

Notes

1. On the other hand, this is one of the reasons that has contributed to the resistance against Kiswahili being selected as a national language in both Uganda and the Democratic Republic of Congo. In both countries Kiswahili has sometimes been seen as a "foreign" language which, like English or French, did not deserve a national status.

2. In Kenya, by 1980, over 65% of the population was estimated to have acquired Kiswahili as a second language (Heine, 1980: 6). Whitely, on the other hand, reported that over 70% of Kenya's rural population claimed competence in Kiswahili at some level, compared to over 40% for English (1974:321-323).

3. This too has created some complications. For example, when Kassim Mwamzandi, the MP for Msambweni, asked a question in Kiswahili about pollution caused by cement dust from the Bamburi Portland Company, the Assistant Minister for Environment and Natural Resources, Mr. Ojwang K'Ombudo pleaded that he be allowed to respond in English contrary to the standing orders. He said, "Mr. Speaker, Sir, I am not good at translating into Kiswahili and since this answer is written in English permit me to read it in that language." This was after the Minister made several attempts to respond in Kiswahili with MPs complaining that he was inarticulate and his Kiswahili was Dholuo in accent *(Daily Nation,* August 6, 1992).

4. It is possible that the Kiswalili which helps define Swahili identity is restricted to what we may call "primary dialects." These are those varieties of the language like Kimvita, Kiunguja, Kiamu, Kitikuu, and so forth, which have existed long before the spread of Kiswahili beyond its traditional coastal borders and prior to the birth of standard Swahili.

5.   According to the 1979 census report, for example, people who can be considered ethnically Swahili in Kenya constitute less than 1% of the total population of the country.

6.   This point concerning the comparative linguistic policies of colonial powers is discussed in a wider context by Ali Mazrui in his "Africa's Experience in Nation-Building: Is it Relevant to Papua New Guinea?" *East Africa Journal,* Vol. 7, No. 11. November 1970, pp. 15-23.

7.   A.W. Smith, *Memo on the Proposed International Bureau of African Languages and Literature,* Edinburgh House, May 1925, p. 7. The missionaries, who dominated the educational system in Uganda at the time, were hostile to Kiswahili because of its strong early cultural links with Islam.

8.   See also James S. Coleman. *Nigeria: Background to Nationalism;* Berkeley and Los Angeles: University of California Press, 1958, p. 254.

9.   This earlier soldier scheme was ill-conceived and badly organized, but not without significance for future developments.

10.   See also Donald S. Rothchild, *The Effects of Mobilization in British Africa,* Reprint Series Number 2, Duquesne University, Institute of African Affairs. Pittsburgh: Duquesne University Press, 1961.

11.   Consult Theodeve Walker's entries for January 1891 and March 1892; G.L. Pilkington for January 4, 1891, as recorded in E.F. Hartford's *Pilkington of Uganda, 1899.*

12.   When he was still President of Uganda, A. Milton Obote showed a keen awareness of these sociological pressures. Consult his lecture, "Policy Proposals for Uganda's Educational Needs," given to the Educational Association of Uganda, *Mawazo,*Vol.2, December 1969.

13.   According to the 1979 census, people who can be considered

ethnically Swahili in Kenya constitute less than 1% of the total population of the country.

14.   "There are over thirty distinct languages and dialect clusters spoken in Kenya. Approximately sixty-six percent of the population speak languages belonging to the Bantu branch of the Niger-Congo family,... Nearly thirty-one percent of the population speak Nilotic and paranilotic languages while three percent speak Cushitic languages... According to initial figures derived from the Kenya Population Census (1969), eight African languages were spoken as first languages by over 1,000,000 people, these being Kikuyu, Luo, Kamba, and Luyia.... The census does not provide data about the number of speakers of Kiswahili as a first language, but I have given reasons elsewhere for estimating that Kisiwahili is spoken as a first language in Kenya by not less than 60,000 persons." (T.P. Gorman, 1974: 385)

15.   Fifty-two percent of the men of Uganda could hold a conversation in Kiswahili, fifty-one percent in Luganda, and twenty-eight percent in the English language. Eighteen percent of the women of Uganda could conduct a conversation in Kiswahili, twenty-eight percent in Luganda, and thirteen percent in the English language. For both men and women the percentage for competence in Kiswahili was thirty-five percent, in Luganda thirty-nine percent, and in the English language twenty-one percent. Consult Peter Ladefoged, Ruth Glick, and Clive Criper, *Language in Uganda*. London and Nairobi: O.U.P., 1972, pp. 24-25.

16.   This constitutional amendment has come under strong attack from many sections of the opposition. Coming just a couple of months before the general elections and within a few months after Kenya became once again, a dejure multi-party state, the move was widely seen as a conspiracy to get Moi back to power. For example, the Law Society of Kenya argued that the clause be deleted because:

    *   It fails to provide country-wide support for a candidate because it treats all provinces as equal in all material respects without regard to the size of the respective populations, ethnic compositions and the number of districts each comprises;

    *   The result is that a province like North-Eastern, with a total number of registered voters approximating Kiambu or Nakuru districts, is equated with such large provinces as Rift Valley, or Eastern, both of which have many more times registered voters of diverse ethnic compositions,

    *   It brings through the back door *majimbo (federalism)* which Kenyans have rejected;

    *   It possibly will precipitate a constitutional crisis and political instability likely to endanger peace and security in that there is no safeguard against repetitive presidential elections in an effort to get a candidate who satisfies the requirements while power is being exercised by a person in whom Kenyans may already have expressed lack of confidence in his rule or misrule, and

    *   It is questionable whether or not it serves the interest of a poor country like ours to create a need for spending scarce public funds in holding repetitive countrywide elections when there are so many other essential services in need of funds. *(The Daily Nation,* September 26, 1992)

17.   See Appendix II (Mazrui, Alamin M., "African Languages in the African American Experience.")

18.   Personal conversation between Idi Amin and Ali Mazrui in 1971.

19.   For a comprehensive study of the language situation in Uganda, consult Ladefoged, Glick and Criper, *Language in Uganda*, op. cit. Table 1.2 gives percentages of Ugandans able to hold a

conversation in Kiswahili, Luganda, and English. The following are the percentages given in the book on page 25.

	Swahili	Luganda	English
Men	52	51	28
Women	18	28	13
Total	35	39	21

20. Originally presented at the seventh symposium of the East African Academy, held at Makerere University College, Uganda, in September 1969. See also: Ali Mazrui (1972).

21. The distinction between Swahili as a culture and Swahili as a language is also discussed in A.Mazrui, "National Language Question in East Africa," *East Africa Journal,* June 1967 and A.Mazrui, "Islam and the English Language in East and West Africa," paper presented at an international seminar on Problems of Multi-Lingualism in Eastern Africa, organized by the International African Institute, and held at University College, Dar es Salaam, December 15-18, 1968.

22. For some of Blundell reminiscences, see his book *So Rough a Wind.* London: Weidenfeld & Nicholson, 1964.

23. The East African child was in the end offered a place at Nakasero, but the parents declined the offer. Meanwhile, debate on language policy continued across the border. In the debate on the Constitution of Kenya(Amendment) Bill, on February 12, 1969, Mr. Ronald Ngala (KANU) suggested it was time Swahili became the official Parliamentary Language. Told by a Member, "It will be like the House of Babylon" he replied, "That may be so, but we are an independent country." Mr. Ngala lamented "we are becoming more English than the English themselves."

In July and August 1969 the language controversy erupted once again in Kenya. The National Assembly passed a resolution recommending to the Government the adoption of Swahili as a joint-parliamentary language with English in the National Assembly.

24.   Originally published in Blackshire-Belay, C.A. Ed. *Language and Literature in the African American Imagination.* Westport: Greenwood Publishers. 1992.

25.   Throughout the medieval period Europe belonged to a regional tributary system which included Europeans and Arabs, Christians and Muslims. The greater part of Europe, however, was located at the periphery of this system. Its center was Latin Europe lying around the Mediterranean basin. It is in this center of the European tributary system that early forms of capitalism began to emerge. The degree and forms of accumulation engendered by the capitalist mode of production led to a tremendous concentration of material power. One of the central components of the legitimating ideology of this emergent capitalism was its materialism and racialism which became the fundamental basis on which European cultural unity was constructed.

From the Renaissance onwards, however, the center of the world capitalist system shifts towards the shores of the Atlantic; and Mediterranean Europe gets relegated to the periphery. European culture now reconstructs itself around an ideological myth that creates an opposition between an alleged European geographical and cultural continuity with the world south of the Mediterranean. "The whole of Eurocentricism," according to Amin, "lies in this mythic construct" (1989: 11). It is at this point that Europe becomes conscious of its power and that its conquest of the world was a possible objective. And it is around this possibility that racialist notions of identity of "self" and "other" begin to crystallize in Europe, especially in Germanic Europe which had become the center of world capitalism.

26.   It has been estimated by Juma Mutoro of the State University of New York, Albany, that in 1988, for example, there were over a

hundred African language programs in American universities, and
that almost invariably Swahili was one of those languages.

27.   This policy was developed by the Conference on College
        Composition and Communication (CCCC) - an affiliate of The
        National Council of Teachers of English (NTE) — and adopted
        during its Executive Committee meeting on March 16, 1988. The
        other two main objectives of the policy, are specified as:

        (a)   To provide resources to enable native and non-native
        speakers to achieve oral and literate competence in English, the
        language of wider communication.
        (b)   To support programs that assert the legitimacy of native
        languages and dialects and ensure that proficiency in the mother-
        tongue will not be lost.

28.   The anthropologist Lucy Mair, for example, made the following
        observation with regard to slavery among the Baganda of East
        Africa:

                Certain duties, it is true, were specifically allocated to
                slaves, but for the greatest part, they shared in the
                ordinary life of the household, were described by the
                head as "his children" and a stranger would not be
                aware that they were his slaves unless this was
                expressly explained by him. (1934: 31)

29.   The idiom includes principles like *umoja* (unity), *kujichagulia* (self-
        determination), *ujima* (collective responsibility), *nia* (intention),
        kuumba (creativity), *ujamaa* (socialism/ communalism), and *imani*
        (faith). Molefi Asante's *Afrocentricity* (1989) also, to some extent,
        relies heavily on an African linguistic idiom. Swahili concepts like
        Kawaida (Tradition), *Nija* (The Path), *Msingi* (Foundation), and

others, form important pillars of his philosophy.

30.   This idea of intra-African sharing as a way of establishing a continental cultural foundation for pan-Africanism was originally proposed by Ali Mazrui.

References

Abdalla, A. Sau*ti ya Dhiki*. Nairobi: Oxford University Press, 1973.

Abdulaziz, M.H. "Tanzania's National Language Policy and the Rise of Swahili Political Culture." W.H. Whitely and Daryll Forde, eds. *Language Use and Social Change: Problems of Multilingualism with Special Reference to Eastern Africa.* London: Oxford University Press, 1971.

Abdulaziz, Mohamed H. "Development of Scientific and Technical Terminology with Special Reference to African Languages." *Kiswahili* 56, 1989: 32-49.

Alexandre, Pierre. "Linguistic Problems of Contemporary Africa." *Presence Africaine* 13.41, 1963.

Amin, Samir. *Eurocentricism.* New York: Monthly Review Press, 1989.

Asante, M.K. and Kariamu Welsh Asante, eds. "The African Essence in African American Language." *African Culture: The Rhythms of Unity.* Trenton: Africa World Press, 1990.

Asante, Molefi Kete. *Afrocentricity.* Trenton: Africa World Press, 1988.

Austin, Dennis. *West Africa and the Commonwealth.* London: Penguin African Series, 1956.

Bennet, George. *Kenya: A Political History: The Colonial Period.* New York: Oxford University Press, 1963.

Blackshire-Belay, C.A. ed. *Language and Literature in the African American Imagination.* Westport: Greenwood Publishers, 1992.

Blundell, Michael. *So Rough a Wind*. London: Weidenfeld and Nicholson, 1964.

Churchill, Winston. *Great War Speeches*. London: Transworld Publishers, 1959.

Clatworthy, F.J. *The Foundation of British Colonial Education Policy: 1923-1948*. PhD Dissertation: University of Michigan, Ann Arbor, 1971.

Coleman, James. *Nigeria: Background to Nationalism*. Berkeley and Los Angeles: University of California Press, 1958.

Davis, Ossie. "The English Language is My Enemy." Robert H. Bentley and Samuel D. Crawford, eds. *Black Language Reader*. Glenview, Indiana: Scott, Foresman and Company, 1973: 71-77.

Deane, Seamus. "Introduction". Terry Eagleton, Fredric Jameson, and Edward Said, eds. *Nationalism, Colonialism, and Literature*. Minneapolis: University of Minnesota Press, 1990: 3-19.

Dillard, J.L. *Black English*. New York: Random House, 1972.

Duke, Lynne and James Rupert. "Power Behind Kabila Reflects Congo War's Tutsi Roots." *International Herald Tribune*, 29 May, 1997.

Eagleton, Terry. "Nationalism: Irony and Commitment." Terry Eagleton, Fredric Jameson, and Edward Said, eds. *Nationalism, Colonialism, and Literature*. Minneapolis: University of Minnesota Press, 1990: 23-39.

East African Royal Commission 1953-1955 Report. London: HMJO, 1955.

Gadsden, Fay. "Language Politics in Uganda: The Search for a Lingua Franca 1912-1944." USSC Conference, Makerere University. December 14-17, 1971.

Gorman, T.P. "The Development of Language Policy in Kenya with Particular Reference to the Educational System." W.H. Whitely, ed. *Language in Kenya*. Nairobi: Oxford University Press, 1974.

Gowers, W.F. Memorandum, "Development of Kiswahili as an Educational and Administrative Language in the Uganda Protectorate." November 25, 1927.

Hall, John Whitney and Beardsley, Richard K., eds. *Twelve Doors to Japan*. New York: McGraw-Hill Books Company, 1965.

Heine, Bernd. "Language and Society." Bernd Heine and N.J.G. Mohliy, eds. *Language and Dialect Atlas of Kenya*. Berlin: Dietrick and Reimer Verlag, 1980: 59-78.

Hodgkin, T. "The Islamic Literary Tradition in Ghana." I.M. Lewis, ed. *Tropical Africa*. London: Oxford University Press, 1966.

Hyder, Mohamed. "Swahili in the Technical Age." *East Africa Journal* 2.9, 1966.

Iliffe, John. *Tanganyika Under German Rule 1905-1912*. Nairobi: East African Publishing House, 1969.

Iliffe, John. "The Creation of Group Consciousness Among the Dock Workers of Dar es Salaam 1929-56." Richard Sandbrook and Robin Cohen, eds. *The Development of an African Working Class: Studies in Class Formation and Action*. Toronto: University of Toronto Press, 1975.

Inatomi, Eijiro. *The Japanese Mind: Essentials of Japanese Philosophy and Culture*. Charles A. Moore, ed. Honolulu: East & West Centre Press, 1967.

Jones, J. *Education in East Africa: A Study of East, Central, and South Africa by the Second African Education Commission.* New York: Phelps-Stokes Fund, 1925.

Jones, LeRoy. *Blues People.* New York, 1963.

Kabwegyere, Tarsis. *The Politics of State Formation: The Nature and Effects of Colonialism in Uganda.* Nairobi: East African Literature Bureau, 1974.

Kahn, Herman. *The Emerging Japanese Super State: Challenge and Response.* Englewood Cliffs, New Jersey: Prentice Hall, 1970.

Karenga, Ron. *Essays in Struggle.* San Diego: Kawaida Publications, 1978.

Kasfir, Nelson. *The Shrinking Political Arena.* Berkeley and Los Angeles: University of California Press, 1976.

Kenya, Republic of. *The National Assembly. House of Representatives Official Report.* Monday, December 14, 1964.- Wednesday, May 12, 1965. Volume IV. Nairobi: Government Printers.

Kenya, Republic of. *The National Assembly Official Report.* Volume XVII, Part II. June 27, 1969 - August 19, 1969. Nairobi: Government Printers.

Kenya, Republic of. *Kenya Educational Commission Report,* (The Ominde Commission Report), Part I. Nairobi: Government Press, 1964.

Kenya, Republic of. *The Kenya National Committee on Educational Objectives and Policies* (The Gacathi Report). Nairobi: Ministry of Education, 1976.

Kiango, S.D. and Sengo, T.J.Y. "Fasihi." *Mulika* 4, 1972: 11-17.

Krapf, J.L. *Outline of the Elements of Kiswahili Language with Special Reference to the Kinika Dialect.* Tubingen, 1850.

Ladefoged, P., Glick, R., and Criper, C. *Language in Uganda.* London: Oxford University Press, 1972.

Livingston, George J. "Forward." Newbell Niles Puckett ed., *Black Names in America: Origins and Usage.* Boston: G.K. Hall and Company, 1975.

Lodhi, Abdulaziz Y. "Language and Cultural Unity in Tanzania." *Kiswahili* 44.2, 1974: 10-13.

Louis, W.M. Roger. *Rwanda-Urundi: 1884-1919.* Oxford: Clarendon Press, 1963.

Lulua, Asaf. Origins and Development of Kiswahili in Uganda with Special Reference to the Question of National Language. Unpublished MS, 1976.

Mackay, A. *Eighteen Years in Uganda and East Africa.* Volume 2, 1908.

Mackay of Uganda, 8th Edition. 1898.

Mair, Lucy. *An African People in the Twentieth Century.* 1934.

Massamba, David P.B. "An Assessment of the Development and Modernization of the Kiswahili Language in Tanzania." Florian Coulmas, ed. *Language Adaptation.* Cambridge: Cambridge University Press, 1989: 60-78.

Mazrui, Ali A. "Africa's Experience in Nation-Building: Is it Relevant to Papua, New Guinea?" *East Africa Journal* 7.11, 1970: 15-23.

Mazrui, Ali A. "National Language Question in East Africa." *East African*

Journal. June 1967.

Mazrui, Ali A. "Political Sex." *Transition* 4.17, 1964: 19-23.

Mazrui, Ali and Zirimu, Pio. "The Secularization of an Afro-IslamicLanguage: Church, State, and Marketplace in the Spread of Kiswahili." *Journal of Islamic Studies* 2, 1990: 25-53.

Mbaabu, Ireri. *Language Policy in East Africa*. Nairobi: Educational Research and Publications, 1996.

McLuhan, Marshall. *Understanding Media: The Extension of Man*. New York: The New American Library, 1964.

Moore, Robert B. *Racism in the English Language*. New York: The Racism and Sexism Resource Center for Educators, 1976.

Msanjila, Y.P. "Problems of Teaching Through the Medium of Kiswahili in Teacher Training Colleges in Tanzania." *Journal of Multilingual and Multicultural Development*, 11.4, 1990: 307-317.

Mulokozi, Mugyabuso M. "English versus Kiswahili in Tanzania's Secondary Education." Jan Blommaert, ed. *Swahili Studies*. Ghent: Academic Press, 1991: 7-16.

Mutabiirwa, Dale E.W. "Kiswahili Proposed as National Language." Feature article in *The New Vision* (Uganda), January 12, 1989: 4.

Nuffield Foundation and Colonial Office. *African Education: A Study of Educational Policy and Practice in British Tropical Africa*. Oxford: Oxford University Press, 1953. (The Binns Report entitled "Report of the East and Central Africa Study Group" is on pp. 58-141.)

Nurse, Derek and Spear, Thomas. *The Swahili: Reconstructing the History and Language of an African Society, 800-1500*. Philadelphia:

University of Pennsylvania Press, 1985.

Nyerere, Julius. *Freedom and Unity: A Selection of Writings and Speeches, 1952-1965*. Dar es Salaam: Oxford University Press, 1966.

Nyerere, Julius. "The Basis of African Socialism". *Uhuru na Umoja:Freedom and Unity*. Nairobi: Oxford University Press, 1966: 162-171.

Obote, Milton. "Language and National Identification". *East Africa Journal*, April 1967.

Obote, Milton. "Language and National Integration". *East Africa Journal*, April 1964.

Ohly, Rajmond. "Dating of the Swahili Language". *Kiswahili* 42.2 and 43.1, 1973: 15-23.

Pike, Charles. "History and Imagination: Swahili Literature and Resistance to German Language Imperialism in Tanzania, 1885-1910". *International Journal of African Historical Studies* 19.2, 1986: 201-234.

Polome, Edgar C. "Aspects of Language Contact in Africa". Fishman, Joshua A.; Tabouret-Keller, Andree; Clyne, Michael; Krishnamurti, Bh; and Abdulaziz, Mohamed eds. *The Fergusonian Impact*, Vol. 1. New York: Mouton de Gruyter, 1986: 387-398.

Polome, Edgar C. "Tanzania: A Socio-Linguistic Profile". Edgar C. Polome and C.P. Hill, eds. *Language in Tanzania*. London: Oxford University Press, 1980: 103-138.

Polome, Edgar. "The Choice of Official Languages in the Democratic Republic of The Congo." Fishman, J.A.; Ferguson, C.A.; and Das Gupta, J. eds. *Language Problems of Developing Nations*. New York: John Wiley & Sons, Inc., 1967.

Puckett, Newbell Niles. *Black Names in America: Origins and Usage.* Boston: G.K. Hall and Company, 1975.

Pyle, L. "Engineering in the Universities and Development". Paper presented at the conference on "The Future Relationships Between Universities in Britain and Developing Countries" held at the Institute of Developmental Studies, University of Sussex, England. March 17-20, 1978.

Rothchild, Donald S. *The Effects of Mobilization in British Africa.* Pittsburgh: Duquesne University Press, 1961.

Roy-Campbell, Zaline M. *Power or Pedagogy: Choosing the Medium of Instruction in Tanzania.* PhD Thesis, University of Wisconsin, Madison, 1992.

Senkoro, F.E.M. *Ushairi: Nadharia na Tahakiki.* Dar es Salaam: Dar es Salaam University Press, 1988.

Shiner, Cindy. "Kabila: A Study in Paradox". *The Washington Post,* 19 May, 1997.

Steere, Edward. *A Handbook of the Swahili Language as Spoken at Zanzibar.* London: Sheldon Press, 1870.

Stichter, Sharon. "The Formation of a Working Class in Kenya". Richard Sandbrook and Robin Cohen, eds. *The Development of an African Working Class: Studies in Class Formation and Action.* Toronto: University of Toronto Press, 1975.

Tanzania, United Republic of. *Mfumo wa Elimu ya Tanzania 1981-2000.* Volume 1. Dar es Salaam: Government Printers, 1982.

Tanzania, United Republic of. *Recent Educational Developments in the*

United Republic of Tanzania 1981-1983. Dar es Salaam: Government Printers, 1984.

Tanzania, United Republic of. *Second Five-Year Plan for Economic and Social Development. 1 July 1969 - 30 June 1974.* Dar es Salaam: Government Printers, 1969.

Turner, Lorenzo D. *Africanisms in the Gullah Dialect.* Chicago: University of Chicago Press, 1949 and New York: Aro Press, 1969.

Twiggs, Robert D. *Pan-African Language in the Western Hemisphere,* North Quincy, Massachusetts: The Christopher Publishing House, 1973.

Uganda, Republic of. *Parliamentary Debates.* Hansard, Second Series, Volumes 6-8. National Assembly Official Report, First Session, 1962-1963; third meeting, 4-26 February 1963.

Whitely, W.H. "Patterns of Language Use in Rural Kenya." W.H. Whitely, ed. *Language in Kenya.* Nairobi: Oxford University Press, 1974: 319-350.

Whitely, W.H. *Swahili: The Rise of a National Language.* London: Methuen, 1969.

Whitely, W.H. "The Classification and Distribution of Kenya's African Languages". W.H. Whitely, ed. *Language in Kenya.* Nairobi: Oxford University Press, 1974: 13-68.

Williams, Robert L. (ed.) *Ebonics: The True Language of Black Folk.* St. Louis, Missouri: Institute of Black Studies, 1975.

Wright, Marcia. *German Missions in Tanganyika: 1891-1941.* Oxford: Clarendon Press, 1971.

Index

Religious purposes, 2
Religious revolutions, 178
Religious roles,
    Non-, 34
Religious sense, 33
Religious studies, 34
Religious symbols, 54
Religious systems, 35
Religious terms, 171
Religious vocabulary, 75
    Significance of, 30
    Universalistic, 31
Reservations, 76
    Tribal, 19
Reservoir,
    of Islamic spirit, 56
    of religious concepts, 74
Restratification, 26
Ricardo, 180
Rich province,
    Mineral-, 16
Richter, Julius, 72
Robert, Shaaban, 170, 186
Role of the Ex-Soldier in Kenya's
    Political History, 68
Roman,
    Roman alphabet, 174
    Roman Catholic, 80
    Roman Empire, 133
        Holy, 133
    Roman script, 57, 58, 74
Romantic terms of loyalty, 203
Roosevelt (President), 146
Royal Technical College Keyne,
    203
Rufiji valley, 54
Rural areas, 6, 92, 93, 198
    Rural counseling, 41
    Rural cultivators, 5
    Rural development,
        Basic needs for, 179

Rural ethnic behavior, 6
Rural misfits, 91, 92
Rural newspapers, 201
Rural production, 41
Rural readership, 202
Rural-to-urban migration, 95
Rwanda, 15, 36, 100, 121, 128-
    9, 143, 145, 148, 153
    Bloody conflicts in, 143
    Language of, 101
    Rwanda army, 100
    Rwanda Patriotic Front, 100
    Rwandan immigrants, 101

S

Sacleux,
    Father, 74
Sahara, South of, 204
Satellite transmission, 41
Sauti Ya Mvita, 170, 199, 200
    Sauti Ya Mvita broadcasting
        programme, 169
Sauti Ya Mvita broadcasting
    programmes, 199
School,
    School books, 46
    School curriculum, 72
        Kenya's, 84
    School education,
        Primary, 62
        Secondary, 83
    School materials,
        Secondary, 62
    School subject, 147
        Compulsory, 135
        Optional, 83
    School system 84, 85
        Integrated, 86
Science,

    Scientific age,
        Challenge of, 40